JAZZ MAVERICKS OF THE LONE STAR STATE

UNIVERSITY OF TEXAS PRESS, AUSTIN

JAZZ
Mavericks of the
LONE STAR STATE

Dave Oliphant

First edition, 2007

Requests for permission to reproduce material from this work should be sent to:

    Permissions

    University of Texas Press

    P.O. Box 7819

    Austin, TX 78713-7819

    www.utexas.edu/utpress/about/bpermission.html

⊖ The paper used in this book meets the minimum requirements of ANSI/NISO Z39.48-1992 (R1997) (Permanence of Paper).

Library of Congress Cataloging-in-Publication Data

Oliphant, Dave.

    Jazz mavericks of the Lone Star State / Dave Oliphant. — 1st ed.

      p.   cm.

    Includes bibliographical references (p.   ) and index.

    ISBN-13: 978-0-292-71495-3 (cloth : alk. paper)

    ISBN-10: 0-292-71495-5 (alk. paper)

    ISBN-13: 978-0-292-71496-0 (pbk. : alk. paper)

    ISBN-10: 0-292-71496-3 (alk. paper)

1. Jazz—Texas—History and criticism. I. Title.

    ML3508.7.T4O44 2007

    781.6509764—dc22

                                      2006034389

CONTENTS

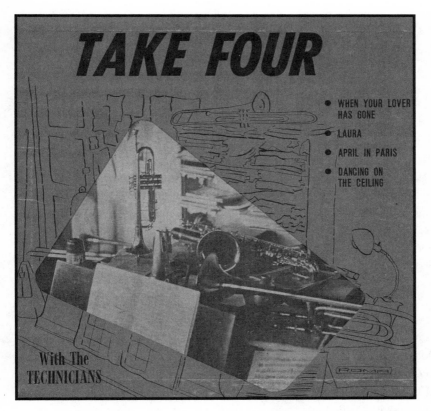

TAKE FOUR

- WHEN YOUR LOVER HAS GONE
- LAURA
- APRIL IN PARIS
- DANCING ON THE CEILING

With The
TECHNICIANS

ROMA

TUNING UP WITH A
FEW INTRODUCTORY NOTES

Funky Butt Hall, Deep Ellum, the Cherry Blossom, the Grand Terrace, Minton's, the Lighthouse at Hermosa Beach. Mister Jelly Lord, I thought I heard Buddy Bolden say, Open up that window and let the bad air out. O play that thing! Hello Central, give me Doctor Jazz, he's got what I need, I know he has. Struttin' with some barbecue. I'm coming Virginia. It don't mean a thing if it ain't got that swing. Born in Texas, raised in Tennessee, no one woman's gonna make a fat mouth outta me. I'd rather drink muddy water, live in a log, than be up here in New York treated like a dirty dog. Mercy. Your feet's too big. Hey Charlie, let's play the blues in B. I'm gonna move way out on the outskirts of town; don't want that iceman comin' round. Salt peanuts, salt peanuts, ooh bop shebam. Freedom's the shape of jazz to come.

These legendary places, names, lines from lyrics, and song and record titles are, for those who know the story of jazz, some of the music's most famous historical touchstones, among which are those connected with Elm Street in Dallas and with native Texas musicians Jack Teagarden, Charlie Christian, and Ornette Coleman. Concerned with these and other celebrated moments and figures in the history of jazz, the present gathering of articles, book-review essays, talks, and ruminations expands on and adds to my book *Texan Jazz*, published by the University of Texas Press in 1996. Although the sixteen pieces collected here were written during a fourteen-year period, from 1992 to 2005, they represent but a fraction of the time that I have been fascinated by jazz. My love for the music began over fifty years ago in 1954, when, as a sophomore, I formed part of the dance band at Beaumont's South Park High School. In that year I purchased my first jazz recordings in local shops and learned something about the early periods of the music, especially the work of Jelly Roll Morton and Duke Ellington from the 1920s and 1930s. In 1955 I heard recordings by the great Charlie Parker, who, without my being aware of the fact, would die during that same year at the age of thirty-five. At the time I could hardly have imagined that I would spend the rest of my life listening to, rejoicing in, and marveling at a music that has become for me an endless source of aural pleasure, historical and cultural insights, and even regional pride, once I discovered the many Texans who were crucial to the creation of this art form admired around the globe.

Shortly after publication of *Texan Jazz*, I was invited by Norbert Carnovale to contribute one of six projected volumes in a series on jazz that he was editing for Greenwood Press of Connecticut. I had been recommended to this general editor by Dr. Richard Burkart, my college trumpet instructor, to whom I am indebted not only for making possible the writing and publication of my second book on jazz, *The Early Swing Era, 1930 to 1941*, but also for having introduced me to the music of Count Basie, Miles Davis, and Les Brown when, in 1957–1958, I became a member of the Technicians, the dance band that Dr. Burkart directed at

PREVIOUS PAGE: Album jacket of 45 rpm record album produced in 1958 by Professor Richard Burkart and his then Lamar State College of Technology Technicians. Line drawings by Roma Newton. Reproduced by permission of Richard Burkart.

Beaumont's then Lamar State College of Technology. Prior to my college career, it had been my high school orchestra teacher, Harold Meehan, who had first opened me up to the panorama of jazz with its invigorating rhythms, tonal richness, and complex system of improvisation. Almost from the beginning of my jazz education, I was aware that Texans had been active at high levels in the music's history, including Beaumont's own Harry James, a star trumpeter of the Benny Goodman Orchestra. In fact, I learned early on that the James home had been moved from downtown Beaumont to Florida Street, the very street on which I lived when I first began to listen to jazz. Coincidentally, the first important album that I acquired, entitled *I Like Jazz*, contained an impressive example of James's trumpet virtuosity: his solo on the 1937 Goodman radio broadcast of "Jam Session." Also in high school I discovered that multi-reedman Jimmy Giuffre was a native of Dallas, this after having heard him on a number of albums participating as a key member of the group known as Shorty Rogers and His Giants. While still in high school I was fortunate enough to hear Dr. Burkart's Lamar Tech jazz octet perform several of the pieces that had been recorded by the Giants, two of which, "The Pesky Serpent" and "Indian Club," were composed by Giuffre. Later in the early 1960s I would encounter the music of other Texas jazzmen, among them Vernon's Jack Teagarden and Fort Worth's Ornette Coleman. It was this early exposure to Texans in jazz that eventually led me to write *Texan Jazz*.

But the publication of my first book would by no means signal the end of my jazz education in terms of a Texas contribution. Even though my second book was devoted primarily to non-Texas musicians of the swing era, in researching that volume I unearthed a number of native Texas jazzmen whose work I had overlooked in writing *Texan Jazz*. One example was a Beaumont-born drummer, Oliver Coleman, who in the late 1930s was an outstanding member of the Earl Hines Orchestra. Even though I discussed Coleman's work in *The Early Swing Era*, I remained unaware that he was a Texan until after the book was published. On the other hand, I did discover at the time of writing this second book that I had left out of *Texan Jazz* multi-reedman Clarence Hutchenrider from Waco, who was an important member of the Casa Loma Orchestra throughout the 1930s. Later, in "The Roots of Texan Jazz," I would cover the career of Hutchenrider, as well as that of cornetist Tom Howell of Cameron, also discovered after the publication of *Texan Jazz*. Thus, each of the essays in the present collection examines further the important roles played by Texans in jazz history. Even after more than fifty years I find that I am far from exhausting this captivating subject. Indeed, the essays collected here strike me as having but inaugurated an investigation into this unlimited field of study. One wish that I have for this selection of essays is that it may encourage others to explore Texan jazz in new areas and from new perspectives.

Today I can recognize the potential for future articles and books on Texans in jazz primarily because the high school and college that I attended in Beaumont permitted the teaching of jazz as a legitimate part of the educational curriculum. Without my understanding it at the time, my high school and college teachers were preparing me for a lifetime of enrichment, both in terms of aesthetic enjoyment and of a growing knowledge of the significant position occupied by jazz in the history of the nation, and even the world. Although native pride may not have been a lesson that my teachers tried to instill in me as one of the values of learning about jazz through listening to and trying to perform the music, being able to identify Texas musicians—and even a folklorist like Austin's Alan Lomax—as significant figures in its creative and critical record was yet another benefit accruing from my early instruction in the history of jazz.

One professional consequence of my introduction to jazz over a half-century ago is the great satisfaction that I now take in sharing my enthusiasm for this music with new generations of students. For several years I have had the privilege of teaching, at the University of Texas at Austin, a freshman seminar on Jazz and Literature. Although the field of my degrees is not music but literature, I have long cultivated an interest in the relationship between the two art forms. A number of world-class writers of poems, short stories, novels, and plays have created works based on the lives of jazz musicians, the impact of the music itself, or its symbolic meaning in terms of ideas of freedom, hero worship, and integration. In conjunction with reading such works of literature, as well as biographies and autobiographies of the musicians, my students listen to jazz and discover the musical and extramusical meanings that the writers on jazz have heard in live or recorded performances, have observed in seeing the musicians play, sing, and interact with their fellows, and have described in such revelatory and stimulating poetry and prose.

The essay-review included here on Alfred Appel's book *Jazz Modernism* reveals among critics and commentators a growing awareness of the links between jazz and the twentieth-century movements of modernism and postmodernism in world art and literature. Once again, Texans, as musicians, authors, and artists, have figured significantly in the connections created and observed between jazz, art, and literature, including, for example, trombonist Jack Teagarden, writer Donald Barthelme, and painter Robert Rauschenberg. The aesthetic, cultural, and historical reach of jazz has truly been global in its impact and appeal, and this fact makes the inclusion of jazz studies in public schools and higher education a valid and commendable development. It is of course ironic that this music, which was originally denigrated and even condemned for its wicked origins and for being a crude, corrupting influence on youth, has proven one of the most respected products of American civilization. Personally I am eternally grateful to my schools and teachers for having brought this music and its legacy to my attention during the formative years of my education. I am hopeful that these sixteen essays will help to bring an appreciation for jazz—its cultural and historical dimensions as well as its Texas connections—to all those with ears to hear and hearts and minds willing to experience the allure of this enduring music.

JAZZ MAVERICKS OF THE LONE STAR STATE

JAZZ MAVERICKS OF THE LONE STAR STATE

Known for many different types of music, Texas is perhaps least recognized for its crucial contributions to the history of jazz. Even devoted fans of this music can be surprised to find that a prominent jazz musician was or is a native Texan. This is largely owing to the fact that most Texas jazz musicians have had to leave the state in order to earn a living by playing their music. Although it was to Kansas City, New York, Chicago, or Los Angeles that many of these jazz musicians migrated, it was in the state's small towns and cities that they first heard the music they were drawn to, where they began to learn its art, and where they performed with territory bands before eventually landing spots in such name big bands of the day as those of Count Basie, Duke Ellington, Benny Goodman, Jimmie Lunceford, Glenn Miller, or Stan Kenton. Texas jazz musicians also joined the ranks of smaller groups led by such stars as Jelly Roll Morton, King Oliver, Louis Armstrong, Charlie Parker, Dizzy Gillespie, and Charles Mingus. But how musicians in outlying towns like Jefferson, Rockport, Wichita Falls, Amarillo, or Texarkana first heard the infectious sounds of jazz and later became members of major outfits and even bandleaders themselves still remains something of a mystery. In Jefferson in 1930, the family of Steady Nelson (1913–1988) owned no radio, and yet by 1940 this trumpeter was a featured soloist in the Woody Herman Orchestra. Kenny Dorham, born in tiny Post Oak in 1924, would become one of the preeminent bebop trumpeters of the late 1940s and of the hard bop movement of the 1950s. Indeed, during every period of jazz history, Texans have played important roles in the development of this music that has captured the imaginations of listeners around the world.

In some ways, the roots of jazz were planted early on in Texas soil. The blues, which forms one source for jazz, had perhaps its earliest exponents in Texas, including Blind Lemon Jefferson (ca. 1880–ca. 1930) of Couchman, referred to as the King of the Country Blues. Likewise, ragtime, the other musical tradition from which jazz drew its inspiration, had its first great composer in Scott Joplin (1868–1917) of Texarkana. Joplin's 1899 "Maple Leaf Rag" was a landmark of ragtime, and "The Entertainer," made famous by the 1973 movie *The Sting,* starring Paul Newman, brought to Joplin's music, if not to his name and birthplace, universal acclaim. In order to aid listeners from within the state and those from outside its borders to remember or recognize the importance of Joplin, Texarkana has established in his memory an annual Jump Jive & Jam Fest, held at the site of the Scott Joplin mural in downtown Texarkana. Other towns and cities have also begun to pay tribute to their native musicians who were vital figures in the history of jazz. In 2003 several events were held around the state to celebrate Texas jazzmen: in San Marcos, the mayor of the city proclaimed

PREVIOUS PAGE: Eddie Durham, photographed by Val Wilmer in 1976 in New York City. Photograph copyright © Val Wilmer. Used by permission.

August 16 Eddie Durham Day; in Dallas, the Marshall Agency and the South Dallas Cultural Center presented its Annual Jazz Legends Festival, whose inaugural fete in 1999 had honored native son Red Garland; in Fort Worth, the first annual Jazz by the Boulevard Festival took place in September 2003 and featured the city's own Dewey Redman; and in November, Corpus Christi hosted its forty-third annual Texas Jazz Festival, with hometown pianist-trombonist Joe Gallardo among the lineup of locally born talent. Other cities like Houston and Denton have honored any number of native musicians, with Houston even laying claim to having held the first jazz festival on record in 1922.

Although it would be possible to mention men and women from every large Texas city and many a small town who have advanced the cause of jazz, the careers of six Texas musicians can represent many parts of the state as well as most of this music's principal periods, from hot to swing, from bebop and hard bop to harmolodics.

Eddie Durham (1906–1987) of San Marcos was one of the first and most influential Texans in jazz. A member of the Oklahoma Blue Devils that recorded in 1929 and of the Kansas City band of Bennie Moten during the late 1920s and early 1930s, Durham was on Moten's milestone recording of 1932 and helped create the riff style that became a fixture of the swing era. A composer-arranger who had taken correspondence courses in music theory while a boy in San Marcos and performed in groups with his brother Joe and his cousin Allen, Eddie Durham played a central role in establishing the popular swing-era style of the Jimmie Lunceford Orchestra from 1935 to 1936, with arrangements of tunes like "Avalon" and "Pigeon Walk" and his own originals like "Lunceford Special" and "Harlem Shout." Later Durham contributed classic compositions to the Count Basie Orchestra from 1937 to 1938 with tunes like "Topsy," "Blue and Sentimental," "One O'Clock Jump," and "Swinging the Blues," the latter considered the epitome of the Basie style. In addition to serving as a composer-arranger, Durham played trombone in the brass sections of the Moten, Lunceford, and Basie bands as well as amplified guitar, the instru-ment he pioneered and later introduced to the greatest of all electric gui-tarists, Charlie Christian (1916–1942) of Bonham. In 1939, at the height of Glenn Miller's renown as a swing-era celebrity, Durham wrote several fine musical charts for the Miller organization, including "Glen Island Special" and "Wham (Re Bop Boom Bam)," and has even been credited in part with one of the most famous Miller arrangements of all, "In the Mood." During

World War II, Durham trained an all-girls orchestra, one of the first and most successful, the International Sweethearts of Rhythm. An unassuming figure, Eddie Durham was at the center of the swing era and left his indelible print on this period, during which jazz was more popular than at any other time in its history.

Another Texas trombonist, one who would revolutionize the playing of this rather awkward slide instrument, was Jack Teagarden (1905–1964) of Vernon. Like Durham, Big T, as Teagarden was called, belonged to a family of musicians (his brother Charlie was a superb swing trumpeter) and was active in jazz circles in the state in the early 1920s, after which he made a huge splash in the big pond of the New York jazz scene. Arriving largely unheralded, Teagarden unveiled to musicians in the East his phenomenal technical skills and his blues-tinged Texas voice with its languid, soothing lullaby of a drawl. His first recordings in 1929 reveal him already to be a master improviser, as he maneuvers on "That's a Serious Thing" with seemingly effortless leaps, from one register of his horn to another, tossing off ornamental turns as if the instrument were equipped with valves, when in fact he executes them almost entirely with his lips. In the same year of the market crash, Big T recorded with Louis Armstrong in one of the first integrated recording sessions in jazz. In the 1940s Teagarden would become a member of the Armstrong All-Stars, but before that, between 1934 and 1939, he was the star soloist with the Paul Whiteman Orchestra and afterward led his own big band.

One of Teagarden's most impressive performances came in 1933 when he participated in the first recording session for jazz vocalist Billie Holiday. His rip-snorting solo on "Your Mother's Son-in-Law" has all the earmarks of his Texas open-range upbringing. From 1936, I would single out his rendition of Johnny Mercer's "I'm an Old Cowhand" as an example of his trombone virtuosity and his delightful vocal treatment of the witty lyrics, which include such lines as "I'm a ridin' fool who is up to date. / I know every trail in the Lone Star State, / For I ride the range in a Ford V8." Mosaic Records reissued this recording in 2001 in a CD box set that includes among several photographs of Teagarden one from 1926 when he was touring in El Paso with Doc Ross and His Jazz Bandits.[1] This box set illustrates the serious attention that continues to be paid to Jack Teagarden, who has been called by critic Gary Giddins "the best trombone player in the world."[2]

Born six miles from the town of Fairfield, Kenny Dorham (1924–1972) was introduced to jazz through his pianist sister, who commented to their parents that KD would one day be a great musician like Louis Armstrong because he "jumps around when he hears music."[3] But only after he moved to Austin did Dorham pick up the trumpet, playing it first in high school and later at Wiley College in Marshall. During World War II he joined various outstanding bands, including those of Dizzy Gillespie and Billy Eckstine, but it was in 1948 that he had his big break when he replaced Miles Davis in the Charlie "Bird" Parker Quintet. In 1949 Dorham appeared with the Bird at the Paris Jazz Festival, the first international gathering of its kind. Dorham's boyhood dream had been to become a cowhand, and in fact in his youth he did drive cattle to the dipping vats. But as a musician he was destined instead to achieve a worldwide reputation as a fleet-fingered trumpeter whose "running" style exhibits a remarkable melodic and logical gift. His solos rarely repeat the same musical ideas, although they are immediately identifiable as his own, full of half-valve effects, unexpected twists and turns, and a mellow tonal quality that makes his sound endlessly appealing.

As a member of Charlie Parker's bebop quintet, Dorham demonstrated his ability to keep pace with one of the greatest jazz musicians of all time. Later, as a founding member of the Jazz Messengers, he was at the forefront of the hard-bop movement, with its gospel-intoned, soulful "preaching" of the word of jazz. In 1960 Dorham recorded his own version of Johnny Mercer's "I'm an Old Cowhand," turning it into an exemplary piece of hard-bop Texana and in a way fulfilling through this piece his early ambition to be a real Texas cowboy. Not only was Dorham one of the most outstanding jazz trumpeters of any era, but he contributed to the jazz repertory such classic compositions as "Blue Bossa" and "The Prophet," the former inspired by his appearance at a jazz festival in Brazil in 1961. In 1960 and 1963, he was invited to Norway and Denmark to record with local Scandinavian musicians. Some ten years before his untimely death, the Texan composed "Dorham's Epitaph," a lovely piece lasting only one minute and nine seconds but played with his inimitable blend of secure technique and passionate expression.[4]

Both Dorham and Teagarden were on occasion referred to as Texas mavericks. They certainly shared a Texas brand of jazz through their rugged individualism and their pride in place. Just as Teagarden would sing in the lyrics to "I'm an Old Cowhand," "Look out Texas, here I come, / Right back where I started from," Texans have tended to congregate with their fellow natives, to choose tunes that remind them of their roots, and to return to Texas at the end of their careers. Two of the many Texans who eventually returned to their home state were Dallas reedman Buster Smith (1904–1991) and pianist Red Garland (1923–1984). Prior to resettling in Big D, these men made a profound impact on jazz history, with Professor Smith, as he was called, serving as a direct influence on Charlie Parker, the seminal figure in the bebop revolution. But perhaps no other Dallas musician was so closely associated for such a long period of time with the careers of major jazzmen as was Red Garland. The pianist's recorded work with Miles Davis and John Coltrane, from the mid- to late 1950s, typifies the fundamental supporting role that many Texans have played in jazz, whether their style has been identified as Texan or not.

Red Garland first joined forces with Miles Davis in 1955, some five years after the trumpeter had worked his way from bebop into a cooler, more nuanced style, with a greater emphasis on introspection. In this regard, Davis had moved away from bebop's largely technical exhibition-ism that had left many listeners unable to respond emotionally to the sheer speed and number of notes reeled off by Parker and his imitators. In form-ing his own quintet that would eventually include new star tenor saxo-phonist John Coltrane, Davis found in Garland a pianist whose relaxed rhythmic sense and expansive chords fit perfectly with the hauntingly inti-mate sounds that Davis was beginning to explore. In a series of historic recordings by the Davis Quintet, Garland not only backed up two of the most daring horn soloists of the 1950s but contributed as well his own swinging solos full of his trademark block chords and long, single-note runs. Typical of his role in the Davis Quintet was his "comping" and solo-ing on driving pieces like the 1956 "I Could Write a Book" and "Bye Bye Blackbird." After leaving Davis in 1958, Garland recorded extensively on his own, forming groups that on several occasions included fellow Texans, among them trumpeter Richard "Notes" Williams (1931–1985) of Galveston and alto saxophonist–flutist Leo Wright (1933–1991) of Wichita Falls. If not the innovator that Davis and Coltrane proved, Garland was one of the most influential pianists of his generation, creating on the keyboard what has been described—in the work of Texas saxophonists like Arnett Cobb (1918–1989) and Illinois Jacquet (1922–2004) of Houston and David

"Fathead" Newman (b. 1933) of Dallas—a sound as big and bright as the wide-open spaces of the Lone Star State.

More of an originator than Red Garland is another Dallas product, multi-reedman and composer Jimmy Giuffre (b. 1921). Educated at what is now the University of North Texas in Denton, Giuffre studied music there before the creation of the school's nationally famous jazz program, established by Gene Hall (1913–1993) of Whitewright. Like two of his classmates, fellow Dallasites Gene Roland (1921–1982) and Harry Babasin (1921–1988), Giuffre emigrated to Los Angeles where he became a leader in 1950s West Coast jazz, with its lower-keyed exuberance. As a member of Shorty Rogers and His Giants, Giuffre experimented with various new techniques, such as huffing on his clarinet without vibrating the instrument's reed. He also utilized unusual instrumental combinations in the groups he formed, such as his piano-less quartet and trio, the latter featuring himself on clarinet, tenor sax, or baritone sax along with guitarist Jim Hall and bassist Ralph Peña. Recognized originally for his arrangement entitled "Four Brothers," written in 1947 for the big band of Woody Herman, Giuffre primarily composed for small groups throughout the 1950s but also wrote a piece entitled "Suspensions" for Brandeis University's 1957 Modern Jazz Concert featuring a fourteen-piece orchestra performing so-called Third Stream music, a fusion of jazz and classical strains. But undoubtedly Giuffre's greatest success came through his folksy trio compositions, especially "The Train and the River," a work representative of his down-home approach that generated a subdued yet pulsing swing in the best jazz tradition.

As late as 1993, Giuffre was still exploring new musical realms, as on his CD entitled *Conversations with a Goose*, where he plays both clarinet and soprano saxophone. Included on this CD is "Watchin' the River," a piece composed jointly by Giuffre and the two members of his trio, pianist Paul Bley and bassist Steve Swallow, a group that originally recorded together in 1961 and 1962 and reunited in 1989.[5] This work might be considered a more classical version of "The Train and the River," for here Giuffre's clarinet is slightly folksy but more often distantly akin to the far-out multiphonics of his fellow Texan John Carter (1929–1991) of Fort Worth, who in the 1980s recorded on clarinet his markedly avant-garde epic series, *Roots and Folklore*.[6] On Giuffre's "Calls in the Night," also on his 1993 CD, he creates on soprano sax eerie sounds that evoke vividly and

at times tenderly the title of his original composition. Many of the titles
of tunes on this CD (all chosen by Giuffre) depict the western outdoors,
as in "Echo Through the Canyon," "Among the High Rocks," and "White
Peaks," with the last of these offering an example of Giuffre's classical-jazz
soprano sax at its most touching. In "Jungle Critters" he shows off his
most advanced conception on soprano, as he matches trills and appropriately dissonant pitches with those played by the pianist and bassist.[7]
Another in a long line of Texas mavericks, Jimmy Giuffre stood out from
the first as his own musician, and ever since he has gone his own way on
every reed instrument on which he has performed and through every
composition he has penned.

   If Teagarden, Dorham, and Giuffre were mavericks, Ornette Coleman
(b. 1930) of Fort Worth, even though a latecomer, is the father of them all.
Playing a white plastic alto saxophone in 1959, he recorded in Los Angeles
his third album, presciently entitled *The Shape of Jazz to Come*. Through
this album, Coleman turned the jazz world on its ear with his unorthodox
sound and technique, odd intervals, piercing saxophone cries, and angu-
lar themes delivered in something of a Texas twang. The "hick" riff-theme
in "Congeniality" was once described by a friend as seeming to say "I'm
goin' tooooo Foat Wuth." On the other hand, tunes like his "Lonely
Woman" and "Peace" represent the deeply probing nature of Coleman's
music, which belies any characterization of the composer-improviser as
either a naif or a yokel. Now in his seventies, he continues—when he
makes one of his rare public appearances—to amaze with the originality of
his musical conception. Over the years he has tried every imaginable
approach to the music, even teaching himself to play the violin and trumpet in an effort to realize the unique sounds that he has heard in his head
from the beginning of his career. An iconoclast of the first order,
Coleman—whose many Cowtown classmates, including Dewey Redman
(b. 1931), have followed his lead into the Free Jazz movement, or what he
calls "harmolodics"—still maintains his position as the most avant-garde
figure in jazz, which he has held since he began recording over forty-five
years ago.

   From Scott Joplin's ragtime to the swing of Eddie Durham and Jack
Teagarden, from the bebop and hard bop of Kenny Dorham and Red
Garland, to the Third Stream of Jimmy Giuffre and the harmolodics of
Ornette Coleman, America's world-class art form can truly be said to bear,
in every period of its evolution, a definite Texan stamp.

THE ROOTS OF TEXAN JAZZ

Although the most prominent Texas jazz musicians have traditionally left the state for greater exposure in the urban centers of Kansas City, Chicago, New York, and Los Angeles, this should not obscure the fact that it was within the state that they received their early training as musicians, responded to the live, recorded, or broadcast sounds that they heard around them, and associated with their fellow Texans in local or territory bands. It has been particularly important to such musicians that African American music in Texas reaches back to its earliest forms, including work songs, chants, spirituals, gospel, blues, ragtime, and boogie-woogie. Indeed, all of these musical forms were known and performed in the state in the nineteenth or the early twentieth century. Consequently, after leaving Texas, an impressive number of native musicians were able to contribute significantly to every period in the entire history of jazz.

In the case of ragtime and boogie-woogie, these highly influential piano styles are thought to have originated to some extent in East Texas, with Scott Joplin of Texarkana considered the greatest of all ragtime composers and best known as the creator in 1899 of "Maple Leaf Rag," and with Hersal Thomas of Houston deemed a boogie-woogie prodigy from the early and mid-1920s.[1] The blues were likewise something of an indigenous product of Texas, developed especially by such rural singer-guitarists as Blind Lemon Jefferson and Huddie Ledbetter (known as Leadbelly), who brought their country blues to the urban settings of Dallas and Houston. In the 1920s Blind Lemon was even billed as "The King of Country Blues." Female blues singers in Dallas and Houston were also active in the 1920s, including Sippie Wallace and Victoria Spivey. Even before these better-known vocal stars had recorded in the mid- and late 1920s, Fae Barnes of Hillsboro was the earliest Texas blues singer to be recorded, under the name of Maggie Jones, in New York City on July 26, 1923.

As to the rise of jazz in Texas, a number of musicians emerged from towns and cities throughout the state and eventually exerted a national impact on this American music. The first jazz recording was made in 1917 by the Original Dixieland Jazz Band, but jazz had been in existence a decade or more prior to this event, and some of its founding figures, such as Bunk Johnson, Sidney Bechet, Jelly Roll Morton, and Joe "King" Oliver, reportedly had ventured into Texas between 1904 and 1914.[2] The presence of these four jazzmen in Texas may well have stimulated a local interest in the music, and yet a major instrumentalist like Jack Teagarden of Vernon was playing jazz around 1921 without even knowing that it had a name. While the white ODJB members and the four black musicians (Johnson, Bechet, Morton, and Oliver), who are now recognized as jazz masters, were all from Louisiana, and while both the bordering states of Louisiana and Oklahoma figure prominently in the development of jazz, Texas is perhaps unique in having produced vital exponents of the music for every period and style in its historical record.

Jazz musicians in Texas were unquestionably aware of blues, ragtime, and boogie-woogie, since these forms of African American music could be

PREVIOUS PAGE: Howell Brothers Moonshine Dance Orchestra, photographed in 1922 by the Jordan Co., Austin, Texas. Pictured from left to right are Lee on trombone, Jay on clarinet, Bill on drums, Hilton on piano, and Tom (the youngest at sixteen) on cornet. Used by permission of Pat Howell Crutsinger.

heard in most every part of the state. But none of these forms was jazz as it is thought of today. That is, these musical forms were not played primarily with wind instruments (with the exception of ragtime bands and the jazz musicians who accompanied female blues singers), did not develop the contrast or harmonization of brass and reeds, did not emphasize improvisation as an essential feature of the form (although both blues and boogie-woogie did involve improvisation to a limited degree), did not normally include a rhythm section devoted to supporting and stimulating a band's sections and soloists, and did not create a sound and rhythmic drive that are identifiable as distinctive to jazz (even though all three of the earlier forms did contribute to the creation of jazz's rhythms, structures, and tonal colors). However, given the relationship between jazz and the earlier forms of African American music, it is somewhat surprising that jazz ensembles developed in areas of Texas that are not generally associated with ragtime, blues, or boogie-woogie. This is certainly true of such groups as Gene Coy's Happy Black Aces of Amarillo and the Real Jazz Orchestra of Laredo, which were active as early as 1921 and the mid-1920s, respectively. Of course, jazz had by this time already spread internationally, as indicated by the fact that in Chile a group called the Royal Orchestra had formed in 1924 and that circa 1926 a recording was made in that South American country of a "shimmy" entitled "Y tenía un lunar" (And She Had a Mole).[3] In Houston in 1925, Fatty Martin's Orchestra also recorded a "shimmy" foxtrot entitled "End O'Main," on which composer Earl Church takes two fine muted trumpet breaks.[4] Pablo Garrido, the organizer in Chile of the Royal Orchestra, noted in an article published in 1935 that Chilean jazz musicians were influenced by Paul Whiteman's recordings, which had first appeared in 1920 with his "Whispering" and "Wang-Wang Blues."[5] The Whiteman recordings represented something of a watered-down version of black jazz, while Gene Coy's Happy Black Aces of Amarillo were playing original tunes "built on the structure of the blues" and at tempos slower than those typical of the one- and two-step dances of the period.[6] Obviously the blues were fundamental even to a group located in an area known more for cattle ranching than for an African American musical form. Indeed, this reveals that even in Amarillo a black jazz group at the beginning of the 1920s was performing in the blues mode that would be characteristic of the work of most all Texas jazz musicians, but especially of the many black Texans who would have such a marked influence on the evolution of jazz.

White musicians in Texas, like their black counterparts, were playing jazz at least by 1920, and probably much earlier.[7] In 1922 "almost certainly the first jazz festival on the books" was held in Houston, where pianist Peck Kelley and his Bad Boys had been performing since 1921.[8] Trombonist Jack Teagarden, born in 1905, left his Vernon home in 1921 at age sixteen and joined his uncle's band in San Angelo. In that same year Teagarden moved on to San Antonio, where he played with Cotton Bailey's band at the Horn Palace, afterward working in Shreveport, Louisiana, before becoming a member of Kelley's Bad Boys in Houston.[9] Like his black colleagues, Teagarden had been affected by hearing the blues, in his case as sung by the Empress of the Blues, Bessie Smith—not on her recordings but rather in person in Galveston. Also, as a boy, the trombonist heard spirituals and reported being able to sing them "with no trouble at all."[10] After touring the Southwest as far as California and into Mexico, first with R. J. Marin's Southern Trumpeters and then in 1924 with Doc Ross and his Jazz Bandits, Teagarden headed for New York City in the fall of 1927. As they say, the rest is history, for "Big T" revolutionized the role of the trombone in jazz through his recordings with any number of prominent groups in New York, from the orchestras of Roger Wolfe Kahn and Ben Pollack to studio bands led by Red Nichols, Benny Goodman, and even Louis Armstrong.

With respect to technique, Teagarden was the most advanced player on his instrument. When he arrived in New York, he brought with him a smoothness of execution on the trombone that had not been seen or heard before. Not even trombonist Jimmy Harrison of the Fletcher Henderson Orchestra, who was simultaneously developing a similar technical facility, was in the same category with Teagarden, who had been advertised even five years before as "The South's Greatest Sensational Trombone Wonder."[11] Teagarden's advanced, blues-based conception has even been compared with the revolutionary melodic and harmonic developments of bebop as conceived by Charlie Parker in the 1940s. In terms of the sheer number of recordings, Teagarden's more than 1,000 sides makes his discography "one of the most extensive in jazz, comparable to Louis Armstrong, Fats Waller, Duke Ellington, and Coleman Hawkins."[12] And as a vocalist, Teagarden has been considered the greatest white singer of the blues in all of jazz history.

Teagarden's career spanned the period from 1921 to his death in 1964 and took him around the world to acclaim in Europe and the Far East.

Future research into the development of Teagarden's jazz artistry will be aided significantly by an archive of the jazzman's life and music, compiled assiduously by Canadian Joe Showler of Toronto. Working with Robert Gibbona and Stephen La Vere, Showler spent two years in producing a 121-minute documentary of Teagarden's career, entitled *It's Time for "T": The Story of Trombonist Jack Teagarden* (1996), which was shown in the spring of 2001 to interested viewers on the campus of the University of Texas at Austin. One particular segment of the Showler film is representative of the kinds of materials in the collector's archive that are unknown to most students of jazz: a radio series played by the Ben Pollack Orchestra

Jack Teagarden (trombone) with Louis Armstrong (trumpet) and Bobby Hackett, from a rehearsal for a concert by Armstrong's All Stars at Town Hall, New York City, May 1947. Reproduced from *The New Grove Dictionary of Jazz*, vol. 2, edited by Barry Kernfield (1988).

for the Whiz anti-freeze company of Canada.[13] On the classic dixieland number "That's a Plenty," both Jack and his trumpet-playing brother Charlie contribute the finest solos on this 1930 side. Jack's extended ride is filled with his trademark turns that no other trombonist of the period could quite duplicate. His improvisation begins with a held and then repeated note that swings with the greatest intensity, and his virtuosity is exhibited through phrases that shift direction abruptly, even as he main-tains a tremendous drive and phenomenal control. It is to be hoped that the Showler archive will eventually come to the trombonist's home state as a resource for the study of the history of jazz as it developed in Texas and in particular through one of the music's major artists.

Charlie Teagarden, like his older brother Jack, also made a name for himself in the story of jazz. As demonstrated by the Whiz radio program recording from 1930, Charlie was by that year already a full-fledged jazz trumpeter. In addition to recording with his brother as part of the Ben Pollack Orchestra, the Mills Merry Makers, and some of the many Five Pennies aggregations led by Red Nichols, Charlie also joined Jack in the Paul Whiteman Orchestra, for which both men were featured soloists dur-ing the mid- to late 1930s. Charlie Teagarden is said to have never taken a bad solo, and in the 1950s he was playing as well if not better than he had in the 1930s when even then he could at times upstage his more famous sibling. This is true, for example, of Charlie's playing on *Jack Teagarden and His Band—1951, Live at the Royal Room, Hollywood,* one of several CDs produced by Joe Showler.[14] Clois Lee, another member of the Teagarden family, was a drummer known as Cub, who joined his oldest brother Jack in the orchestra that the latter formed in 1939. Sister Norma, a pianist, performed with her brothers on occasion, including the 1951 Royal Room appearance, at which even "Mama" Helen Teagarden was present as a guest pianist. Jazz was clearly a family affair with the Teagardens, as it was for many other Texas musicians, both white and black, among them brothers Budd and Keg Johnson as well as Eddie Durham and his cousins Allen Durham and Herschel Evans. But before moving on to black jazz musicians like these who made a name for them-selves in the 1930s, I would like to mention a few other figures in the 1920s, black and white, who, though not in the same class historically with the Teagardens, Johnsons, and Durhams, lend additional insight into the early awareness of jazz by Texas musicians and their ability to create this type of music on a level comparable with—or at least imitative of—that of such legendary jazzmen as King Oliver, Louis Armstrong, and Bix Beiderbecke.

Like Scott Joplin, cornetist-trumpeter Lammar Wright was born in Texarkana and made his reputation in Missouri, where Wright was a key member of the Bennie Moten band. Recording in 1923, the first year that both King Oliver and Louis Armstrong were immortalized on wax, the Moten band cut two sides, "Crawdad Blues" and "Elephant Wobble," on which Wright performs with a cup mute after the manner of King Oliver. Since Wright was only sixteen at the time and Oliver had been a major figure for a decade, it seems clear that Wright was aware of the King either from having heard him on riverboats or during the older musician's reported trips through Texas and Missouri. But even if Wright was influenced by Oliver, the younger musician could hold his own, especially in terms of a blues-inflected sound and style. Of Wright's playing on the 1923 "Crawdad Blues," one critic has declared that "it is doubtful if anything he has done since 1923 can surpass the beauty of the cornet work on this record; even the poor recording possible at this time cannot dim the immediacy of his searing, stabbing style."[15] Later, in 1929, Wright would record with the Missourians, a group that in the next year became the orchestra of singing star Cab Calloway. On the Calloway unit's recording of "Some of These Days," from December 23, 1930, Wright is the featured soloist on this side that critic Gunther Schuller has considered "amazing to this day for its hell-bent break-away tempo, upwards of 300 to the quarter-note beat . . . a staggering technical achievement . . . and . . . the fastest tempo achieved by any orchestra up to that time."[16] Wright remained with the Calloway organization until 1947, contributing throughout the 1930s a number of powerhouse solos in the King Oliver vein and serving throughout his years with Calloway as a strong section leader.

After King Oliver, the next great cornetist-trumpeter was Louis Armstrong, who is considered by many the most important figure in jazz history, owing to his role in making the music primarily an art of the improvised solo. On June 28, 1928, Armstrong and pianist Earl "Fatha" Hines recorded King Oliver's "West End Blues," and Armstrong's cadenza on this occasion demonstrated his up to that moment unmatched virtuosity. On December 5, 1928, Leroy Williams and his Dallas Band recorded "Going Away Blues," on which Williams plays a cornet cadenza that, as discographer Brian Rust has noted, "suggests that we have a potential rival to Louis Armstrong," although Rust goes on to assert that Williams's "other known records by no means bear this out."[17] As a matter of fact, another recording of a tune entitled "Tampa Shout," on which Williams leads the same ensemble and solos to fine effect, reveals that what Rust calls an "effortless introduction" to "Going Away Blues" was no fluke, that indeed on more than one occasion Williams was an impressive soloist in the New Orleans tradition.[18] Williams and his band may well have come from the Crescent City to Dallas, for the style of their jazz is in keeping with that of New Orleans, both from the point of view of their note choices and phrasing and of the group's instrumentation, which included banjo and brass tuba. The other soloists include alto saxophonist Lawson Brooks, who may have been related to Alva Brooks, an altoist in the 1930s with the outstanding San Antonio band of Boots Douglas, and Octave Gaspard, the brass tuba player who the year before, in December 1927, had recorded with Dallas blues singer Lillian Glinn.[19] The name Gaspard, like that of trombonist Fred Millet, is of French derivation and again suggests that this group probably originated in New Orleans. Their presence in Texas certainly must have contributed to an early awareness in the state of the grand tradition of New Orleans jazz, and especially in Dallas, which already by 1927 was the home of a number of future impact players at the national level, including saxophonists Budd Johnson and Buster Smith and trumpeter Oran "Hot Lips" Page.

While Austin has never been thought of as a jazz center, the state's capital city was in fact the birthplace of two notable jazzmen, pianist Teddy Wilson and bassist Gene Ramey, and the home for an important early period to two others, trumpeters Hot Lips Page and Kenny Dorham. Although a native of Dallas, Page was discovered working in Austin in 1927 by the Oklahoma Blue Devils band, which hired him away from Eddie and Sugar Lou's Hotel Tyler Orchestra. During 1929 and 1931 Eddie and Sugar Lou's orchestra recorded several sides, but it is clear from the group's recording of "There'll Be Some Changes Made," of October 1929, that the trumpeter who replaced Page, either Henry Thompson or Stanley Hardee, was neither technically nor imaginatively on a par with Hot Lips.[20] Fortunately, in 1929, Page, with his powerful drive and highly inventive, blues-tinged improvisations, would also be captured on wax when the Blue Devils made their only recordings, of two tunes entitled "Squabblin'" and "Blue Devil Blues."

Hot Lips Page's opening solo on "Blue Devil Blues" has been acclaimed for exhibiting "great rhythmic freedom" and as "a remarkably cohesive solo built on two ideas, both constantly varied."[21] In 1932 Hot Lips would record with the Bennie Moten Orchestra on a session that produced what critics have judged to have been "one of the dozen or so most thrilling single sessions in this history of jazz. Here is the epitome of the Kansas City big band sound before it became absorbed into the swing movement."[22] As one of the principal soloists in the Moten unit, Hot Lips can be heard in a classic, blues-inflected performance on the "hair-raising, exciting 'Toby,'" a Kansas City-style riff by Texan Eddie Durham "certainly known to all the black musicians of the day." Also on "Moten Swing," a piece arranged by Eddie Durham, Hot Lips has been praised for producing a solo of "pure melodic essence" and limiting himself to "a minimum of activity with a maximum of expression, a lesson Lester Young was to extend several years later."[23] In 1937 Page led his own short-lived band at Smalls' Paradise in New York, being promoted at the time as another trumpeter-singer in the Louis Armstrong mold by none other than Armstrong's own manager, Joe Glaser. Later, in 1941, Page would become the featured soloist for the highly popular white swing-era orchestra of Artie Shaw.

In the year following Hot Lips Page's first recording date of 1929, Tom Howell, another trumpet (or cornet) player, and his brother, trombonist Lee Howell, recorded in San Antonio with a group billed as Fred Gardner's Texas University Troubadours. On June 9, 1930, the Howells took part in the Troubadours' recording session that produced four tunes: "Loveless Love," "Papa's Gone," "No Trumps," and "Daniel's Blues."[24] Of Tom Howell, little was known, except for the suppositional information provided by Brian Rust in his discography for recording sessions from 1929 and 1930 and in his notes to a 1997 CD:

> Many years ago, someone in a defunct magazine tried a leg-pull suggesting that British reedman Freddy Gardner, on holiday in Texas, had gathered a band together in a recording studio and made these four numbers—and the cornetist was Bix Beiderbecke. It was in fact Tom Howell, a brilliant musician who later worked with Sunny Clapp and his Band o' Sunshine, and who may well have been a student at Texas at the time, along with his colleagues in the band.[25]

Although the registrar's records at the University of Texas at Austin are not complete, it is clear that Howell was on the campus as early as 1924. In 1929 he was photographed for the university's student annual, *The Cactus*, as part of Steve Gardner's Hokum Kings, which was composed of "university students, the pick of the campus musicians, and each man master of numerous instruments." Steve Gardner is identified in the photo caption as the "manager and director of the Hokum Kings," which, according to the annual, is "well known in musical circles. [Steve Gardner] is master and teacher of all instruments and head of the Department of Band, Orchestra and Public School Music in the University Conservatory of Music."[26] Other members of the unit were Chester Seekatz, who played saxophone, clarinet, soprano sax, and double clarinet; J. V. (Jaybird) Thomas on drums and traps; F. N. "Tommy" Howell on saxophone, clarinet, soprano sax, banjo, trumpet, and piano; Leland H. "Freshman" Adams on banjo, trombone, bass, trumpet, and piano; and Fred Gardner on saxophone, clarinet, soprano sax, and banjo.[27] Adding to the confusion in the historical record is the presence among this group of two musicians with the name Howell, the one referred to as "Tommy" and the other Thomas A., both able to play the trumpet. But it is obvious that the principal instrument of Thomas A. was the trumpet or cornet, and it seems evident that the trumpeter-cornetist on the 1930 recordings made in San Antonio was the same Thomas A., who was born Thomas Alva Howell Jr. in Belton, Texas, on May 6, 1906, and died on July 5, 1989, in Bexar County. Howell's father, Thomas Alva Sr., owned a music store in Cameron, a town midway between Temple and Bryan, and Tom Howell Jr. was the youngest of five brothers who in 1921 formed the Howell Brothers Moonshiner Orchestra, which played regularly for dances at the University of Texas in Austin and in the Central Texas area.[28]

The idea that Tom Howell was jokingly identified as the legendary cornetist Bix Beiderbecke is not surprising. His performance on "No Trumps" can easily be taken for the work of Beiderbecke, who died on August 7, 1931, slightly over a year after this side was recorded by the Texas University Troubadours. Howell's cornet tone, his upward rips, and his phrasing all recall Beiderbecke on this tune that is itself reminiscent of "At the Jazz Band Ball" as recorded by Bix and His Gang on October 5, 1927. Also, Fred Gardner's bending of his notes on tenor saxophone sounds close to the work of C-melody saxophonist Frankie Trumbauer, who in 1928 had recorded two classics with Bix, "I'm Coming Virginia" and

"Singin' the Blues." Furthermore, either pianist Tom Donahue or Tommy Howell plays in the style of Frank Signorelli, pianist on the 1927 Bix session that produced "At the Jazz Band Ball." While Tom Howell was undeniably influenced by Bix, the Texan has his own peculiar manner within the dixieland style. His notes are cleanly played, as Bix's were, and Howell executes some tricky phrases typical of Bix, even if on a couple of these he does not quite have the latter's control. Howell's second solo break on "No Trumps," on which he uses a mute, is also in imitation of Bix's approach yet contains the Texan's own tonal touches. On both solos, Howell drives with the same forcefulness and swing that were characteristic of Bix at his best. Present as well on the Texas University Troubadours recording is a violin break by Lew Bray, a very proficient soloist who forecasts the coming of western swing in Texas. The brass tuba player, John Gardner, pumps away quite wonderfully, and the overall ensemble renders this a splendid, swinging piece.

Tom Howell, Cameron, Texas, n.d. Used by permission of Pat Howell Crutsinger.

Another of the four sides also merits comment: "Daniel's Blues," with a vocal by drummer Jay "Bird" Thomas. What is striking about this tune (a fact not mentioned by Brian Rust in his notes to the session) is that its opening is the Troubadours' version of Duke Ellington's "The Mooche," which the composer first recorded in December 1928. Obviously Gardner and his men had heard the Ellington tune either through radio broadcasts from the Cotton Club in New York or on a recording, which reveals how up to the minute Texas jazz musicians were, as well as their good taste in picking up so early on this classic Ellington composition. The group captures perfectly the *misterioso* quality of the piece, and even after the side shifts to become more of a straight blues, tenorist Fred Gardner especially echoes the opening strains of Ellington's work. Howell's cornet again sounds like Beiderbecke, even though in more of a blues vein. Another notable feature of this side is that the vocal by Thomas includes the phrase "Honey, raise your window high," which would be made famous by blues shouter Jimmy Rushing of the Count Basie Orchestra, but only much later in the 1930s.

The year before the Troubadours' recording session, Howell also participated in a session with Sunny Clapp and His Band o' Sunshine. The Clapp band, with New Orleans clarinetist Sidney Arodin, recorded several sides on July 23, 1929, also in San Antonio.[29] On two of these sides, according to the Rust discography, there are two trumpeters, Bob Hutchingson and Tom Howell, even though the personnel listed on *Texas & Tennessee Territory Bands*, the CD that reissues the two sides, does not include Howell.[30] Nonetheless, it seems certain that Howell is present on both "Down on Biscayne Bay" and "We Can't Use Each Other Any More," where he must be the cornetist backing up the vocals credited to Hutchingson, who obviously cannot be singing and simultaneously playing the muted obbligatos. Furthermore, the sound of the cornetist behind Hutchingson is clearly in Howell's Bix-inspired style. Shedding further doubt on the reliability of the insert notes for the personnel is the fact that there is no trombone listed, and yet Rust includes in his discography trombonist Lee Howell, who must be the soloist on his instrument who takes breaks on both sides.[31] The Clapp band also recorded in New York in 1931, but the fine trumpet on the two sides from July 1, "Come Easy, Go Easy Love" and "When I Can't Be With You," included on *Texas & Tennessee Territory Bands*, does not at all sound like Howell, or Beiderbecke, and apparently is that of Bob Hutchingson.[32] In the end, however, none of these Texans from the bands of Fred Gardner and Sunny Clapp has survived in the mainstream history of great jazz, unlike a number of the black jazzmen from Texas who would have a profound impact on this music.

Budd and Keg Johnson of Dallas were members in the 1920s of several territory bands in Texas, including the Blue Moon Chasers, Ben Smith's Music Makers, and Gene Coy's Happy Black Aces. Both Budd and Keg had studied music in Dallas with Portia Pittman, the daughter of famed black author and educator Booker T. Washington. By 1929 the brothers were in Kansas City with the band of George Lee, with which Budd recorded in that year his first tenor solo, on "Paseo Street (Strut)."[33] In 1933 the Johnson brothers formed part of the Louis Armstrong Orchestra, which recorded several sides that have been singled out as exceptional, both for Armstrong's solos and for the contributions made by Budd on tenor and Keg on trombone. While critic James Lincoln Collier has lamented that an "excellent jazz player" like Keg Johnson "did not record often enough to receive the recognition he deserved," we do have fine outings by Keg on the 1933 Armstrong recordings of "Basin Street Blues," "Mahogany Hall Stomp," and "Laughin' Louie."[34] Of Keg Johnson's break on "Basin Street Blues," critic Gunther Schuller states that it is a "soulful open-toned, unfancy solo."[35] Keg's solos on the other two Armstrong sides exhibit the trombonist's exceptional work in the upper register of his horn. Keg also recorded impressively with the Benny Carter, Fletcher Henderson, and Cab Calloway orchestras, but of the two brothers, it is Budd Johnson whose name is more fully a part of the history of jazz.[36]

As a multi-reed man, Budd Johnson made a lasting contribution to jazz through his recordings with the Earl "Fatha" Hines Orchestra, for which during the late 1930s and early 1940s he was the straw boss, an important composer-arranger, and a soloist on clarinet, alto, and tenor. Budd also was involved in and helped organize the first bebop recording, made on February 16, 1944. His solo work on tenor resembles at times that of Lester Young, even though the two men developed their styles independently during the mid-1930s. On alto Budd could sound at times like a forerunner of the great Charlie Parker. One of Budd's most unusual and even startling solos was taken on clarinet with the Hines Orchestra on December 2, 1940, on the tune entitled "Jelly Jelly."[37] Budd's no-frills clarinet break has none of Benny Goodman's florid romanticism but delivers rather an intensely direct, penetrating, bluesy sound that goes straight to the soul.

In the mid-1960s, Budd Johnson was still performing at the highest artistic level with an Earl Hines combo that included Budd's fellow Texan Gene Ramey on bass. Having first recorded in 1929, as had the various white university musicians who were active at the time but who were essentially never heard from thereafter, Budd demonstrated his staying power in 1965 by offering a five-minute, master-class solo on "Sometimes I'm Happy," full of his "Texas honks" and his unending variations on the song's timeless theme.[38] Before his death on October 20, 1984, Budd Johnson had performed with a variety of important groups, among them the orchestras of Count Basie, Billy Eckstine, Dizzy Gillespie, Woody Herman, and Gil Evans, but as Gunther Schuller acknowledges, the Texas reedman had gotten his start and "had grown up with all the great Southwestern territory bands," and in many ways *that* is what made him the soulful, straight-ahead, exuberant soloist and the highly adventure-some composer-arranger that he was, qualities he possessed in common with so many of his Texas compatriots.[39]

Another Dallas reedman who would play a decisive role in the devel-opment of jazz was Buster Smith, whom critic Ross Russell characterized as the nearest thing to an "archetypal jazzman of the Southwest."[40] Like the Johnson brothers, Smith was active in the 1920s, but aside from local medicine show bands, he was principally a member of only one unit between 1925 and 1933, the legendary Blue Devils. This group, as we have seen, recorded in 1929, with Hot Lips Page on trumpet. Gunther Schuller has judged Smith's alto solos from this date to be "advanced for their time."[41] After a brief period with the Bennie Moten band in 1933 and with the Count Basie band of 1935, Smith formed his own group, which in 1938 included the soon-to-be major new jazz stylist, alto saxophonist Charlie Parker.

Much has been written about the influence of Buster Smith's alto approach on Parker, who clearly absorbed it from sitting next to "The Professor," as Smith was called. This seems undeniable in light of Buster's solos recorded on June 30, 1939, not with his own band, which unfortu-nately never made a single side, but with Hot Lips Page and pianist Pete Johnson. Smith's performance on "Baby, Look at You" is truly a new sound on his instrument—harder, more pristine, with no vibrato to speak of, unadorned, yet with a flexibility and flow that had not been heard before.[42] Although Smith's alto method would soon be mastered and bettered by Parker, Smith recorded in his groundbreaking style over a year prior to·

Parker's inaugural recording of November 1940. Smith also soloed on another side with Hot Lips Page—on a remarkable version of "I Ain't Got Nobody," recorded January 1, 1940.[43] As Budd Johnson once declared, and the evidence seems to support his claim, "[Charlie] Bird [Parker] really came from Buster Smith. Because when I was a kid Buster Smith was playing like that then. Way before Bird was ever born. In Dallas, Texas."[44] Indeed, Buster Smith, like Budd Johnson and Lips Page, had begun his career in the Southwestern, Dallas tradition of a blues-driven, direct-to-the-heart delivery.

Yet another highly influential jazz musician associated with Dallas was electric guitarist Charlie Christian, who was born on July 29, 1916, apparently in Bonham.[45] Christian first played string bass with the Dallas orchestra of Alphonse Trent, but once he began to concentrate on the electric guitar, in his hands it became a major jazz instrument, capable of long, flowing melodic improvisations filled with a combination of blues inflections and an expanded harmonic vocabulary. In his use of the amplified guitar, Christian was preceded by several performers on this type of instrument, among them Eddie Durham of San Marcos, Bob Dunn of Braggs, Oklahoma, and Leon McAuliffe from the Houston area. Durham was probably the first to amplify a standard guitar, placing a resonator inside it to project his sound, employing this homemade instrument at least by 1932 if not earlier. As a true jazz musician, Durham had first recorded on acoustic guitar in 1929 with Bennie Moten's band, and even then his solos looked forward to some extent to Charlie Christian's long-lined, single-note production. Durham initially recorded on amplified guitar on September 30, 1935, with the Jimmie Lunceford Orchestra, on Durham's own arrangement entitled "Hittin' the Bottle." But his most advanced guitar style can be heard on his arrangement entitled "Time Out," recorded with the Count Basie Orchestra on August 9, 1937.[46]

Prior to Durham's first recorded performance, Bob Dunn had recorded with the Texas Western Swing unit of Milton Brown and His Musical Brownies on January 27 and 28, 1935. On this date, Dunn played an amplified steel guitar, which primarily was utilized for Hawaiian music.[47] "Taking Off," from January 28, features Dunn's honking, trombonelike sound, and while his solo work is in a way swinging, one is hard put to call it jazz in the traditional sense of the word, since it leans toward a more countrified and Hawaiian tonality and phrasing.[48] As early as 1933, Leon McAuliffe also was playing amplified steel guitar, and in 1935 he joined

Bob Wills and His Texas Playboys, recording with the latter his own composition, "Steel Guitar Rag," during a session of September 29–30, 1936.[49] Again, McAuliffe's amplified steel guitar, like that of Dunn, is far from traditional jazz, and certainly McAuliffe's sound is light years away from the smooth drive, rich harmony, and imaginative contours of Charlie Christian's proto-bebop conception.

It is quite likely that Dunn's and McAuliffe's amplified steel guitars were heard by Christian on radio or on record and may have had an effect on his development of the jazz electric guitar. But undoubtedly it was Eddie Durham who served as an early influence on Christian; this is evident from the latter's solo on "Gone with What Draft" (or "Gilly"), from December 19, 1940.[50] Durham reported that Christian had approached him about his interest in learning the electric guitar, but even if this account is unconfirmed by any reference to Durham in Christian's essay on jazz guitar, published in December 1939,[51] the fact that Christian knew Durham's work is clear from his quotation of Durham's break on the latter's own arrangement of "Avalon," recorded with the Lunceford Orchestra on September 30, 1935.[52] Nonetheless, even if Durham is more in the mainstream jazz tradition than either Dunn or McAuliffe, Durham's notes and his overall style are essentially different from Christian's. On amplified guitar, Charlie is simply a more fluent, more imaginative performer than all three of his predecessors.

What critic Bill Simon has said of the contrast between French jazz guitarist Django Reinhardt and Charlie Christian holds true in part for the difference between Christian and his three Southwestern contemporaries: "[Django] brought new, exotic and showy elements into jazz; still he himself never came close to the core of jazz. One has only to compare [Django's] frothy, though fertile, inventions with the driving, earthy improvisations of young Christian to understand the difference."[53] Gunther Schuller has concisely summarized the relationship between Christian and his roots in the Southwest by answering a question asked by Teddy Hill, manager of the original bebop venue, Minton's Playhouse, in Harlem. Hill asked of Christian, "Where did he come from?" and Schuller has replied in print by referring to "the kind of musical origins that could produce such a major innovative talent":

> The simple short answer is that the Southwest is guitar country and
> blues country, the Texas blues tradition particularly being one of the

oldest indigenous traditions and probably much older than the New Orleans idiom that is generally thought to be the primary fountainhead of jazz. And Christian embraced all of that: a guitarist who brought the Southwestern blues into modern jazz—and more.[54]

But one of many recordings that reveals Christian's very bluesy feeling—as well as his ability to quote phrases from various sources, to incorporate them into his improvisation, and to imitate through his electric guitar the sound of the tenor saxophone—is his version of "Star Dust," from early March 1940. This particular performance was taped in Minneapolis with Jerry Jerome on tenor (a regular at the time with the Benny Goodman Orchestra, with which Christian was featured on "Solo Flight" from March 4, 1941, in addition to his many recordings with the Goodman Sextet), Frankie Hines on piano, and an unidentified bass and drums.[55] Here Christian quotes from the pop-tune "Pretty Baby" and Duke Ellington's "I Let a Song Go Out of My Heart," sounding at times like Jerome's tenor, even as Charlie creates his trademark long, melodic lines laced with surprising leaps and swinging runs. Another standout side is entitled "Blues in B," which was a fully improvised performance captured on March 13, 1941, while the Benny Goodman Sextet members were awaiting the leader's arrival for a recording session. One can hear Christian modulate into the unusual key of B at the suggestion of another of the sidemen, and then begin to chord the blues with an extraordinary drive that does, as Gunther Schuller suggests, bring the grand tradition of Texas blues guitar—from Blind Lemon Jefferson through Eddie Durham—to bear on developments in jazz that at the time were characterized by a piece entitled "Swing to Bop" (based on Durham's classic tune "Topsy"), which marked a change to which Charlie Christian fundamentally contributed.[56]

Innumerable other Texans also made important contributions to the swing and bebop movements. To name but a few: Clarence Hutchenrider of Waco, who, during his years with the Casa Loma Orchestra from 1931 to 1943, was "a superb clarinetist" able to take his place "alongside the best jazzmen";[57] Carl "Tatti" Smith of Marshall, who, to judge from his presence on the first recordings by tenor great Lester "Prez" Young in 1936, was unfortunately a rarely recorded trumpeter with an expressiveness and fluidity of execution close to those of the "President";[58] Harry James of Beaumont, who, as a member of the Benny Goodman Orchestra and the leader of his own band, was probably the most popular trumpeter of the swing era;[59] and tenor saxophonist Herschel Evans of Denton, who starred in the late 1930s with the Count Basie Orchestra as a bursting-at-the-seams, big-toned foil to Lester Young's lean, lithe, and ethereal mode.[60]

Clarence Hutchenrider, born June 13, 1908, led his own band at age fourteen and in the late 1920s played at the Adolphus Hotel in Dallas in the band of Jack Gardner, who himself would later in 1939 serve as the pianist in Harry James's first big band. Like so many Texans in jazz, Hutchenrider and Gardner were active early in the history of the music, performing during its first decade in territory bands, and then in the 1930s as members of some of the prominent units of the swing era. In addition to clarinet, Hutchenrider also excelled on alto and baritone; in fact, for my taste, his two highly swinging baritone choruses on "I Got Rhythm," from December 30, 1933, are superior to any solos he took on clarinet.[61] Carl "Tatti" Smith, also born in 1908, was a member of a number of territory bands, including those of Alphonse Trent, Terrence Holden, and Gene Coy. In 1936 Smith became a sideman with the Count Basie Orchestra, serving as well in that year as the nominal co-leader of the group known as Jones-Smith, Inc., which produced the classic Lester Young recording of "Oh! Lady Be Good," with Smith making an impressive contribution on trumpet.[62] Born March 15, 1916, in Albany, Georgia, Harry James got his start in 1931 when his circus family settled in Beaumont and he began playing with local groups like the Old Phillips Friars and the bands of Logan Hancock and Herman Waldman before being picked up by Ben Pollack in 1935 and later joining Benny Goodman in 1937. Herschel Evans, born in 1909, first recorded in San Antonio in 1929 with the Troy Floyd Orchestra, which cut two sides of a tune entitled "Dreamland Blues, Parts 1 and 2."[63] One commentator has noted that even at this early date "Herschel Evans's first recorded solo is a minor landmark in tenor saxophone style and shows that he was securely rooted in the Texas blues tradition."[64] But it was as a member of the Basie band, beginning in 1935, that Evans helped establish what became known as "the Texas tenor" sound.

The Texas tenor tradition that derived from Herschel Evans was principally carried on by tenor saxophonist Buddy Tate of Sherman and two tenorists from Houston, Illinois Jacquet and Arnett Cobb.[65] Tate, born February 22, 1914, took Evans's chair in the Basie band on Herschel's death of a cardiac condition in 1939. Evans and Tate had played together in the San Antonio band of Troy Floyd, and Tate, like both Evans and Carl "Tatti" Smith, had been with a number of territory bands. Tate's solos with the Basie band are perhaps even bigger-toned than Evans's, and much more daring, as evinced by his improvisation on "Seventh Avenue Express" from October 19, 1947.[66]

Both Illinois Jacquet (born in Louisiana in 1922 but from age one a resident of Houston) and Arnett Cobb (born in Houston in 1918) were members of the Houston band of Milt Larkin, who was born in the Bayou City on October 10, 1910, took up the trumpet under the influence of New Orleans cornetist Bunk Johnson, and formed his own unit in 1936. The Larkin outfit has been considered "probably the last of the great Texas bands."[67] Possibly even before Larkin was born, Houston was visited by the self-proclaimed inventor of jazz, Ferdinand "Jelly Roll" Morton, who looked up the piano players in Houston and declared that "they were all terrible."[68] While this may have been true at the time, in the early 1920s Hersal Thomas and his father George W. Thomas of Houston would prove important boogie-woogie pianists, and Houston also would produce a number of vital blues singers who recorded in the 1920s with the leading jazzmen of the era, including King Oliver and Louis Armstrong.[69] By the late 1930s, when the nationally known orchestras of Jimmie Lunceford and Cab Calloway came through Houston, they received "rough treatment" at the hands of the local Milt Larkin band, which battled other units "every Sunday for years at the old Harlem Square Club in Houston."[70] In 1942 Illinois Jacquet left the Larkin band to become the star tenor soloist with the Lionel Hampton Orchestra, with which he recorded in New York a chorus on "Flying Home" that "triggered a whole generation of big-toned, extrovert sax solos."[71] Jacquet also would be a featured soloist with the Count Basie Orchestra from 1945 to 1946.

Following in the same tenor tradition of Herschel Evans, Buddy Tate, and Illinois Jacquet, Arnett Cobb likewise starred with the Hampton Orchestra, soloing on "Flying Home No. 2" in 1944, but adding to Jacquet's honks, squeals, shakes, and stratospheric high notes Cobb's own "vocal and drawling" sound full of "grunts, hoots, and wrenching wails," all of which would characterize the "Texas tenor style."[72] Cobb once described the origins of his full-toned "Texas" sound as deriving from the fact that he would practice in a large field near his home in Houston's Fifth Ward, which required him "to fill up the open space."[73]

Other important figures from Houston who were associated with Milt Larkin include alto saxophonist Eddie "Cleanhead" Vinson, pianist-arranger Cedric Haywood, and altoist Jimmy Ford. Vinson would make a name for himself both as an altoist and a blues singer, principally through his hit song "Kidney Stew Blues," recorded in 1945 with his own band. Vinson's group at the time included tenorist John Coltrane and Dallas pianist Red Garland, both of whom would in the 1950s star with the Miles Davis Quintet. Cedric Haywood's tune "Hot Rod" would be recorded in 1947 by Illinois Jacquet's own group, which included Jacquet's brother Russell, who had also been a member of the Larkin band, and baritone saxophonist Maurice Simon, another Houston native but never a member of the Larkin unit.[74] Jimmy Ford had played the Eldorado, Houston's jazz ballroom, in 1947, and after a short time in New York, he was back in Houston working with Milt Larkin. In 1948 Ford returned to New York and joined the Tadd Dameron band, which included some of the giants of bebop, among them Fats Navarro and Kenny Clarke. Russell Jacquet, like a number of Texans, would study at Wiley College in Marshall, and it was in Russell's own California band that one of the central bebop figures from Texas, trumpeter Kenny Dorham, landed his first important job. Dorham too had studied in Marshall, as had pianist-arranger Wild Bill Davis (who worked with the Milt Larkin band beginning in 1939) and trombonist Henry Coker of Dallas (a soloist in the 1950s and 1960s with the Count Basie band). Galveston also produced two fine musicians in drummer G. T. Hogan and trumpeter Richard "Notes" Williams, the latter featured with the Charles Mingus Jazz Workshop in the late 1950s and early 1960s. Born in Houston between 1938 and 1940, Stix Hooper, Hubert Laws, Wilton Felder, and Joe Sample were students at Texas Southern University before forming their group known as the Jazz Crusaders, which would create a type of early fusion jazz in the 1960s.

After working with Russell Jacquet in California, Kenny Dorham moved on to New York where he joined the Dizzy Gillespie big band in 1945, and in January 1946 he recorded with the Billy Eckstine Orchestra, soloing on his own composition, "The Jitney Man."[75] Dorham, born in Post Oak, Texas, on August 30, 1924, first played the piano at age seven but then switched to trumpet when he attended high school in Austin. Like Arnett Cobb, Dorham seems to have been influenced in his style by the Texas landscape, as critic Doug Ramsey suggests when he comments that "a hallmark of [Dorham's] playing was an expansiveness that reflected the open spaces and freedom of his youth."[76] Dorham's "Fragments of an Autobiography," which appeared in *Down Beat Music '70*, is a revealing account of his early years when he took part in cattle roundups and was subsequently first exposed to jazz through the music of Louis Armstrong. Once in New York, Dorham's style developed quickly, especially under the tutelage of bebop genius Charlie Parker, who took the Texan into his quintet with the departure in 1948 of Miles Davis. During his two years with Parker, Dorham performed in Paris at the first international jazz festival and recorded with many other leaders of the bebop movement, including Bud Powell, Kenny Clarke, Fats Navarro, and Milt Jackson. While with the Eckstine Orchestra, Dorham worked with drummer Art Blakey, with whom in the 1950s Dorham and Horace Silver formed the original Jazz Messengers. Dorham first recorded with a Blakey group in December 1947, when the latter's octet, called simply the Messengers, cut four sides, one of which was Dorham's original tune "The Thin Man."[77] As trumpet soloist, ensemble player, leader of his own group the Jazz Prophets, and composer and arranger, Dorham left a rich legacy that is still being discovered and re-released on countless CDs.[78]

Prior to Kenny Dorham's arrival in Austin in the 1930s, Gene Ramey, born in the capital city on April 4, 1913, had already been active in the local band of George Corley, which in 1930 also included tenorist Herschel Evans. Corley, who was born in Austin on September 12, 1912, played trombone in the high school band, along with his brothers Wilford on tenor sax and John on trumpet, with whom he formed the Royal Aces. Later, in 1937 and 1938, Corley recorded with the San Antonio band of drummer Clifford "Boots" Douglas (born in Temple on September 7, 1908), but the trombonist never made it in the big time as Gene Ramey did.[79] Originally playing sousaphone with the Royal Aces, Ramey moved on to Kansas City in 1932 and studied the string bass with Walter Page, who in 1936 would become part of the Count Basie All-American Rhythm Section. In Kansas City, Ramey regularly practiced with Charlie Parker while serving as the bassist for the Jay McShann Orchestra, the last great Kansas City big band. While with McShann, Parker made his first recordings, accompanied on bass by Ramey and on drums by Gus Johnson, who was born in Tyler on November 15, 1913. Ramey would later perform on some of the first recording sessions of the modern jazz giant Thelonious Monk as well as with a wide variety of big bands and smaller groups, including the combo of Lester Young. Gus Johnson subsequently became the drummer of the Count Basie band in the early 1950s.

Oscar Moore, another Austinite, played a prominent role in the jazz scene of the 1940s. Born on December 25, 1912, Moore was an advanced guitarist who developed independently of Charlie Christian and served as a vital member of the Nat King Cole Trio. As noted earlier, another outstanding Austin-born jazz musician was Teddy Wilson, star of the Benny Goodman Trio and Quartet. Like Oscar Moore, Wilson, born in Austin on November 24, 1912, left Texas at an early age, although in Wilson's case he seemed attracted throughout his career to groups whose members included Texans, among them Budd and Keg Johnson, Harry James, Jack Teagarden, Herschel Evans, and Eddie Durham. Like Gene Ramey and Gus Johnson with the McShann Orchestra, Wilson and other natives of the state often teamed up and seemed mutually inspired by their shared Texas origins.

Along with Dallas, Houston, and Austin, Fort Worth is the other Texas city whose many musicians have made a lasting mark on the history of jazz. One of the earliest natives of Cowtown to figure in the story of jazz was Euday L. Bowman, who was born in Fort Worth on November 9, 1887. Bowman's famous "Twelfth Street Rag" was recorded by almost every important swing band of the 1930s, and on many occasions the recordings involved evolutionary improvisations by such soloists as Louis Armstrong and Lester Young.[80] Other Fort Worth musicians who contributed to various developments in the history of jazz include two members of the Glenn Miller Orchestra: tenor saxophonist and vocalist Tex Beneke (born February 12, 1914) and trumpeter Clyde Hurley (born September 3, 1916). Both of these men were often featured by Miller as soloists, most famously on "In the Mood" in 1939 when Hurley, who had studied music at Texas Christian University in Fort Worth, performed the tune's memorable trumpet solo.[81] Drummer Ray McKinley, born in Cowtown on June 18, 1910, formed part of the Miller organization during World War Two.

The most significant figure in jazz history to hail from Fort Worth is indisputably Ornette Coleman, who was born there on March 19, 1930. Coleman made a profound impact on jazz beginning in the late 1950s, after he had gotten his start at Fort Worth's I. M. Terrell High School, where a number of other figures associated with the so-called Free Jazz movement also began their careers, among them Dewey Redman, born in Fort Worth on May 17, 1931. Coleman was influenced early on by the blues and Mexican American and country-western sounds that he heard around him, but also by the bebop tradition, which he had mastered by 1947. In high school, when Coleman improvised in the bebop vein on John Philip Sousa's "Washington Post March," he was booted out of the band, but would go on to revolutionize jazz through his keyless compositions and extended improvisations full of Southwestern harmolodics. According to another alumnus of I. M. Terrell and a classmate of Ornette Coleman, clarinetist John Carter, who was born in Fort Worth on September 24, 1939, Coleman, Cowtown drummer Charles Moffett (born September 11, 1929), and Carter would practice together in "an upstairs joint" in Fort Worth where they would "work hard on [their] bop repertoire and at the same time develop [their] personal styles." Carter reported that in the 1940s they were "all stone boppers."[82] Dewey Redman similarly worked on his jazz in the area of Rosedale Street on Fort Worth's southeast side where dozens of "uniquely trained young musicians . . . were either born or weaned musically."[83]

Other Texas cities and towns also produced jazz musicians who made a name for themselves. Like so many of the other figures mentioned here, Emilio and Ernie Caceres and their cousin Johnny Gomez of South Texas were relatives who formed a family band, in their case a string trio that created "some of the hottest music around San Antonio."[84] In 1937 the trio recorded in New York City after having appeared on Benny Goodman's "Camel Caravan" radio show. Born in Rockport on November 22, 1911, Ernie would subsequently become an important sideman in the orchestras of Glenn Miller and Jack Teagarden. Yet another musician who would figure prominently in major orchestras was trombonist Tyree Glenn, born in Corsicana on November 23, 1912. Glenn was a featured soloist during his tenure with the orchestras of Cab Calloway, Benny Carter, and Duke Ellington, and during his five years with the Ellington orchestra, beginning in 1946, Glenn not only carried on the tradition of Ellington's earlier trombonists, Charlie Irvis and Tricky Sam Nanton, but he also soloed on vibraharp, notably for the Carnegie Hall premiere of Ellington's *Liberian Suite* on December 26, 1947.[85]

Although this overview has been limited largely to a thirty-year period, from 1920 to 1950, the story of Texans in jazz has continued to the present day with the contributions after 1950 of a number of vital figures. Booker Ervin of Denison and John Handy of Dallas, along with Richard "Notes" Williams of Galveston, were members of and recorded frequently with the important Charles Mingus Workshop, and Leo Wright of Wichita Falls starred with the Dizzy Gillespie Quintet and Orchestra.[86] The part played by these and other Texans has been considerable, and was even indispensable to the types of jazz created by Ellington, Mingus, Monk,

Parker, Basie, and so many other giants of this music. Even without including any discussion here of the Texans who came after 1950, there were, as we have seen, numerous sidemen from Texas who were active from the beginnings of recorded jazz up to mid-century and who deeply affected the artistry and appeal of this American music.[87]

While it is possible to list Texans from almost every part of the state who were members of the leading jazz units from the 1930s on, it is perhaps difficult to determine in many cases how their Texas roots contributed to the kinds of jazz that were produced by the various groups with which they performed. Nonetheless, it seems clear that at the very least the Texas blues tradition has been inherent to the creativity of almost every Texas jazz musician. It also appears evident that the state was in no way isolated from but played a crucial role in the creation of every phase of jazz, from hot to swing to bebop and beyond. High school and college music programs, local jazz units and their inspirational performers, and access to traveling shows, radio broadcasts, and recordings all made it possible for aspiring Texas jazz musicians to imitate the leading musicians and even to excel themselves as creative artists. While Texas may be better known today as a crucible for country-western, conjunto, and western swing music, the state has equally been the home of some of the most remarkable figures in the history of jazz. And once again, almost every section of the state can lay claim to a jazz musician whose roots were formed in its peculiar climate and terrain and whose place in the annals of jazz has been documented by the encyclopedias and histories of this native American music recognized around the world as one of the greatest forms of twentieth-century art.

The Bebop Revolution
in Words and Music

dial

203-B

1. EMBRACEABLE YOU
2. DEWEY SQUARE
3. QUASIMADO
4. SCRAPPLE FROM APPLE

33⅓ RPM   MICRO GROOVE LP

CHARLIE PARKER SEXTET

CHARLIE PARKER......Alto Sax
MILES DAVIS............Trumpet
J. J. JOHNSON........Trombone
DUKE JORDAN.............Piano
TOMMY POTTER.............Bass
MAX ROACH..............Drums

CONTEMPORARY CLASSICS

FROM BEBOP TO HARD BOP AND BEYOND
The Texas Jazz Connections

I n 1955 Harold Meehan, my orchestra teacher at South
Park High School in Beaumont, proved the open sesame
to many a wondrous unknown world, and in particular
to the one of recorded bebop. Pictured on the covers of several albums that Mr. Meehan purchased with district funds
were altoist Charlie "Bird" Parker and trumpeter John Birks
"Dizzy" Gillespie, the two inventors of that challenging 1940s
form of African American music. Long before 1955, the year

of Parker's death at age thirty-five, bebop had already established itself as required thinking for all avant-garde practitioners of jazz. But as an aspiring trumpet player myself, I immediately felt on hearing such music that in terms of theory and technique it was beyond anything I could ever hope to understand or perform.

Dizzy Gillespie's phenomenally fast runs and his stratospheric high notes were to me completely inconceivable. Not even trumpet star Harry James, who had grown up in Beaumont, came close to Gillespie's breathtaking, pyrotechnical brilliance, since James's virtuosic performance of "Flight of the Bumble Bee" was a mere showpiece with nothing of bebop's ingenious improvisational artistry. Indeed, Parker and Gillespie's playing of their intricate "contrafacts"—that is, tunes entitled "Anthropology" or "Ornithology" but based, as I would learn much later, on the pop songs "I Got Rhythm" and "How High the Moon"—was unlike anything James ever attempted in the late 1930s when he recorded with the Benny Goodman Orchestra or even in the 1940s and 1950s with his own big bands. All of this I could recognize even if I could not comprehend the harmonic differences between swing and bebop and was not at that point aware of the evolutionary developments that led to the emergence of the latter's musical language.

What I never suspected in 1955 and did not learn for many years thereafter was the fundamental contribution made to this "new" music by Texans, including even Harry James, but more notably by a number of black musicians: Buster Smith, Gene Ramey, Budd Johnson, Charlie Christian, and Kenny Dorham, among others. All of these jazz figures were alive and active in 1955, with the exception of Christian, who had died in 1942 at age twenty-six. The only one of these figures that I would meet in person was bassist Gene Ramey, who in the 1970s returned from New York to his hometown of Austin. In the early 1980s, my son and I shook hands with Ramey after having viewed him on screen, in Batts Hall at the University of Texas at Austin, talking and performing in *The Last of the Blue Devils*, a documentary film on that vital Southwestern territory band.[1] Also featured in this film are Buster Smith of Dallas and Eddie Durham of San Marcos, two of the Blue Devils' major stars. Early in the career of Charlie Parker, both Smith and Ramey performed with the Bird, and

Ramey recorded with the altoist in the Jay McShann Orchestra. Ramey also recorded with such bebop greats as trumpeter Fats Navarro and baritonist Leo Parker.

In 1955 I knew none of this, and the closest thing to a living bebop musician that I could hear in Beaumont, or anywhere in Texas so far as I was aware, was Harold Meehan, who played "legit" violin in the symphony but jazz alto sax when he could find jobs with local bands. Of course, my awareness of jazz activity in Beaumont was limited at the time by segregation. The black high schools may have produced many gifted musicians, but I never had an opportunity to hear them perform. However, in 1958 at then Lamar Tech, the city's four-year college, there was a trumpeter—the first black musician I ever knew personally and the only one majoring in music—who could play in the style of Clifford Brown, the marvelous second-generation bebopper whose Pacific Jazz album from 1954 I had found in a neighborhood record shop.[2] Unfortunately, this student musician was not a good sight reader and apparently gave up college when he failed to make his grades.

The question of which ability is preferable in jazz—reading or playing by ear—has always stirred up controversy among aficionados of the music. The great white cornetist, Bix Beiderbecke, was a poor reader for most of his life, yet few instrumentalists have ever matched the beauty of his sound or the inventiveness of his melodic improvisations. Even Erroll Garner, the phenomenal pianist, never learned to read music, and pianist Dave Brubeck graduated from college as a music major without being able to read the notes he played! For some jazz enthusiasts, the further an individual or group strays from improvisation and depends rather on written music, the less genuine and inspiring the performance. However, even black jazz musicians who could read "charts" were highly critical of those who were "illiterate." For some listeners, it is a combination of improvised and composed jazz that results in the finest work in this African American musical form—the term itself a reminder that such music is something of a blend of aural African and written European traditions. In the case of bebop, a jazz musician like Budd Johnson of Dallas emphasized the necessity for having bebop themes notated, because otherwise they were too difficult to perform. On the other hand, a jazz composer of the bebop era like the marvelous Thelonious Monk—whose music was recorded with the help of both Gene Ramey and trumpeter Kenny Dorham—would teach his band members a new tune by playing their parts on the piano before he would show them a written score. This would certainly have been the case with Monk's most treacherous composition, "Skippy," which he rarely recorded, the first time in 1952 with Dorham on trumpet.[3]

In 1952, when Harold Meehan moved to Beaumont from his native St. Louis, he brought with him a firsthand knowledge of bebop, from having attended performances by Charlie Parker, trumpeter Miles Davis, and drummer Max Roach. In 1945, while serving in World War Two, Mr. Meehan had heard the Dizzy Gillespie big band in South Carolina at a time when the group would have included Kenny Dorham. In April 1946 Mr. Meehan was discharged and returned to St. Louis where he studied violin at the city's Institute of Music and regularly listened to such bebop classics as "Groovin' High," "Koko," and "Ornithology" on a jukebox at Bal Tabern. On first hearing bebop, Mr. Meehan had wondered why Gillespie played so many weird, dissonant notes, but by 1946 he was a convert to the new music. He would haunt the St. Louis nightspots with other white musicians who "dug" bebop, especially Eddie Johnson, who could scat-sing Bird and Dizzy's most famous solos. Mr. Meehan remembered Parker clowning on stage at the St. Louis Birdland, puffing through his fingers as if he were smoking pot. On one occasion, when Stan Kenton's Orchestra came to the city's Tune Town Ballroom, Mr. Meehan spoke with bop trombonist Kai Winding, and during this same period he also chatted with Max Roach, who told him that a bebop drummer could not be metronomic in his playing because a bop ensemble weaves a little off the beat, so the drummer must go with the band.

Although Mr. Meehan arrived in Beaumont with a keen appreciation for bebop, he soon discovered that there was little in the local music scene to encourage this kind of jazz. Most "gigs" were designed for businessmen dances or a type of polite-society Muzak, not serious improvisation. While he tried to interest us students in bebop, he could not realistically expect us to be anything but intimidated by what we heard. And yet his early introduction of bebop made a lasting impression—at least on me—and would lead to a lifetime of listening pleasure. Eventually this early exposure to the music would stimulate my interest in the role played by Texans in the history of jazz, including the bebop movement. But it was only in the late 1980s that I was struck by the revelation that Texans not only influenced the creation of bebop but also affected all the major forms of jazz music, from ragtime (Scott Joplin of Texarkana), blues (Blind Lemon Jefferson of Wortham, Sippie Wallace of Houston, Lillian Glinn of Dallas), and boogie-woogie (Hersal Thomas of Houston) to hot jazz, swing, and—following from bebop—hard bop and free or harmolodic jazz. Indeed, not only did Texas musicians contribute to the evolutionary developments leading up to bebop but several participated in historic recordings that helped make this form of jazz one of the most profound expressions of African American culture.

Prior to the classic bebop recordings that Parker and Gillespie cut in 1945, these two jazz giants crossed paths with a number of Texans who played crucial roles in Bird's and Dizzy's early careers. In 1932 Parker first met Buster Smith, who would become Bird's mentor on alto saxophone. Born in Alsdorf, south of Dallas, in 1904, Smith was self-taught on clarinet and alto and also as a composer-arranger. Credited with some of the finest and most advanced big-band arrangements of the 1930s, Smith collaborated with two other Texans, Eddie Durham of San Marcos and trumpeter Oran "Hot Lips" Page of Dallas, in the writing of the Count Basie theme song "One O'Clock Jump." Like many other Texas blues-based musicians, Buster Smith got his start on the streets of the Deep Ellum section of East Dallas where guitarist-singers Blind Lemon Jefferson, Leadbelly, and T-Bone Walker entertained along Elm Street and Central Avenue. Smith began with the Voddie White Trio at the Tip Top Club on Central, performed with medicine shows, and by 1925 had been recruited by the Blue Devils out of Oklahoma City. In November 1929, Smith made his first recording, and his alto chorus on the Blue Devils' "Squabblin'" has been heard by jazz critics Ross Russell and Gunther Schuller as a presaging of Charlie Parker's style and conception. The same fluid lines, which were new to saxophone performance at the time, the airy tone, and the floating, bluesy sound of Smith's chorus are all characteristic of Parker's approach to jazz alto.

Buster Smith's impact on the younger Parker came primarily through the fact that Charlie signed up in 1937 as a member of Buster's own band. During this formative period, Bird shared choruses with "Professor" Smith, and he obviously emulated his leader's method and manner. One important effect of working with the Smith band would surely have been Parker's learning from the leader his facility for setting riffs—short, repeated phrases against which soloists would improvise their own melodic lines. An outstanding example of the riff is found in "One O'Clock Jump," which, as noted above, is credited to Smith and his fellow Texans, Durham and Page. Such riffs became the basis of various bebop tunes, like

Gillespie's classic "Salt Peanuts," a riff widely quoted, for example, in "Bop Bounce," a 1948 recording by the Benny Carter Orchestra. The Carter recording includes a trombone solo by Henry Coker of Dallas, who would later become the lead trombonist in Count Basie's "New Testament" band. Although riffs were utilized throughout the swing era, their origins in the blues are documented by 1920s recordings made by the Central Texas "King of the Country Blues," Blind Lemon Jefferson. Territory bands of the Southwest, which included many Texas sidemen, employed Lemon's blues practice of building improvisations over one or a series of memorable riffs. In part, bebop style also derived from riff-like figures, with such repeated patterns allowing for complex and imaginative solo flights that yet remained rooted in a folklike phrase or chord progression.

Charlie Parker's technical virtuosity on alto at age nineteen was owing largely to his early mastery of his instrument through intense practice. One of the secrets to his amazing improvisational skill was his ability to play a tune in any of the twelve keys, whereas most players were limited to those with fewer flats and sharps, such as C or B-flat major. According to Gene Ramey, who knew Parker in the early 1930s and toured with him in the Jay McShann Orchestra beginning in 1939, Parker was encouraged by the bassist to "jam" everyday, with the two men working out together the relationships between notes and chords. McShann, a blues and boogie-woogie pianist, formed his band after the grand tradition of the Kansas City units of Bennie Moten and Count Basie, which featured strong rhythm sections for their bands' shouting, riff-style blues. With Ramey on bass, Gus Johnson of Tyler on percussion, and McShann on piano, the band's rhythm section formed a firm foundation on which Charlie Parker developed his swinging, highly inventive melodic and rhythmic improvisations. Bird's first recordings, made with the McShann Orchestra in 1940, are astonishing displays of his technical and imaginative prowess, even though these performances are still basically in the swing tradition. After some three years with McShann, Parker left for New York City, where he joined the Earl Hines Orchestra, taking the place of Texan Budd Johnson, who, as the leader's straw boss, had already hired Dizzy Gillespie for the Hines organization. It was at this time that Bird and Diz began to experiment with altered chords and to produce what bandleader Cab Calloway characterized snidely as Gillespie's "Chinese music."

Budd Johnson of Dallas has primarily been credited in the history of bebop for his part in organizing the first recording session for the new music, held early in 1944. During this same year, Johnson was a member, along with Dizzy Gillespie and Oscar Pettiford, of the first organized small bebop combo, which performed at New York's Onyx Club on 52nd Street. In addition, Johnson wrote arrangements for and soloed with the Billy Eckstine Orchestra, which also featured Parker and Gillespie and was involved in the transition from swing to bebop. Johnson was an example of the type of Texas jazz musician who received important training as a youngster, in his case through lessons taken with local Dallas music teachers, including Portia Pittman, the daughter of educator Booker T. Washington. Johnson's arrangements and compositions for the Earl Hines, Boyd Raeburn, and Billy Eckstine bands, among many others, were largely in the blues-based riff style, and for the first bebop recording date in 1944, Johnson co-composed with pianist Clyde Hart the "hip" riff tune entitled "Bu Dee Daht." Later, in 1960, Johnson composed and arranged "Trinity River Bottom," a piece for himself on tenor sax, accompanied by four trumpets. Of this composition named after his hometown river, Johnson commented that in Dallas the Trinity River "has caused a lot of trouble and taken a lot of lives so I always associate it with people having a hard time. I therefore thought there ought to be a blues about it."[4] As with so many other Texas jazz musicians, Budd Johnson reflected his Texas background in his writing and playing—in particular a riff tradition deriving from the country blues—whether he was performing swing or bebop, or, in the early 1960s, the experimental orchestrations of Gil Evans, a collaborator with Miles Davis, one of the early proponents of bebop and later of cool jazz during the hard-bop era.

Another Texas composer-arranger noted for his work in the blues-riff mode was Eddie Durham. One of the principal composer-arrangers for the Bennie Moten, Jimmie Lunceford, and Count Basie orchestras, Durham helped give definition to the riff style prevalent in much swing-era dance music. Equally important was Durham's influence as the first jazzman to record on an amplified guitar, which would encourage the career of Charlie Christian of Bonham, who became a major figure in the transition from swing to bebop. From Durham's father, who was an Irish Mexican (his mother part African American and part Native American), Eddie learned the folk-music practice of filling a cigar-box fiddle with snake rattles. Later he would place a resonator with a tin pie plate inside his acoustic guitar in order to amplify the sound as bands became larger and louder. Eventually, Durham found a commercial amplified guitar, with which in 1935 he recorded his own arrangement of "Hittin' the Bottle" with the Lunceford Orchestra.

One reaction to the elephantiasis of the big bands was bebop's return to the five-piece instrumentation of early jazz, as represented by Louis Armstrong's Hot Five of 1925. In 1936, even before bebop reduced the size of a normal jazz ensemble from big band to combo, trumpeter Carl "Tatti" Smith of Marshall was the nominal co-leader for a session of Jones-Smith, Inc., a quintet featuring tenorist Lester Young, whose first recordings on this date significantly influenced Charlie Parker. In 1938 Eddie Durham headed up another recording date with Young, and on this occasion Eddie's electric guitar choruses clearly presage the work of Charlie Christian as well as the more intimate group improvisation of bebop. As an electric guitarist par excellence, Christian came into prominence through his work with the Benny Goodman Orchestra, but more importantly, he also took part in small-group jam sessions held at Minton's in Harlem, where drummer Kenny Clarke and pianist Thelonious Monk began around 1940 to introduce the new rhythms and harmonies of bebop. Among the tunes by Christian, Clarke, and Monk recorded on a home tape machine in 1941 was Eddie Durham's "Topsy," made popular by the Count Basie band but appropriately retitled by the Minton crew as "Swing to Bop."

Charlie Christian's approach to the guitar grew out of the Southwestern tradition of riffed blues and single-string improvised melodies. Blind Lemon Jefferson had mastered the riffed blues combination of guitar and vocal, but Christian developed beyond this style his long, swinging lines that have often been compared to the "cool" manner of Lester Young. In many ways both Christian and Young prefigured the coming of bebop—both lent innovative melodic phrasing to jazz at the same time that they expanded the harmonic and rhythmic dimensions of the music. Christian exhibited the new altered chords, the asymmetrical rhythmic patterns, and the offbeat accents that became the hallmarks of bebop. While still working within the blues-riff tradition, he could reel off his surprising, extended eighth-note improvisations that with their enriched progressions opened up the possibility for bebop's more inventive, wide-ranging explorations into musical time and space. In this way, too, Christian would influence several generations of jazz guitarists, although no other player has ever achieved the special Southwestern blues-riff feeling with which Christian invested his remarkably relaxed but driving lines.

After Charlie Parker had recorded extensively with a group that at first included Dizzy Gillespie and then Miles Davis on trumpet, the altoist chose for the latter's replacement Texan Kenny Dorham. While the Bird's recordings made during Dorham's time with the group (1948–1950) are not quite on the same level with those featuring Gillespie and Davis, the leader found in Dorham a musician with a thorough understanding of the bebop language, which the Texan began to "speak" in his own lyrical mode. Dorham had already made important recordings with beboppers Fats Navarro and Bud Powell before he joined Parker in 1948, but during his stay with the Bird, Dorham learned to match the master bar for bar. While engaging in bebop's penchant for quoting popular songs, Dorham also developed an approach that some have considered unique among jazz trumpeters, a combination of touching warmth and stabbing attack. In common with trombonist Henry Coker of Dallas and Richard "Notes" Williams of Galveston, Dorham attended college in Marshall, he and Williams at Wiley College (a Methodist school) and Coker at Bishop College (a Baptist school) before it moved to Dallas. But whereas Coker and Williams concentrated on music, Dorham took courses in chemistry and physics while playing in the college band. It would be of interest to know more about the Wiley program, which obviously prepared these musicians for making it with the leading beboppers in New York.[5] Of course, neither Parker nor Gillespie was the product of a college education, so bebop's complex artistry was never determined by academic credentials.

Of prime importance to all the beboppers must have been the black music traditions that were shared wherever the musicians were born or congregated, made possible through radio and phonograph, as well as by hearing live bands on tour or traveling with them as sidemen. Most musicians learned through imitation, teaching themselves by listening and applying the styles and techniques they heard to the playing of their own particular instruments. What often made Texas jazzmen distinctive was their blues-riff background, and even Dizzy Gillespie acknowledged that he was not a bluesman in the same class with Hot Lips Page of Dallas, an early member of the Blue Devils and active in New York at jam sessions in the 1940s. Kenny Dorham was deeply immersed in the Texas blues tradition, and this may account in large part for his role in the development away from bebop's more cerebral approach and toward the greater emotive tendency of what became known as hard bop. In fact, Dorham was a founding member of one of the most influential hard-bop ensembles, the Jazz Messengers, which began officially in 1954, headed up by drummer Art Blakey and pianist Horace Silver. The Messengers emphasized an emotional form of communication with their audience that was less characteristic of bebop, even as the hard-bop exponents based much of their musical thinking on bebop phraseology. The difference lay in the intensity of hard bop's almost religious revivalism, which was indicated by Blakey's remark that if members of an audience are not patting their feet and nodding their heads to the music, something is wrong; the band is not getting the "message across."[6]

Ironically, perhaps, some of the finest examples of Kenny Dorham's emotive hard-bop approach are found on four tunes he recorded in January 1960 in Oslo with an obviously inspiring Norwegian rhythm section. Included on a compact disc entitled *Kenny Dorham: New York 1953–1956 & Oslo 1960* are "Con Alma" by Dizzy Gillespie, "Lament" by bebop trombonist J. J. Johnson, and "Short Story" and "Sky Blue" by Dorham. The Texan's playing on these four pieces offers something of a workshop in hard bop, a kind of master class in jazz trumpet. These four tunes also represent a type of mini-history of bebop and hard bop, for the compositions by Gillespie and Johnson, the premier bop trumpeter and trombonist respectively, are interpreted by Dorham through his definitive hard-bop styling.[7]

Like Kenny Dorham, Richard "Notes" Williams of Galveston also participated in this post-bebop movement as a member of one of the foremost hard-bop organizations, the Charles Mingus Jazz Workshop. Along with Williams, two other Texans formed part of the Mingus "Dynasty": tenor saxophonist Booker Ervin of Denison and altoist John Handy of Dallas; a fourth Texan, altoist Leo Wright of Wichita Falls, also served briefly as a member of the Mingus Workshop. Shouting blues-derived performances rooted in black church traditions characterize the Mingus recordings on which Williams, Ervin, and Handy add fundamentally to the ecstatic religious feeling that the leader sought and achieved with such fervid results. In the playing of these Texas musicians, Mingus found exactly the kind of eloquent, heightened expression that hard bop aimed to create, even as it worked largely within bebop's technical and harmonic vocabulary.

By the end of the 1950s, hard bop had, for some, expended most of its dithyrambic energy and was wearing itself down in a sort of tired repetition of what was referred to as funk or soul music. Whether this was entirely true is arguable, but meantime another movement was developing that would extend bebop one step further by eliminating chord progressions as the basis of improvisation and by expressing, as in hard bop, "more kinds of feeling than [jazz] has up to now," in the words of Fort Worth native Ornette Coleman.[8] Denominated free or action jazz, this new phase of bebop was spearheaded by Coleman, who began on alto but became a multi-instrumentalist and a composer of a more flexible type of blues-riff structure within which soloists ventured further into the frontier reaches of musical space. Sounding a bit like a combined version of rhythm and blues, jump, and even at times country-western bands, with a touch of classical music thrown in for good measure, Coleman's brand of free—or what he would come to label "harmolodic"—jazz was greeted with open arms by the Third Stream, that is, jazz-classical composers like George Russell, Gunther Schuller, and Coleman's fellow Texan, Jimmy Giuffre of Dallas. Essentially, Coleman's free jazz of the early 1960s is still the most advanced stage of jazz—and bebop—and yet even his album *Free Jazz* contains overlapping riffs so characteristic of early Texas blues.

Although it would be an oversimplification to suggest that Texans have always had the impact of an Ornette Coleman on the development of jazz, it is nonetheless true that black jazz musicians from Texas have made an enormous contribution to jazz history. White Texans have also left their mark on the music, including reedman-composer Jimmy Giuffre, and especially trombonist Jack Teagarden of Vernon, who, deeply influenced by black blues singers, forecast in his own playing in the late 1920s the technical innovations of 1940s bebop. Undeniably, the Texas legacy to this African American music has been owing to the state's wealth of black folk culture that has formed the subsoil of both durable jazz compositions and performances by the state's native sons and daughters before, during, and after the "Bebop Revolution."

TEXAS BEBOP MESSENGERS TO THE WORLD
Kenny Dorham and Leo Wright

oming as I do to the study of jazz history as a student of literature, I have found that a little-known short story by Edgar Allan Poe aptly presents the "revisionist" attitude that I took toward my historical survey, *Texan Jazz*, soon after it was published in 1996. Having traced the jazz contributions of Texas musicians over a period of almost one hundred years, from Scott Joplin's "Maple Leaf Rag" of 1899 through Blind Lemon Jefferson's 1920s country blues and on to Marchel Ivery and Cedar Walton's 1994 recording of "Every Time We Say Goodbye," I ruefully came to appreciate, after the publication of the book, the views on revising a work of history as expressed by the

Egyptian character in Poe's short story entitled "Some Words With a Mummy."

According to Poe's mummified character, who is literally shocked back to life by a group of American Egyptologists who jokingly apply to his well-preserved body a galvanic charge from a voltaic battery, the Egyptian philosophers of the mummy's distant day—following discovery of the embalming principle—were struck by the idea that it would much advance the interests of science if life were lived in installments. In this way,

> an historian, for example, would write a book with great labor and then get himself carefully embalmed; leaving instructions to his executors *pro tem*, that they should cause him to be revivified after the lapse of a certain period—say five or six hundred years. Resuming existence at the expiration of this term, he would invariably find his great work converted into a species of hap-hazard notebook—that is to say, into a kind of literary arena for the conflicting guesses, riddles, and personal squabbles of whole herds of exasperated commentators.

Poe's mummy goes on to say that the revivified Egyptian historian, after finding his work distorted by annotations and emendations of later historians, would rewrite it and thus prevent history "from degenerating into absolute fable."[1]

What interests me about Poe's short story is not so much its satire of the way that historians question and perhaps distort the work of their fellow scholars, but rather the notion that, were we able to return to our writings five hundred years hence, we would surely see them differently and would feel the need to revise them thoroughly. As a matter of fact, in my own case it took far less than a single year before I ardently wished that I could revise what I had written, and especially what I had said or failed to say about the now cult-status jazz trumpet player Kenny Dorham, who was born in Post Oak, Texas, near Fairfield, on August 30, 1924. After attending high school in Austin and Wiley College in Marshall, Dorham became one of the preeminent figures in the bebop and hard-bop periods of jazz history.

PREVIOUS PAGE: Kenny Dorham (trumpet), Horace Silver (piano), and Percy Heath (bass) at Minton's Playhouse, January 1955, recording rehearsal for the album *Kenny Dorham— Afro Cuban*. Photograph by Francis Wolff. Used by permission of Mosaic Images LLC.

Even though, after finishing *Texan Jazz*, I believed that I had covered Kenny Dorham's career as fully as I could within the limitations of a historical survey filled with numerous important figures, it was not long before I came upon a group of recordings issued on compact discs that had not been available at the time of my writing. Such a discovery of additional material is not unusual in any field of study, since new information often emerges only after a book is in print. And while further data need not change a writer's essential view of an important figure, I immediately saw that the unknown recordings would have been extremely helpful in establishing more substantially a central tenet of my book, namely, that a Texas background influenced the kind of jazz produced by Texas musicians. The newly released CDs also altered my conception of Kenny Dorham as an artist, since they demonstrated to me that I had not given this jazzman the full credit he was due as an instrumentalist and a creative thinker.

What I discovered through one recording—originally made on January 10, 1960, and reissued in 1995 as *The Kenny Dorham Memorial Album*—was that, as a boy growing up on a farm in Post Oak, the trumpeter had had "aspirations of becoming a top cowhand and being able to yodel and sing songs like the horsemen of the West." As Dorham goes on to say, "The Gene Autry-type yodelers and the local cowboys were mostly white. I had a black satin two-year-old pony with a white, diamond-shaped spot in the middle of his forehead. He was equipped with a Sears & Roebuck western saddle, bridle and halter."[2] One of the tunes included on the 1960 memorial album is entitled "I'm an Old Cowhand," and the appeal of this piece for Dorham may be accounted for in part by his early attraction to ranch life, which, as he seems to suggest, was unusual for a black in the Fairfield area, even though there had always been black cowboys in Texas.[3] But more importantly, Dorham's performance of "I'm an Old Cowhand" reveals much about the jazz artistry of this native Texan who traded his bridle for bebop.

Written by Johnny Mercer, a native of Savannah, Georgia, "I'm an Old Cowhand" was conceived in 1936 during a trip that Mercer and his wife took across the state of Texas. Reference in the lyrics to the Rio Grande establishes the specific setting, and this must have been significant to Dorham as a Texan. Yet the melody itself—the only one ever composed by lyricist Mercer—was undoubtedly the most attractive feature of the piece. Curiously, Mercer's melody is based on a famous English tune,

"Westminster Chimes," which was itself inspired by the clock in the tower of the Parliament building in London. Dorham possibly heard Mercer's song when it was sung first by Bing Crosby in the 1936 film *Rhythm on the Range* (with the Jimmy Dorsey Orchestra), or later by Roy Rogers in a 1941 movie, *Red River Valley*, but certainly it seems that the combination of the cowboy connection and the traditional English tune stimulated the trumpeter's musical imagination.[4] Dorham's improvised variations on the Mercer tune are pure jazz, with his glissandoed and flutter-tongued notes lending to the melody a unique quality that is so different from the song's British source or the lyricist's comic treatment of Dorham's Lone Star State. Indeed, the Texan's inventive handling of the theme represents vital features of the art of jazz.

What makes jazz so special is difficult to define, but hearing Kenny Dorham perform this type of music makes it clear that any definition would include the blend of varied sounds that has gone into its creation. As played by Dorham, this one piece, "I'm an Old Cowhand," brings together two continents and a wide range of human expression, from joy and playfulness to technical and intellectual ingenuity. And this was characteristic of Dorham's work as a jazz artist by the time he spent two years as the trumpeter in the Charlie Parker Quintet, which in May of 1949 traveled to Europe for the first Paris International Jazz Festival, where it proved to be "one of the greatest and purest bop units . . . producing . . . some of the finest small-group bop ever heard in France."[5] It was then that Dorham incorporated into his recorded solo on "Out of Nowhere" a phrase from Australian composer Percy Grainger's *Country Gardens*.[6] During this same visit to Paris, Dorham recorded on May 26 with a group of American jazz musicians that included drummer Max Roach, trombonist J. J. Johnson, and tenor saxophonist Sonny Rollins. One of the tunes they recorded was Rollins's "Hilo," during which Dorham quotes a phrase from "On the Trail," a movement forming part of Ferde Grofé's *Grande Canyon Suite*.[7] The trumpeter's quotations from Granger and Grofé indicate something of the reach and all-encompassing nature of jazz, its openness to all sources in any and every culture. It is this coming together of different types of music that accounts in part for the worldwide impact of jazz, which, as "the most democratic music on this planet" and a symbol of freedom, has even been credited in some quarters with the Glasnost movement that revolutionized the Soviet Union.[8]

On a smaller scale we can witness the effect of jazz abroad through recordings that Kenny Dorham made in Norway and Denmark with jazz musicians from those two Scandinavian countries.[9] In 1960 Dorham recorded in Oslo and in 1963 in Copenhagen. On the second of these visits the trumpeter composed a piece entitled "Scandia Skies" as a tribute to the region that received him so warmly.[10] On the earlier trip to Norway, Dorham recorded with three Norwegians a tune entitled "Lament," by jazz trombone virtuoso J. J. Johnson.[11] "Lament" had already been recorded in 1957 by trumpet legend Miles Davis on a landmark album entitled *Miles Ahead*, which brought widespread recognition to Davis's introspective, elliptical style of playing.[12] Dorham's 1960 performance of Johnson's tune thus represents a jazz tradition that the Texan shared with his fellow musicians in Norway. However, Dorham's own interpretation of "Lament" is different from the Davis version but equally moving, a very personal approach that is characteristic of Kenny's more direct statement of feeling (an attribute of hard bop as well) and that also exemplifies the individual expression possible within the larger jazz tradition. The highly expressive, emotive power of Dorham's playing comes through fully on this 1960 performance, despite the fact that the recording is marred by distortion from the taping and reproductive process in Oslo.

Even before Dorham traveled to Scandinavia in the 1960s, the trumpeter apparently had already exhibited a musical connection with this part of the world. On yet another tune by trombonist J. J. Johnson, entitled "Opus V" and recorded during the same May 26, 1949, session on which Dorham worked in the phrase from Ferde Grofé's "On the Trail," the trumpeter quotes from what sounds to me like Norwegian composer Edvard Grieg's incidental music to Henrik Ibsen's *Peer Gynt*.[13] Four years later, on December 15, 1953, Dorham again quoted from Grieg on "Osmosis," a tune by Osie Johnson.[14] As I discovered after the publication of *Texan Jazz*, Dorham often incorporated in his trumpet solos the same phrase that seems to derive from the "Anitra's Dance" section of Grieg's *Peer Gynt Suite*. This phrase can be heard in the Texan's solo on his own tune, "Minor's Holiday," and also on "Basheer's Dream," both from March 29, 1955; on his own tune, "The Theme," recorded on November 23, 1955 (with Art Blakey and the Jazz Messengers); on "Man of Moods," from May 22, 1956; on his own tune, "Mexico City," from May 31, 1956; and on "Why Not?" from March 13, 1961.[15] I hasten to add, however, that this is unusual in Dorham's playing, since in the dozens of solos that I have heard on his recordings, the trumpeter never really repeats himself; his solos are all quite different in conception and style, ranging from his flowing, lyrical choruses to short, jabbing phrases, half-valve effects and flutter-tonguing, dazzling runs, sudden leaps to piercing high notes, and everything in between. One of the finest examples of Dorham at the top of his form is his solo on "The Theme," where the trumpeter's virtuoso performance finds him reeling off flawless melodic runs at breakneck speed.

Dorham's awareness of and fondness for the Grieg-like phrase could have come from any number of sources. Trombonist Jack Teagarden, a fellow Texan, recorded "Anitra's Dance" with his own big band in June 1941.[16] Female trombonist Melba Liston, who was with the Dizzy Gillespie orchestra in 1949—Dorham having been a member of the first Gillespie big band in 1945—also arranged the Grieg piece at the suggestion of the trumpeter-leader.[17] My own father heard Grieg's music through a public school program in Fort Worth around 1930, and Dorham may well have first known the work while in secondary school or while attending Wiley College in Marshall in the early 1940s. Of course, it may simply be a coincidence that the phrase that I hear in Dorham's solos is much like a passage in Grieg and that in fact the phrase was of the trumpeter's own invention, for he was an original improviser and a prolific composer. Whether Dorham echoes a Grainger or a Grieg, his adoption of the bebop penchant for musical quotation is an indication of the Texan's capacity for interlacing his blues-based jazz with a world-music heritage, which makes of him a regional artist with an international latitude. Just as his incorporation of motifs from classical works demonstrates his ability to utilize such repertoire for his own jazz objectives, a tune like his "K. D.'s Blues" makes evident the significance of his own Texas background to his creation of hard bop during the 1950s—that is, what jazz critic James Lincoln Collier has referred to in calling the state "a blues hotbed."[18] Of course, the blues have long enjoyed in themselves a universal appeal, but Dorham's combination of the blues mode with his witty quotes from Grainger and Grieg achieves an intellectual blend that lends to bebop its typically all-inclusive quality.

The notion of a connection between jazz and a world-music (classical or folk or both) tradition is close in spirit to the recent work of black historian Robin D. G. Kelley, who, through his consideration of polyrhythms in jazz, has conceived of the importance of polyculturalism in black history, an idea that he elaborated during a lecture entitled "People in Me: On the Polycultural Nature of Blackness."[19] Kelley's point was that black culture has drawn upon other cultures to develop its own way of life, with the historian's particular examples limited to the black use of Mao Tse-tung's *Little Red Book* and the folk traditions preserved by Australian aborigines. Although Kelley did not mention Kenny Dorham, he may eventually do so, since this historian is reportedly writing a biography of jazz pianist Thelonious Monk, with whom in 1952 Dorham recorded three Monk compositions: the difficult and rarely performed "Skippy"; the early jazz waltz "Carolina Moon"; and the classic "Let's Cool One."[20]

But to return to Dorham's Scandinavian connection. The motif that I have heard as deriving from Edvard Grieg's "Anitra's Dance," which Dorham worked into a number of his solos, was either evoked somehow in the trumpeter's mind while he was playing or was simply a favored phrase that served him in the construction of his solos, whether based on the melody and chords of a tune related or unrelated to the *Peer Gynt Suite*. Such motifs can be the building blocks or linking devices of any music, and certainly the appropriation of others' lines or phrases is not unheard of among jazz improvisers. Charlie Parker frequently quoted from Bizet's *Carmen* and used the opening of Percy Grainger's *Country Gardens* as a coda.[21] But so far as I am aware, Dorham is the only bebopper to have drawn upon Grieg's "Anitra's Dance," although in doing so he was clearly working within the bebop tradition practiced by Parker, whose tendencies Dorham obviously absorbed during his time with the Bird's quintet between 1948 and 1950. This assimilation of world-music sources in jazz was but one aspect of the bebop message that Dorham carried with him to Scandinavia.

Just as Charlie Parker had been stimulated by his visit to Sweden in 1949 to create his piece entitled "Swedish Schnapps," so too was Dorham inspired by his stay in Norway and Denmark to compose his "Scandia Skies."[22] Other American jazzmen were also inspired by their visits to Scandinavia—for example, Duke Ellington composed his "Serenade to Sweden" during his trip there in 1939, and in 1951 tenorist Stan Getz toured Scandinavia, picking up on a Swedish folk tune entitled "Dear Old Stockholm," subsequently recorded so memorably by the Miles Davis Quintet with tenorist John Coltrane and Texas pianist Red Garland.[23] But more than Parker or Ellington or Getz, Dorham, in visiting Scandinavia, forged in a way a more direct, personal bond between his own form of bebop and one of what I take to have been its sources in the music of Grieg, which had figured structurally in his solos for more than half a dozen years prior to his trip to Oslo.[24]

All of Dorham's highly melodic solos that contain the Grieg-like motif are long-lined, in what has been called his "running" style, which critic Michael James has suggested was an influence on Charlie Parker, who "tended to use longer phrases when partnered by Dorham."[25] As for Dorham's impact on the Scandinavians, this is evident not only from the fact that Allan Botschinsky—who joined Dorham on fluegelhorn for the 1963 Copenhagen recording session—had long admired the Texan, but also from the fact that on "My Funny Valentine" Botschinsky "picks up the mood [from Dorham's solo] so completely as to maintain a virtually uninterrupted melodic flow." Dorham's "elegant melodic powers" were a large part of his contribution to bebop and hard bop, and this too he took with him on his Scandinavian trip.[26]

In addition to Dorham's "Scandia Skies," another tune that he recorded both in Oslo and in Copenhagen, with Norwegian and Danish jazz musicians, respectively, was his tune "Short Story."[27] Reportedly this piece derives from "Tickle Toe," a composition by the great tenor saxophonist Lester Young, first recorded by the Count Basie Orchestra in 1940. Young was an important influence on Charlie Parker, and this and the practice of basing a tune on the chords of an earlier work (referred to in bebop parlance as a "contrafact") were again part of the jazz legacy that Kenny Dorham carried with him to Paris and the Scandinavian capitals as well as to Rio de Janeiro, where in 1961 he recorded with an all-star group that included saxophonists Zoot Sims and Al Cohn.[28]

Dorham's effect on the Scandinavian jazz scene seems apparent from the inspired performances by the musicians with whom he recorded: among them, Botschinsky, trumpeter Rolf Ericson, pianist Tete Montoliu, drummer Alex Riel, and bassist Niels-Henning Ørsted Pedersen. While many countries have built up substantial jazz traditions, the presence of a vital figure like Dorham among musicians of another culture always brings out the best in those native or immigrant players. As for the impact of Dorham's appearance in Rio on the Brazilian jazz scene, it may not be possible to gauge this so directly, since he did not record with local musicians but only with a group from the United States. What is evident, however, is the strong impression made on the Texan by Brazilian music, for after hearing Brazil's highly infectious rhythmic styles, Dorham composed a number of pieces that "helped shape several schools of jazz for the next decade."[29] In addition to recording Brazilian composer Heitor Villa-Lobos's "Prelude" in an unusual duet with pianist Bobby Timmons (a combination that harks back to recordings by Joe "King" Oliver and Jelly Roll Morton in 1924 and Louis Armstrong and Earl "Fatha" Hines in 1928), as well as Brazilian Luis Bonfa's "Manha de Carnaval," Dorham wrote and recorded two quite popular tunes based on his South American tours of 1960 and 1961, "Una más" and the remarkable "Blue Bossa."[30] Other Latin-based pieces by Dorham include his "São Paulo," "El matador," "Afrodisia," and "Pedro's Time."[31] Both the Scandinavian and South American trips undertaken by Dorham suggest the reciprocal nature of his international experience, which in itself represents the openness that jazz has always fostered, regardless of its origins or where it has gone. This too was a message that Dorham, on his travels abroad, "preached"—to employ a favorite "gospel" analogy of hard-bop adherents like brothers Nat and Cannonball Adderley and Horace Silver of the Jazz Messengers.

Beginning with his first trumpet lessons in Austin and continuing with his college experience in the Wiley Collegians dance band, Kenny Dorham slowly and steadily developed his musical talents, later playing with most of the seminal groups and individual stars of the bebop and hard-bop periods and eventually serving as a jazz ambassador to the world. As my own research has continued into his life and artistry, I have realized that there is a more profound, imaginative, and substantive expressiveness to the work of this modest, highly dedicated musician than I had previously recognized. It has been especially revealing to learn that as a boy he took part in cattle roundups, helping drive the herds to the dipping vat for five dollars a day, and that his most cherished dream was to become a hobo, thinking "it would be very exciting to . . . hitch rides on freight trains and [go] as far west as San Francisco and southwest to the border towns of Mexico."[32] Little did he suspect, perhaps, that one day by means of his own music—both through such compositions as his "Mexico City," "São Paulo," "Monaco," "Bombay," "Tahitian Suite," and "Scandia Skies" and by virtue of his long-lined, "running"-style, solo-trumpet "rides," at what often has been identified as a Texan's "loping" trot—he would traverse the globe in the astonishing saddle of blues and bebop.[33]

Like Kenny Dorham, his fellow Texan Leo Wright, who was born in Wichita Falls on December 14, 1933, also conveyed his native musical heritage and his own "brand" of bebop to a world audience. Wright's father,

Mel, an alto saxophonist, played at the end of the 1930s with the San Antonio band called Boots and His Buddies,[34] and also "gigged" professionally with the father of Buddy Tate, a tenor saxophonist from Sherman, Texas, who was featured with the Count Basie Orchestra.[35] Leo, the son, first studied the alto with his father when they moved to California in the early 1940s; on returning to Wichita Falls, he was instructed during his senior year of high school by Texas tenorist John Hardee, who had been recorded in the 1940s by Blue Note, Savoy, and the newly formed Atlantic label.[36] Leo earned a scholarship to Huston-Tillotson College in Austin and later attended San Francisco State College before being drafted into the army. While stationed in Germany, Leo was in charge of a jazz group and met up with a number of important jazz musicians, including Dallas pianist Cedar Walton. On returning to the United States, Leo Wright enrolled again at San Francisco State, but when the money from his G.I. Bill ran out, he headed for New York to try his luck in the big time.

At New York's Half Note nightclub and at the Newport Jazz Festival, Wright performed with the Charles Mingus Jazz Workshop, which included three other Texas sidemen: tenorist Booker Ervin, altoist John Handy, and trumpeter Richard "Notes" Williams. Although Wright did not record with Mingus, he would appear on albums with Dizzy Gillespie, whose unit Wright joined in 1959, traveling in September to Copenhagen where the group was recorded in concert. Just as Kenny Dorham had formed part of the Charlie Parker Quintet, Leo Wright, as a member of the Gillespie quintet, also worked with one of the two masters of the bebop movement.[37] Gillespie was especially attracted by Leo Wright's talents as both an alto saxophonist and a flutist. Wright had studied the flute at San Francisco State, but "he had begun to resent the instrument," until Dizzy started featuring him on flute on such pieces as "I Found a Million Dollar Baby" and the trumpeter's classic tune, "A Night in Tunisia."[38] Whether on flute or alto, Wright's performances add tremendously to Gillespie's bebop jazz. Even though Gillespie recorded "A Night in Tunisia" innumerable times over the years following his first recording of the piece in 1946, with Don Byas on tenor and Milt Jackson on vibraphone, every Gillespie performance of this work differs from all his other versions. While the Copenhagen performance is similar to the one recorded by Gillespie and Wright at Newport in 1960, it yet differs from that recording and also from their version recorded on February 9, 1961, at the Museum of Modern Art, and especially from the big-band orchestration by Argentinean pianist-composer Lalo Schifrin, entitled "Tunisia Fantasy," recorded at Carnegie Hall on March 4, 1961, with Wright as usual on both flute and alto.[39] In every instance, Gillespie's classic remains an appealing, stirring piece, and Leo Wright contributes strikingly on his two instruments, as he aids in projecting the exotic flavor of this masterful composition.

Although Kenny Dorham and Leo Wright may not have been on the same level of originality or expressive power as Parker and Gillespie, both of these Texans had their own voices and from the beginning of their careers had been drenched or baptized in the blues tradition, which invested their playing with a soulful, hard-bop feeling. Gillespie himself

Leo Wright on the CD insert of his *Soul Talk* (Water Records, 146, 2005). Photograph by Lee Friedlander. Used by permission of Runt LLC.

confessed that he was not a blues man, contrasting his playing with that of Texas trumpeter Oran "Hot Lips" Page; Wright, on the other hand, was definitely a blues man.[40] On alto Wright at times sounds more like a tenor, his tone gruffer than Parker's and his ideas fiercer, more ferocious. While Wright does not offer Parker's complex bebop locutions, he does at times rip off strings of precipitant runs that are reminiscent of the Bird's phenomenal musical flights. In tandem with Gillespie on "A Night in Tunisia," Wright flawlessly negotiates on alto the demands of the composer-trumpeter's complex rhythms and harmonic changes. On flute Wright evokes the Middle Eastern (or is it Caribbean?) mood of "Tunisia," as he does on "Kush," Gillespie's self-described "African rhythm and tone poem," written on the quintet's trip to Africa and performed at the 1961 MOMA concert.[41] Just as Poe's Egyptologists revived their 500-year-old mummy, Gillespie's "Kush" brings to life the rediscovered ancient lost Nile city of that name, and Wright's flute once again sets the mood for this African composition. On alto Wright not only enters the spirit of the piece with his primitivistic screams but also at one point recreates something of an Arabic-sounding motif. Both "A Night in Tunisia" and "Kush" illustrate the comment by bassist Bob Cunningham that playing Gillespie's music showed him "the world," and "Kush" underscores the view of Lalo Schifrin that this piece demonstrates Dizzy's interest in "other cultures, and his African roots."[42] For his part, Wright assisted Gillespie in exploring and evoking in music such cultures and roots so vital to jazz.

Another work performed by the quintet at the MOMA concert was Duke Ellington's "The Mooche," originally recorded by the composer and his orchestra on October 1, 1928, and characterized variously by Ellington as "a stylized jungle . . . a sex dance."[43] Surely this is the source of much of Gillespie's own exotic music, for Ellington's piece remains a modern-sounding "African" work and was therefore a natural choice for the MOMA program, along with Gillespie's own African-inspired "A Night in Tunisia" and "Kush." As for Leo Wright, one of his personal inspirations on the alto was reportedly Ellington's star altoist, Johnny Hodges, who dialogues on the 1928 recording of "The Mooche" with growl-trumpeter Bubber Miley. However, Wright's alto solo on the quintet version is stylistically quite different from Hodges's approach, and although both alto players share a certain austerity and clarity of tone, Wright's style is more "crackling," a term several commentators have used to describe his attacking, even somewhat tormented, cry. There is also a blues quality to

Wright's sound that is rather more aggressive than the easeful, lilting style of Hodges. These differences in approach serve to point up the contrast between earlier saxophonists and those of the hard-bop persuasion who were often more anguished and even perhaps more bitter than Hodges ever was in his solo or ensemble work. Such a distinction also makes evident the fact that Wright, through his playing of Ellington's and Gillespie's music, brought to audiences here and abroad the more aggrieved manner of sixties jazz as it had developed out of the bebop revolution.[44]

In 1960 Lalo Schifrin would write a suite for the Gillespie big band entitled *Gillespiana*, with the quintet serving as soloists in something of a concerto format.[45] In the 1940s, Gillespie had incorporated Latin American elements in his music, especially through the percussion work of Cuban bongo player Chano Pozo. For the Gillespie big-band concert at Carnegie Hall in 1961, Wright solos along with the leader on the Gillespie-Pozo Afro-Cuban classic entitled "Manteca," and Wright is the featured soloist on the ballad "This Is the Way," which he performs on alto with a magisterial sound and technique. *Gillespiana* would serve as a continuation of the jazz tradition of including a "Spanish tinge"—a phrase used by Jelly Roll Morton to describe the Latin American ingredient that he considered essential to any recipe for jazz. Leo Wright, the only reedman on the recording, solos on alto with intense swing in the Prelude, Panamericana, and Toccata sections, as well as adding his lovely flute voice to the Blues and Africana sections, which combine Latin American rhythms with a jazz blues feeling. Wright can be heard *and* seen performing the Toccata section of *Gillespiana* with the trumpeter and his quintet, including Lalo Schifrin, on a video from the Ralph Gleason television program *Jazz Casual*, aired from Los Angeles on January 17, 1961. To view Wright playing on this video is to lament how "obscure" this "brilliant Texas reed-and-flute master" remains but to feel fortunate that Gleason captured him live on a film that reveals his remarkable versatility, control, inventiveness, and drive.[46]

In 1962 Wright left Gillespie and recorded with his own group a composition by Lalo Schifrin entitled "Dionysos," which the Argentinean created for and dedicated to the Texan, thus bringing together—through the music and the musicians—a meeting of South America and the American Southwest. But prior to going off on his own in 1962, Wright had already helped to bridge the music worlds of the two Americas, touring the southern continent with the Dizzy Gillespie Quintet. From this experience he necessarily came to share with Kenny Dorham an affinity for Brazilian music, later recording his own version of bossa nova with the Antonio Carlos Jobim tune "A Felicidade," which was written for the prize-winning 1959 film *Black Orpheus*.[47] Both Dorham and Wright were two of the earliest exponents of Brazilian-based jazz, which in the 1960s became all the rage.

In *Texan Jazz*, I focus almost exclusively on Leo Wright's work with his fellow Texan and trumpeter Richard Williams of Galveston, whose first and only album under his own name, *New Horn in Town*, was recorded in November 1960. Wright in turn would enlist Williams for the altoist's own first album, his 1960 *Blues Shout*.[48] The title tune of the album, by Gigi Gryce, shows most clearly Wright's blues roots as well as what Leonard Feather calls his manner of cutting "through with knife-like clarity, his dynamics more flexible, more a part of his personality than on flute."[49] Wright's version of Gillespie's "A Night in Tunisia" has him playing the accompaniment figure to Williams's theme statement in a rhythmic, phrasal manner that is unlike any of the renditions that he recorded with Gillespie. "The Wind," a beautiful tune by pianist Russ Freeman, reveals Wright's ability to slip convincingly from a very touching ballad mood into bluesy, twisting, boplike lines. The final tune on this first album, a Wright original entitled "Two Moods," likewise shows the altoist moving from something of a ballad feeling to a boppish jump style. Capable of a wide range of expression, on both flute and alto, Wright was certainly a master of the bebop genre, yet he was equally effective on a lush, more mainstream touchstone like "Body and Soul," which was given its classic reading by Coleman Hawkins in 1939. Wright's rendition of "Body and Soul," accompanied by another fellow Texan, pianist Red Garland, was recorded in San Francisco in 1978 and is a tour de force performance that exhibits the altoist's total control of his instrument and his amazing musical imagination.[50]

Leo Wright emigrated to Europe in 1963, and apparently his wife, Sigrid, with whom he performed duets and from whose name he derived the title for his composition "Sigi," was German or Scandinavian.[51] Living first in Berlin and later in Vienna, Wright became a member of the Radio Free Berlin Studio Band, performed at festivals in Germany, Switzerland, and Finland, and appeared with jazzmen like Lee Konitz in Paris, continuing in all of these venues to spread the good word of bebop and his own native Texas blues. Like Dorham, Wright played a significant role in the creation of jazz during the late bebop period, although both were over-shadowed at the time by the startling arrival of their fellow Texan Ornette Coleman and his avant-garde Free Jazz.

Both Kenny Dorham and Leo Wright have been described as quiet-mannered, cooperative men, even as their jazz comes across as urgent, dynamic, assertive. Both musicians also shared a sense, as Wright put it, that "jazz is the greatest medium for bringing people together—here, and all over the world."[52] To what degree their Texas upbringing determined either their admirable personal qualities or their impressive and treasured music making may remain an open question, but what seems important to bear in mind is that after their early years in Texas they went on to partic-ipate in the creation of a world-renowned art that continues to be valued beyond the borders of their own southwestern state. Hopefully, the contri-butions to jazz history by Kenny Dorham and Leo Wright (and their fellow Texans) will become more fully appreciated now and in the future—not just abroad, as they already are, but here in their own "stomping grounds."

BRITISH ACOLYTES OF JAZZ AND ITS TEXAS CONTINGENT

In the realm of literary fiction, Edgar Allan Poe is credited with creating the art story, and two of his best-known works in this genre, "The Fall of the House of Usher" and "The Cask of Amontillado," concern, as do other of his short stories, a premature burial. In the field of jazz criticism, British art critic Clive Bell has the dubious distinction of being the earliest commentator to call for a premature burial and obituary of jazz.[1] In September 1921, two years before the classic jazz recordings by King Oliver and Louis Armstrong, as well as by Bennie Moten and Texas cornetist Lammar Wright, Bell published an article in the *New Republic* entitled "Plus de Jazz" (later included in *Since*

Cezanne, his 1922 collection of essays).[2] In this piece Bell declares that even though in the preceding ten years jazz "had dominated music and coloured literature,"[3] "Jazz art is soon created, soon liked, and soon forgotten."[4] In another piece in *Since Cezanne*, entitled "Negro Sculpture," Bell remarks that because blacks "lack intelligence they are incapable of profound conceptions," and because they hardly attempt "a personal vision," this implies "a definite want of creative imagination."[5]

Despite these perverse views and Bell's precipitate pronouncement that "Jazz is dead," this British critic must be accorded his due for having traced at an early date the impact of jazz on some of the twentieth century's greatest creative artists, among them Pablo Picasso, Igor Stravinsky, T. S. Eliot, and James Joyce.[6] Speaking of the writings of his sister-in-law, novelist Virginia Woolf, Bell observed that through the influence of jazz's predecessor, ragtime, and its syncopated rhythms, Woolf "'leaves out' with the boldest of them: here is syncopation if you like it. I am not sure I do."[7] (Since the relationship between Texas jazz musicians and British criticism will be referred to throughout this essay, it should be remembered in passing that the King of Ragtime was Scott Joplin [1868–1917] of Texarkana, Texas.) If Clive Bell did not like ragtime and jazz, there were plenty of British listeners who did. And if Bell was stupendously mistaken in sounding the death knell for jazz in 1921, he was clairvoyantly correct in recognizing that if "one may, for excellent reasons, dislike a movement," one would have to be a fool "to deny that experimenting" with a syncopated style had led artists like Picasso and Braque to produce "works of the greatest beauty and significance."[8] After having announced in "Plus de Jazz" that this music "is dying" and even "dead," Bell, near the close of his essay, allows that there are jazz-influenced artists whose "extraordinary merit" deserves "the most careful attention" and that "he, at any rate, who comes to *bury* [emphasis added] Jazz should realize what the movement has to its credit."[9] If grudgingly, Clive Bell did just that.

Although from the beginning of my own passion for jazz in the mid-1950s I had been aware of the vital role played by British critics in promoting and promulgating the music, it was not until I read Jim Godbolt's *A History of Jazz in Britain 1919–1950* that I discovered an unknown connection between Texas and Britain's jazz enthusiasts. In fact, there was even a

---

PREVIOUS PAGE: Cover of the CD box set of *Jazz in Britain, 1919–1950*, compiled and annotated by Jim Godbolt (Properbox 88, 2005). Used by permission of Proper Records Ltd.

connection between Texas and the copy of Godbolt's book that was given to me by my former Latin teacher and longtime friend Christian Smith, who picked it up at a sale when the San Antonio Public Library discarded the volume. It was ironic that Christian had bought the book, since he happens to consider jazz little more than kitsch. Nonetheless, thanks to his generosity, I found reproduced in the Godbolt book the contents page of a 1944 issue of *Jazz Music*, which, according to Godbolt, was "arguably Britain's most informed specialist jazz magazine."[10] Among the contributors I noted the name Jake Trussell, which I recognized as that of the host of a jazz radio program in Kingsville, Texas, during the 1940s and 1950s. I knew of Jake Trussell through his son, Philip, an Austin artist whom I first met in 1965. In revealing that Jake Trussell had contributed a record review to a British jazz magazine, Godbolt demonstrated that Texans have long been interested in what British reviewer-interviewer-photographer Valerie Wilmer has claimed is "the most vital and heart-rendingly emotional of all the arts."[11] Godbolt's book also vividly reminded me of the fact that without the British jazz critics, my own book, *Texan Jazz*, would not have been so comprehensive in its discussion of the Texas contribution to jazz and would not have developed so effectively my thesis that Texans were prominent figures in every period of the music's history.

Jazz Music, the "specialist magazine" that first appeared in 1935 and bore a typical British subtitle, "Bulletin of the Jazz Sociological Society," was co-edited by Albert McCarthy, whose book, *Big Band Jazz*, proved indispensable to me in learning of the territory bands in Texas and the Southwest during the big-band era.[12] McCarthy supplied me with the personnel of little-known touring orchestras and the individual members' birth dates and places, and he also furnished discerning commentary on the recordings made by a number of the territory bands. In Jim Godbolt's second volume, *A History of Jazz in Britain 1950–1970*, he quotes John Postgate on Albert McCarthy and his later publication entitled *Jazz Monthly*, which McCarthy launched in February 1955.[13] Postgate, who wrote for *Jazz Monthly*, observes that

> The collective dedication of its contributors to a cause; its tolerance of affectation and pretentiousness in the quest of critical standards; the individualism; the fury with which we attacked each other in print; the willingness of [Albert McCarthy] the anarchic editor to publish anything unedited; these attitudes were relics of an earlier expansive

era: low-circulation, high brow magazines dedicated to poetry, art, literature and so on, most of which died in the Second World War. Commercialism never entered our (or Mac's) head: the idea of rejecting a poor [i.e., negative] record review so as not to offend the advertiser, now commonplace, was unthinkable. And the idea of pulling one's punches because someone was a fellow contributor was also unthinkable: the reverse was true.[14]

Postgate recalls attending occasional gatherings of the contributors to *Jazz Monthly*, and in listing the attendees by name, he brought to my mind other British critics who had made possible my book on Texans in jazz, in particular Charles Fox, of whom presently I will have something to say.

Speaking of yet another British publication from the 1950s, *Jazz News*, Godbolt regards this as undoubtedly "one of the raciest, most informative and stimulating magazines"; he then goes on to remark that "the quality of the newsprint was suggestive of low-grade lavatory paper, but the magazine took jazz seriously, not solemnly."[15] Godbolt's last phrase echoes in its way Clive Bell's comment in 1921 when he wrote that "art, though it need never be solemn, must always be serious."[16] Contributors to *Jazz News* included two writers, Charles Fox and Paul Oliver, who had figured prominently among the contributors to McCarthy's *Jazz Monthly*, and it was to Oliver, a blues specialist, that I was deeply indebted for his work on such early Texas bluesmen as Henry "Ragtime Texas" Thomas and Blind Lemon Jefferson. As for Charles Fox, he and his fellow Brits, Max Harrison and Eric Thacker, compiled *The Essential Jazz Records*, toward which I have mixed feelings.[17] On one hand, this book too was vital to my writing on Texan jazz, but on the other, I cannot quite forgive Charles Fox for preempting one of the few "original" discoveries that I thought that I had made with regard to the two tunes entitled "Pigeon Walk" and "Time Out," arranged by Eddie Durham of San Marcos, Texas. A guitarist, trombonist, and composer-arranger, Durham had scored these pieces in the 1930s for two entirely different swing bands, those of Jimmie Lunceford and Count Basie. Although the authoritative American composer–jazz historian Gunther Schuller had discussed both of these tunes in his monumental study *The Swing Era*, he had not mentioned the fact that "Time Out" was based in part on James V. Monaco's "Pigeon Walk," and so I was quite pleased with myself for what I took to be a true contribution to scholarship. Only later would I read in *The Essential Jazz Records* a review by

Charles Fox of an album by the Lunceford band, in which Fox had already noted that Durham's arrangement of "Pigeon Walk" includes a brief sequence that later appeared in his "Time Out." I was devastated, even though this did confirm what my own amateur ear had correctly heard.

More significant than any tracing of a musical source is the fact that these two 1937 charts by Texan Eddie Durham, for the Lunceford and Basie bands, were singled out both by Fox and Schuller as among the finest arrangements for and performances by those two great swing-era units. Not incidentally it should be mentioned that the first brief tenor solo on the Basie version is by Herschel Evans, a native of Denton, Texas, and a cousin of Eddie Durham; also, that the fine guitar solo on this same recording is by Durham himself. In addition to aiding me in my writing on these two swing-era Texas musicians, Max Harrison and other British jazz critics, through their volume entitled *Modern Jazz: The Essential Records*, also supported me in the writing of an article on Texas bebop trumpeter Kenny Dorham.[18] Harrison himself reviewed a book that I edited in 1992, *The Bebop Revolution in Words and Music*, and although his criticism was quite severe, and rightly so in a number of instances, he did praise one of the contributors to this volume, Douglass Parker, for his article on Miles Davis and his tune entitled "Donna Lee."[19] Harrison finds it "something of a relief that somebody else has at last noticed Davis's incorporating a literal quotation from Fats Navarro's solo in 'Ice Freezes Red,' also based on 'Indiana' and recorded four months before the Charlie Parker date that gave us 'Donna Lee.'"[20] Here Harrison is indirectly patting himself on the back for having noticed the "literal quotation" long before Douglass Parker. There is a particular pleasure that comes with being the first to notice something about a work of art, or even to notice something on one's own without knowing that others were aware of the fact and had already commented on it in print.

While all of this is relevant to my own indebtedness to British jazz criticism, it has gotten me ahead of the story, which begins, as Jim Godbolt retells it, in 1919. In that year the *Times* of London, following "a list of forthcoming marriages and condolences from their Majesties King George V and Queen Mary," first acknowledged the existence of jazz in the form of a show then running at the Coliseum. The *Times* observed that the unnamed orchestra had tried to "convert itself into a jazz band, one of the many American peculiarities that threaten to make life a nightmare."[21] Similar charges were repeated for years from England to Australia, as well as in the music's own native land, where in December 1921 the *Ladies Home Journal* published an article under the title "Unspeakable Jazz Must Go! It is Worse than Saloon and Scarlet Vice, Professional Dance Experts—Only a Few Cities are Curbing Evil."[22] In the second volume of Godbolt's history of jazz in Britain, he even cites a letter to the editor of the *Church Times* that appeared as late as an October 1957 issue, which condemns the performance of a folk mass because it used popular rhythms and modern musical styles. Alluding to the corruptive influence of jazz, the writer, a certain Charles Cleall, asks,

> How can one discuss an interest that boasts only three books published in the United Kingdom? It has no literature because its devotees can hardly read a book from cover to cover.
>
> There is an unpleasant correlation between jazz and drug-taking: between swing fanatics and juvenile delinquency. Let jazz inside our church and our music will rot.[23]

Godbolt counters such charges by merely noting that in Britain as of 1957 there were hundreds of books on jazz and that "for a music appealing to a minority, jazz was documented by a disproportionately large volume of literature."[24] The beginnings of this outpouring of jazz literature in Britain had in fact taken place almost forty years earlier after the arrival on April 1, 1919, of the ODJB (short for Original Dixieland Jazz Band) onboard the *RMS Adriatic,* which docked at Liverpool with this all-white American group that had made the first jazz recordings in history only two years before in 1917.[25]

Traveling on to London by train, the ODJB would perform at the Hippodrome, and when it unleashed its barnyard sounds on the British public and a large aggregate of American doughboys, the *London Daily News* reported that "the fever spread throughout the theatre until every last man and woman was on his feet, shouting and clapping in a manner that was peculiarly un-British."[26] From this moment on, Britain, in many ways, was never the same; indeed, the British would welcome jazz with greater enthusiasm, devotion, and even reverence than its American audiences. Not only this, but the British would treat black musicians as a new kind of royalty. After first thinking that whites played the real jazz and that blacks were only primitive and barbarous, their style designated as "nigger" or "coon" music, British devotees would begin to construct elaborate genealogies for jazzmen, especially for the early black musicians from New Orleans.[27]

By January 1926, a serious critical approach to the study of jazz was under way with the publication of the first issue of *Melody Maker* magazine, which, as Godbolt puts it, was "the bible of jazz and dance-band enthusiasts in those palmy days."[28] As more and more recordings reached England, jazz fans recognized the vast difference in the level of inventiveness and virtuosity between the members of the ODJB and the great black trumpeter Louis Armstrong. However, when Armstrong gave a concert at the Palladium on July 18, 1932, the response was mixed. A columnist for the *Daily Herald* quoted one listener as having declared that Armstrong "did everything with the trumpet but play it," and of Armstrong's now world-famous gravelly voice the writer quoted a theater manager as having stated that he "couldn't understand one word he said."[29] The same columnist reported on Armstrong's July 25 performance that the "pale aesthetes were lily-like when he appeared and the young Jewish element at the back were enthusiastic."[30] Perhaps unwittingly, even this latter statement revealed early on the great attraction to jazz and the significant contribution made to it by Jewish musicians, among them Mezz Mezzrow, clarinetist and author of one of the finest jazz autobiographies, *Really the Blues*; Benny Goodman, clarinetist and leader of probably the most popular swing orchestra of the mid-1930s; Arthur Arshawsky (a.k.a. Artie Shaw), yet another clarinetist and leader of a highly popular swing orchestra of the 1930s; and Milton Rajonsky (a.k.a. Shorty Rogers), a trumpeter, composer, and bandleader vital to West Coast jazz.

Also perhaps without realizing or appreciating it at the time, this same *Daily Herald* journalist put his finger on something of the improvisatory nature of jazz artistry—that is, the musician's ability to create his own melodic lines based on a tune's chordal structure—when he observed that Armstrong, "making [his instrument] do things I've never heard a trumpet do before, emits from it a rapid succession of notes which have nothing to do with the melody."[31] Once again, Clive Bell had in 1921 already identified, from a likewise rather adverse perspective, this art of "ragging" a popular tune, of syncopating it, of altering its rhythms "out of easy recognition," which he related to T. S. Eliot's "black and grinning muse" and to James Joyce's deliberately "break[ing] up the traditional sentence, throwing overboard sequence, syntax, and, indeed, most of those conventions which men habitually employ for the exchange of precise ideas."[32]

With regard to a reciprocal impact of British audiences on Louis Armstrong, Godbolt suggests that "the British experience probably made him realize that he was playing a major role in the evolution of jazz."[33] Comments by British musicians clearly acknowledged Armstrong as "a great and inspiring artist and genius," a "guiding star," and even as "definitely the artist of the century."[34] Yet true to their very serious valuation of jazz, the British could also criticize the music's trumpet master when he would "descend to low comedy" or play "too many meaningless top notes."[35] But in the end, Godbolt believes that Armstrong must have left the country "buoyed up with the knowledge that for the first time he was accepted as a celebrity and a player of rare ability."[36]

It was, however, the next great jazz visitor, Duke Ellington, who received on June 12, 1933, the most enthusiastic welcome ever. The performances by Ellington and his band were heralded as the work of "the greatest jazz orchestra the world has ever known" and as "an ensemble unique in the history of all music."[37] As Godbolt reports, the reaction to the Ellington orchestra exceeded anything that it had experienced in the States, and he accounts for this in part by the fact that "there were more jazz enthusiasts per capita in Britain than in the country of its birth. . . . These British jazz enthusiasts worshipped this almost unbelievable constellation of stars and marveled at the instrumental settings in which they glittered."[38] Of Ellington, the *Daily Express* had already announced on June 10 that "He's good-looking, tall and the high priest of the new syncopation."[39] As will be noted from the excerpts above, Godbolt and the *Express* writer employ words and phrases that underscore the religious fervor of the British listeners, as does Godbolt in the following snippets: "The doubting Thomas had become a fervent convert!"; "it was a revelation"; "non-believers as well as the enthusiasts . . . gaped and gasped at the sheer brilliance of the performances."[40] Just as with Armstrong's warm British reception, Godbolt claims that with Ellington too his was an entirely new experience for the bandleader, since, "for the first time ever, he had an audience that, for the most part, had studiously collected his records and studied and argued about their meaning and their differing personnels; people who intellectualized his music as well as reacting emotionally to its incredible fecundity."[41] The Duke himself would recall in 1974 that "we were absolutely amazed at how well informed people were in Britain about us and our records. They had magazines and reviews far ahead of what we had [in America] and everywhere we went we were confronted with facts we had forgotten and questions we couldn't always answer."[42]

Jazz fans of every walk of life attended the Ellington performances, including the Prince of Wales, who sat in and played a Charleston beat on the drum set of the Duke's percussionist, the marvelous Sonny Greer. Godbolt avers that "it must have been a heady experience for a second-class citizen in his own country being so royally feted—and perhaps, just as heady an experience for a Royal who, as events proved, was patently a non-conformist."[43] In the second volume of his history, Godbolt returns to the theme of second-class citizenship for American blacks when he concludes his sequel with a quote from the penultimate paragraph of the first volume of his *Jazz in Britain*: "That jazz should have emerged in its own breeding ground is one phenomenon. That it should permeate the musical activity and public consciousness of so many other countries and Britain in particular is another, and is quite incredible in its extent and ramifications. The history of jazz in Britain is a remarkable story of *missionary zeal* [emphasis added]."[44]

Among the many British missionaries of jazz, I count especially those who have been central to my own education in the field of jazz studies. Jim Godbolt, in referring to the work of his fellow Brit, John Chilton, author of *Who's Who of Jazz*, points out that "it was an incredible achievement for a Britisher who had never been to America, to elicit, by dint of intensive correspondence and diligent research, a mass of information on over a thousand American jazz musicians, the data including their geographical movements, various employers and associates."[45] Not only was Chilton's *Who's Who* crucial to my research on little-known Texas figures, but later, in preparing my second book, *The Early Swing Era, 1930 to 1941*, I would rely heavily on Chilton's *The Song of the Hawk: The Life and Recordings of Coleman Hawkins* (1990) for information on this great tenor saxophonist. However, the first British critic whose biographical work I encountered at the beginning of my career as a jazz enthusiast was that of Leonard Feather, author of *The Encyclopedia of Jazz*. In 1962 my parents purchased for me the first American edition of Feather's encyclopedia, which has since gone through a number of editions, adding entries for each decade since its initial appearance in 1955. Reading in this encyclopedia would awaken me to the history of jazz and initiate my interest in knowing who was who in the music. Like Chilton and other British critics, Feather wrote a number of books on jazz and contributed countless record liner notes. In addition, he even performed on piano in an important recording session with the great Dallas trumpeter and blues singer Oran "Hot Lips" Page and was responsible for arranging and directing the background jazz for a recording with Langston Hughes reading his jazz-inspired poetry.[46]

Other significant British jazz authorities on whom I have depended for information and insights include Brian Rust, compiler of the basic jazz discography *Jazz Records, 1897–1942* (2 vols., 1975); Brian Priestley, author of a critical study of Charles Mingus and his Jazz Workshop, which included at least four important Texas sidemen; Sinclair Traill, editor of *Jazz Journal*, which celebrated its fiftieth year of publication in 1997, "a world record for an English-language jazz magazine";[47] and poet Philip Larkin, whose record reviews

> admitted to adroitly using words that would not give offence to "demonstrative devotees of modern jazz", but which cloaked his true feelings, and those who read jazz literature would have been deprived of a rare facility of expression had he been genuinely true to himself. After all, what does a little dissembling matter if the upshot was prose of such excellence for so long a period in the jazz column of a quality daily?[48]

The career of Sinclair Traill represents one of the curious ironies of the British zealot, since Traill's lifestyle seems far removed from the "disreputable" jazz world, even as it reveals the "internecine warfare" that has raged and still rages continuously "between the various jazz factions" in Britain. As Godbolt observes,

> There was no love lost between Traill and [Albert] McCarthy. Traill, with his middle-class upbringing, his banking career, five years in the officers' mess, and many assiduously cultivated hours in the company of the Marquis of Donegall, the Honourable Gerald Lascelles, Sir Edward Lewis and Lord Montagu, was hardly a person who would have time for a working-class anarchist who adopted literary airs and graces.[49]

As for Philip Larkin, not only his record reviews, reprinted in his *All What Jazz: A Record Diary* (1970), but his poetry—notably his poems on New Orleans clarinetist and soprano saxophonist Sidney Bechet and on not attending a dance where he hears a trumpet's "rough-tongued bell / (Art, if you like) whose individual sound / Insists I too am individual"— have added immeasurably to an understanding of the impact that jazz can have on any alert listener.[50]

Yet another important British jazz critic, who, like Leonard Feather, emigrated to the United States and became a seminal figure in the promotion of jazz appreciation in America, is Stanley Dance, who has authored, along with an array of informative record liner notes, at least three fundamental works: *The World of Duke Ellington, The World of Count Basie*, and *The World of Earl Hines*. Dance's interviews with the sidemen of these three illustrious bandleaders documented the early lives in music of such major jazz stars as Ellington's Cootie Williams, who revealed in his interview how he discovered that the trumpet was his true instrument when he played on it the "Twelfth Street Rag" by Fort Worth composer Euday L. Bowman; Basie's arranger-composer-instrumentalist Eddie Durham of San Marcos; and Earl "Fatha" Hines's straw boss, arranger-composer-reedman Budd Johnson of Dallas. Dance, who first visited the United States in 1937 and moved permanently to the States in 1959, published in 1970 *The World of Duke Ellington*, which was actually a collaborative work prepared with the assistance of his wife, Helen Oakley. Born in Toronto in 1917—as noted earlier, the first year of recorded jazz—Oakley also assisted her husband with his work on *The World of Count Basie* by conducting in part the interview with Eddie Durham, to which she contributed significantly by asking the Texan questions about his siblings and their own musicianship.[51] Prior to her marriage in 1947, Helen Oakley moved first from Canada to Chicago in 1933, when she became a reviewer for *Down Beat* magazine, as well as for the *Chicago Herald* and *Examiner*. By virtue of her early reviews she was at the time one of the few women in the field of jazz studies, and in 1935 she was responsible for staging the first jazz concert. After moving to New York in 1936, Oakley worked with Duke Ellington's manager, Irving Mills, to produce a number of important Ellington small-group dates. She also talked Benny Goodman into including Texas-born pianist Teddy Wilson in the first public integrated jazz concert.[52] In 1987, Oakley would write *Stormy Monday*, a biography of Dallas blues singer and guitarist T-Bone Walker.

In my writings on any number of swing-era bands and their recordings I have found Stanley Dance's liner notes invaluable sources for the identification of solo performances by Texans who were members of such orchestras as those of Jimmie Lunceford and Count Basie. Also valuable to my writing were Dance's descriptions of trombone solos by Vernon native Jack Teagarden included on the outstanding album entitled *The Golden Horn of Jack Teagarden*. As for Helen Oakley Dance, a review that she wrote in 1936 for the American jazz magazine *Metronome* remains one of my favorite reviews ever, principally because it reinforced my own high regard for the Ellington orchestra's 1935 recording of "Merry-Go-Round." In covering the Ellington unit's appearance at New York's famed Apollo Theatre, Oakley reports that the opening number consisted of a group of five of the Duke's biggest hit tunes, which she calls a "potpourri of all that is to follow."[53] She goes on to say that "Duke now presents one of his greatest numbers, written several years ago, a recorded masterpiece, recently revised during his Chicago stay at the Congress Hotel, where it proved to be a 'killer.' Duke announces it himself, 'Ladies and Gentlemen, *Merry-Go-Round.*'" The reviewer continues with these very discerning observations:

> Very few of Duke's compositions show to any greater advantage the magnificent team work of which his reed and brass sections are capable. The intonation and power in the brass section are consistently amazing to even those most familiar with the band, and the blend and flexibility of the reeds could not be bettered by any unit playing today.

I cite this early review for three reasons: first, because I could not agree more; second, because it was this one performance more than any other that inspired my deepest attraction to jazz when I first heard it around 1955 on the album entitled *I Like Jazz*, which I purchased as a high school sophomore (and even after all these years this recording still sends chills up my spine, especially the trombone solo by Lawrence Brown and the baritone sax solo by Harry Carney); and third, because I see Helen Oakley's review as the work of a woman jazz critic who paved the way for British writer Valerie Wilmer, whose writings on jazz represent some of the most personal and engaging responses to the music of any non-playing male or female author.

At this point I would note that, despite the very crucial roles played by such English and Canadian jazz critics as Albert McCarthy, John Chilton, Stanley Dance, and Helen Oakley, and the fact that early on the British recognized Ellington's consummate artistry, it was an American by the name of R. D. Darrell who actually contributed a landmark piece of Ellington criticism: an article entitled after Ellington's tune "Black Beauty" and published in 1932 in the magazine *disques*. Not only is Darrell's essay still considered "one of the most important articles ever written about Ellington," but in it the critic comments that in Ellington's "Black and Tan Fantasy," recorded on April 7, 1927,

> at last I had found the answer to Clive Bell's [1921] accusation that jazz had a childish horror of the noble and the beautiful; the answer to his demand for "thought rather than spirits, quality rather than color, knowledge rather than irreticence, intellect rather than singularity, wit rather than romps, precision rather than surprise, dignity rather than impudence, and lucidity above all things."[54]

Following Darrell's lead, Constant Lambert, an English composer-critic, likewise paid tribute to Ellington in what Mark Tucker has called Lambert's "quirky, patronizing, bigoted, occasionally insightful discussion of jazz."[55] In 1934 Lambert observed in his book *Music Ho! A Study of Music in Decline* that "the best records of Duke Ellington . . . can be listened to again and again because they are not just decorations of a familiar shape but a new arrangement of shapes," that Ellington's works "are the only jazz records worth studying for their form as well as their texture," and that Ellington

> is definitely a *petit maitre*, but that, after all, is considerably more than many people thought either jazz or the coloured race would ever produce. He has crystallized the popular music of our time and set up a standard by which we may judge not only other jazz composers but also those highbrow composers, whether American or European, who indulge in what is roughly known as "symphonic jazz."[56]

Aside from evidence of British jazz idolatry in books and magazines published in England itself, such evidence is also present in a rather malicious article that appeared in the *Philadelphia Record* of May 1935. The writer for the newspaper reported that Ellington was "taken up by the musical intelligentsia of the British capital" and that "Duke" enjoyed "the greatest British triumph since Dr. Livingstone's adventures in Darkest Africa. . . . Constant Lambert . . . practically [smothered] the jazz boy's

'Blues' in an admiring avalanche of fancy critical verbiage," while "the
fashionable and ultra-sophisticated Sitwells blew perfumed critical kisses
in Duke's direction" and "Percy Grainger went overboard with a splash,
comparing Duke's melodic line to that of Bach. Others followed with tributes to the jazz composer that ranked him with Stravinsky and Ravel."[57]

All such laudatory and near-reverential praise of the music of Duke
Ellington is but one aspect of the attention bestowed by the British on
American jazz. In her 1989 autobiography, British photographer and music
critic Valerie Wilmer reveals that even in 1955, at the tender age of thirteen,
she was aware that "among British jazz enthusiasts there was a general
interest in Afro-American culture," but that

> by and large . . . the music press offered no indication of the move-
> ments of change taking place internationally and the idea that Afro-
> American music could in itself function as a kind of resistance was
> unknown. Yet the music would lead me to discover the literature of
> protest and struggle and to go beyond, eventually to recognize how
> the Afro-American oral tradition has, as one writer put it, offered a
> radical alternative to Western literary values.[58]

Predictably, Clive Bell had already touched on protest in jazz, yet
rather than applauding it, he abhorred such a tendency in art and congrat-
ulated Virginia Woolf, despite her "taste for playing tricks with traditional
constructions," on having "no note of protest" in her writing.[59] In contrast,
Valerie Wilmer seems to have been intent from the first not only to hear
the protest in jazz and blues but to register her own dissatisfaction with
British attitudes toward Afro-American and African music that she would
denounce with fervid invective. She records early in her autobiography
that a researcher who had aided her from the beginning of her interest in
jazz had "sadly . . . become infected by the racist fantasies of Nick La
Rocca, leader of the Original Dixieland Jazz Band—generally referred to as
the first jazz band to record but now identified by some researchers as in
fact a non-improvising 'novelty' band (thereby allowing credit for the hon-
our to pass to a Black band, Kid Ory's)." To Wilmer, both La Rocca and her
British friend were deranged in thinking that "only white men played the
'true jazz.'" Eventually, whether precociously or by hindsight, Wilmer
came to view the British jazz world's enthusiasm for the music as a means
"to defeat Black self-determination." [60]

Valerie Wilmer thus presents another side to the very genuine coin of British jazz criticism, differing in many ways from its more traditional approach. For example, whereas John Chilton never visited the United States in compiling his *Who's Who of Jazz*, Wilmer traveled not only to New York and interviewed, listened to ("women have always been good listeners; that's been one of our ways of getting by"), and lived among jazz musicians, but over a period of ten years during the 1970s and early 1980s she journeyed into the hinterlands of the Deep South to tape-record, photograph, and learn firsthand of the culture and folk art of black blues singers. She also visited many of the African countries, interviewing musicians and artists and entering as fully as a white woman could into their everyday lives.[61] Often she observes that she realized that she could never truly be a part of a culture into which she was not born, recalling on one occasion that a trumpet player from Mississippi suggested that she "might have got a better idea of what life was like down there if [she'd] had to pick cotton under the sun."[62] Not only was being a white woman talking to and taking photographs of blacks in the South frowned upon by white Southerners, not to mention dangerous, but Wilmer recognized that in the States "women were expected to take a back seat in the music world." Nevertheless, Wilmer was not one to back off; instead, she "developed the courage to challenge, something few women are brought up to do."[63]

Cover of *Mama Said There'd Be Days Like This: My Life in the Jazz World* by Valerie Wilmer (1989). Pictured in the photograph by John Hopkins are, from left to right, trombonist Vic Dickenson, Valerie Wilmer, and singer Big Joe Turner. Used by permission of Val Wilmer.

If Wilmer could feel out of place and even question her motives in seeking to know black music and musicians in the States, in Britain she found her views on Afro-American and African cultures to be those of an outsider even in her own homeland. In beginning her career as a journalist, she approached white newspapers and magazines with an idea for writing on black "artists who were household names" but was "met with incredulity that anyone would be interested in reading about Black endeavor and achievement." Although "Ellington and Basie could always be sure of some coverage, especially when Princess Margaret graced one of their concerts," this was the exception, since "the prevailing media belief was that Black people had nothing to say."[64] Unlike most of the traditional British jazz critics, Wilmer consistently expresses a concern for the social implications of black music. In the case of Ellington, for example, she takes special interest in his trumpeter, Rex Stewart, who had written an article, later collected in his *Jazz Masters of the Thirties* (1972), on band mate and wa-wa trombonist Tricky Sam Nanton, whom Stewart revealed was not only a "key figure in the Ellington Orchestra" but "a scholar, a fierce nationalist and devoted follower of Marcus Garvey in the 1930s."[65] In holding her sociopolitical views on the music and musicians, Wilmer found that she was "nothing like the hip and flashy people around the jazz scene," and as a result she realized that "to support Black creativity meant being treated with amusement or disdain by our peers."[66]

Wilmer began her "life in the jazz world" by listening to pre–World War Two jazz classics, and she recalls that she was led to many important recordings through the discography of Brian Rust. While her schoolmates were "immersed in rock 'n' roll," Wilmer was drawn to the sounds recorded decades earlier, and she reports that she still owns the 78s she collected of greats like Bessie Smith doing "Empty Bed Blues" and "the ebullient Fats Waller, recorded in London."[67] Years later, when she was in the States, she found that having been involved with discography meant that she "automatically knew the identity of the most obscure player" and that, consequently, "at a jam session in New York," she experienced "a thrill of recognition when an older trumpeter climbed on the bandstand and turned out to be Herman Autrey, who'd cut dozens of sides with Fats Waller before [she] was born."[68] Reading of Wilmer's recollection of Autrey was particularly meaningful to me because of a Waller recording from June 24, 1935, a rendition of Euday L. Bowman's "Twelfth Street

Rag," with Autrey on trumpet supplying what I have described elsewhere as his "own brand of jovial jazz."[69] This rag by the Fort Worth pianist-composer has been referred to as ubiquitous, owing to its having been recorded some 300 times by a wide variety of groups, including the Duke Ellington version, which was listed by R. D. Darrell in his landmark 1932 article as among Ellington's thirty "best and most characteristic recordings."[70]

Although Wilmer was astutely, perhaps even precociously, aware of the early masterpieces of jazz and blues, her writing would focus more especially on the music and musicians of the 1960s with their more overtly political and social messages. After having her first article printed in Sinclair Traill's prestigious *Jazz Journal* in 1959 at age eighteen, Wilmer published five years later in Chicago's *Down Beat*, which brought to the Brit her first real recognition among this country's jazz musicians and critics. Wilmer's 1964 appearance in the leading American jazz magazine was in the form of an interview that she conducted with saxophonist Joe Harriott concerning his new concept that he called Abstract or Free Form. Wilmer also interviewed the revolutionary Texas saxophonist Ornette Coleman of Fort Worth, who almost single-handedly established the Free Jazz movement, beginning in 1959. In fact, Wilmer lived for five weeks in Coleman's "large, spacious loft . . . on Prince Street in the heart of SoHo."[71]

Although Ornette Coleman objected to being photographed and at times made fun of Wilmer's being "pretty wide-eyed around him" and at heart "a kid for the music," he kindly took her in and made it possible for her to associate with other Texas jazzmen, including tenorist Dewey Redman, also a native of Fort Worth.[72] Coleman, Redman, and other musicians in their circle were not the only Texans that Wilmer knew on fairly intimate terms. Indeed, her book mentions over the course of its 316 pages an impressive number of Texans whose music she listened to through recordings or heard in live performance. In addition to Coleman and Redman, the Texans named in her book include Ernestine Anderson and Arnett Cobb of Houston, Henry Coker and Cedar Walton of Dallas, Kenny Dorham of Post Oak, Eddie Durham of San Marcos, Gus Johnson of Tyler, William "Prince" Lasha of Fort Worth, and Gene Ramey of Austin. In her book *The Face of Black Jazz*, she also includes her photograph of Dallas baritone saxophonist Leroy Cooper, whom she interviewed in 1975 when he was touring with the Ray Charles Orchestra. Her photograph of Eddie Durham is an especially historic document, since it pictures him in a lounge chair accompanied by his trombone and his electric guitars.[73]

Of all the Texans that Wilmer photographed and knew personally, the two that she was closest to were Henry Coker, the lead trombonist with the Count Basie Orchestra, and Gene Ramey, a bassist who was with the great Charlie Parker at the beginning of Ramey's and the Bird's careers in Kansas City. An interview Wilmer conducted with Coker, published in *Jazz Journal* in 1961, first brought to my attention her significant work.[74] In her autobiography she recalls having met the trombonist in London in 1959 when he came there for the second time with the Basie band.[75] She credits Coker with showing her the ropes as an eighteen-year-old aspiring journalist, calling him her "buddy, a real gentleman who treated me with respect whatever the circumstances." She even asserts that without the friendship of a musician like Coker "I doubt whether I would have survived" in the world of journalism and "man-made music."[76] In the late 1970s, Coker was with the Ray Charles Orchestra, and Wilmer reports that "the last time he was in London I was tied up the night of the concert, but I rushed to the hotel early so that we could have breakfast together before the band left. I'm glad that I did see him then, for it was not long afterwards that Henry's big heart gave out."[77]

Of Gene Ramey, Wilmer has written that she first met this Texan in London when he was on tour with former Basie trumpeter Buck Clayton's band. At the group's departure, she had tears in her eyes and Ramey "chided [her] fondly and from then on addressed her as 'CB' ('Cry-Baby')." Later, when they met again in New York, Wilmer remembers that she was drawn to Ramey "immediately, a comfortably older man with white gunfighter moustache and an easy manner. Despite the flirtation that loomed in the air, he cast himself in the role of protector." In New York it was Ramey who introduced Wilmer to Harlem and "soul food."[78] Ramey and Coker and so many other jazz musicians come alive in the photographs and writings of Valerie Wilmer, who, as the title of one of her books aptly puts it, has taken black music "as serious as your life."[79] How seriously she has taken her role as a writer on black music is indicated by some of her thoughts toward the end of her autobiography, which indict her own society, culture, and race for their lack of any real concern for the black world:

The history of white writing on jazz has been filled with misunderstanding and misapprehension. . . .

Few Whites emerge from short contact with Black society with other than superficial burns. Whether there for the music or other sensual attractions, the pervading mood is consumerist. . . .

Among even the most open-minded of Whites, men and women, I've found an unfailing tendency to disbelieve the extent of racism. The psychological dislocation it can create remains unknown. Feeling themselves to be blameless as individuals, they can see no need to take on board situations created by "others." Tell them that if they're not part of the solution, they're part of the problem and they grow uneasy. Tell them that they, too, are racist because they benefit from an unjust and unequal society, and they go off into paroxysms of protest. Such people cannot conceive that there are others who have challenged themselves and come to terms with the realization that they are participants in the system, that there are some of us who have been torn apart by that realization, that there are those among us who have endeavoured to do whatever we can to change the status quo.[80]

There have been, then, different facets to the British ministrations on behalf of jazz and the people who made it perhaps the most widely and perennially admired music of the twentieth century. All aspects of British criticism have in one way or another effected change, if not of the status quo, at least in terms of an appreciation for the artistic and human values of a music still associated in certain minds with bordellos and bars, with anti-religion and the corruption of youth. It is to the great credit of the British that they have devotedly and even zealously valued an American import, which came to the New World and to the Old by way of an African diaspora. But then for whatever reason, as even Valerie Wilmer has allowed, the British have always been enthusiastic about other cultures and in particular African and American art and literature. And thanks to the work of scores of British commentators, discographers, interviewers, record collectors, dancers, and concertgoers, the history of jazz, of the music and its makers, is better known, better understood, and more highly esteemed than it would have been without Godbolt, Wilmer, and a host of acolytes who have served to render to an African American art form the homage it so richly deserves.

THE WISCONSIN-TEXAS JAZZ NEXUS

As jazz critic Gunther Schuller has commented, it is surprising to discover the "diverse regions of the country" from which jazz musicians have arisen.[1] It is especially surprising that such musicians, with differing geographical, political, social, religious, ethnic, racial, and economic backgrounds, have been able to band together to perform a music that requires a very particular spirit, peculiar technical skills, and a sensitivity to and an appreciation for musical forms and traditions that owe their origins to conditions rarely endured by the musicians themselves. Few if any of the first black jazzmen and certainly none of the early white jazzmen had ever known the often inhuman servitude borne by those who sang the chants, spirituals, and blues that would form the basis of jazz from its beginnings right up to the present time. The institution of slavery had, of course, divided the nation, and on opposite sides in the Civil War were the states of Wisconsin and Texas, both of which sent troops into the bloody, decisive battle of Gettysburg. Little could the brave men of the Wisconsin 6th who defended or the determined Rebels of the Texas Regiments who made an assault on Cemetery Ridge have suspected that one day musicians of their two states would join forces to produce the harmonies of jazz, which have depended so often on the blues form that is native to the Lone Star State yet has been loved and played by men from such Wisconsin towns and cities as Fox Lake, Madison, Milwaukee, Waukesha, Brillion, Monroe, and Kenosha.[2] Around the world, jazz has proven a magnet for the meeting of minds and the free exchange of musical ideas, through melancholy or fast-paced blues and the swinging, bopping, driving rhythms that have appealed to players and listeners in every corner of this country and those perhaps in every nation on earth.

In defeating the South in the Civil War, Wisconsin and the other Union states helped make possible in many ways the rise of blues, ragtime, and boogie-woogie, forms of black music whose origins have been traced in part to freed slaves who migrated to Texas. In East Texas the railroad lines especially provided employment for men who had been able to do little more than labor away relentlessly as sharecroppers on the same southern lands where they essentially remained in bondage during the postwar Reconstruction. As Texas folklore scholar Alan Lomax has pointed out, more American music has referred to or been related to the railroad than any other form of musical inspiration.[3] Certainly the railroad as a source of sound and sorrow is at the roots of blues rhythms and lyrics and the chugging, swaying patterns of boogie-woogie as well as a sophisticated jazz composition like Duke Ellington's "Daybreak Express." A songster's constant reference to a honey or momma going away, or a singer's urge to leave in the face of lost love, is standard blues fare. But more important to the emergence of jazz was the fact that the railroad gave to blacks in Texas relatively more freedom to travel, to work at jobs that allowed for greater economic well-being, and the ability to purchase instruments, to hear radios and recordings, and to develop their music in association with their fellow blacks who began to congregate in cities like Dallas and Houston. While the Deep South languished to a large degree under the burden of what William Faulkner refers to as a reliving of "the moment before Pickett's charge, as if the outcome [of Gettysburg] could be changed," Texas moved on and developed a cattle industry in the 1870s and then in

PREVIOUS PAGE: Box set of *The Woody Herman Story* (Properbox 15, 2000). Used by permission of Proper Records Ltd.

the early 1900s an oil industry, both of which offered jobs and a peripatetic lifestyle for blacks, which eventually led to their creation of jazz in many parts of the state.[4]

By 1918 black musicians from New Orleans had begun to migrate west and north, many ending up in Texas, California, and Chicago. Texas blacks had earlier followed the cattle trails north, but in the 1920s they also felt the lodestone pull of entertainment centers in Kansas City and Chicago that catered to musicians who could perform the new music called jazz that had begun to crop up from New Jersey to Los Angeles, beholden to but superseding the guitar-accompanied country blues and the repetitive piano rags. The first jazz recordings began to appear in 1917 and by 1923 classic jazz ensembles developed in Kansas City, Chicago, and New York, led by such seminal figures as Bennie Moten, King Oliver, Fletcher Henderson, and Duke Ellington. Texans had been at the forefront of black music, beginning with Scott Joplin of ragtime fame and continuing with Blind Lemon Jefferson, the King of Country Blues, and some of the earliest boogie-woogie pianists who recorded in Chicago in 1924.[5] And Texans were also present on some of the earliest and most vital jazz recordings, including several made in 1923 by Bennie Moten, Jelly Roll Morton, and Fletcher Henderson.[6]

At the end of the 1920s, two of the most important Wisconsin jazz musicians appeared on the scene: trumpet star Bunny Berigan of Fox Lake and clarinetist Woody Herman of Milwaukee.[7] Around 1928, contact between Wisconsin and Texas occurred in jazz terms when Woody Herman reportedly toured the state of Texas with the Joe Lichter band, with which he had played during high school.[8] This marked the first in a fascinating series of musical intersections between the two states, but rather than through musicians visiting one another's region, such intersections came primarily through their participation in recording sessions that took place elsewhere, usually in Chicago, New York, or Los Angeles. For at least five decades, from the 1930s into the 1970s, a number of Wisconsin and Texas sidemen worked together to create a wide variety of jazz, frequently based on the blues form. Indeed, during the 1930s, 1940s, and 1950s, Wisconsin and Texas jazz musicians would take part in recording sessions that produced outstanding examples of the prominent jazz styles of those periods, from swing to bop to the cool West Coast sound.

Although there were no Wisconsin musicians present—at least so far as I have been able to ascertain—on a recording of "Bugle Call Rag" made in Los Angeles in 1923 by the group called Jimmie's Joys, this early piece is a remarkable example of jazz style and technique in a year marked by an outpouring of jazz recordings that included the first by King Oliver and Louis Armstrong.[9] Jimmie's Joys was a group of musicians from Austin who regularly played for dances at the University of Texas, and their rendition of "Bugle Call Rag" already contains many if not all the characteristics of jazz, including the use of a well-known natural or man-made sound as the basis for a piece of music—in this case a bugle call; breaks, in which a soloist inserts a phrase or passage while the rest of the band stops playing; quotations from popular songs, here the University's anthem, "The Eyes of Texas," and "Yankee Doodle Dandy," the latter quoted by the trombonist; jazz techniques like flutter-tonguing by the cornetist and smears by the trombonist; and some swinging group improvisation. The breaks in this piece are taken by the cornetist, saxophonist, trombonist, and pianist, with each contributing a brief solo or a quote from another tune, and such breaks derive largely from the blues, since at the end of each line of verse when the blues man or woman is not singing, an instrument fills in the remaining beats in a bar with musical comments on what has been sung, which is the origin of jazz improvisation. Eventually jazz solos could extend over the entire side of a long-playing record, but on this cut of "Bugle Call Rag" each solo break is quite brief yet still represents an important aspect of any instrumental blues or jazz performance.

Leaping ahead twenty-one years to 1944, we find a recording of a live performance of the very same "Bugle Call Rag," featuring members of the group billed as Jazz at the Philharmonic.[10] On this date, the JATP musicians include tenor saxophonist Illinois Jacquet from Houston and guitarist Les Paul from Waukesha, Wisconsin. Like the trombonist on the 1923 recording by Jimmie's Joys who quotes from "Yankee Doodle Dandy," here bass player Red Callender quotes from the same song, which struck me as either a strange coincidence or some type of connection between the notes in "Bugle Call Rag" and those in "Yankee Doodle Dandy." The musical link between the two pieces may be part of the explanation, but in fact on the first recording of "Bugle Call Rag," made in 1922 by the New Orleans Rhythm Kings (NORK), trombonist George Brunis quotes from "Yankee Doodle Dandy," and it is clear that much of this 1922 jazz version was copied by Jimmie's Joys the following year.[11] But why would an advanced group like the JATP, in the same year as the first bebop recording session (reportedly organized by Texan Budd Johnson), resort to quoting a rather corny, flag-waving tune like "Yankee Doodle Dandy"? It would seem unlikely that Callender would have imitated the NORK recording, since later practicing musicians tended to reject so much early jazz as out of date. But this would probably be unfair to Callender, who may well have been quite familiar with a tradition established by NORK and carried on by Jimmie's Joys. In fact, in 1944 Callender recorded with New Orleans trumpeter Bunk Johnson's V-Disc Veterans, on such traditional tunes as "Ballin' the Jack," "Careless Love," and "Panama." In 1946 Callender would appear in the movie *New Orleans*, with Louis Armstrong and Billie Holiday. Of being hired to perform in that movie, the bassist commented, "I was the bebopper in the old-timer's band, but who cared? I had fun and to me music was always music; I didn't care what style it was as long as I could handle it."[12]

More to the point is the solo electric guitar work of Les Paul, who later achieved his greatest fame in 1951 with singer-guitarist Mary Ford on their version of "How High the Moon," which pioneered the use of overdubbing. Paul would have known the work of Texas-born electric guitarist Charlie Christian, who influenced every subsequent performer on his instrument, and certainly a number of Paul's pinged notes and his guitar phrasing recall Christian's sound and style. Following Paul's break is Illinois Jacquet's solo, which includes his suddenly playing a low note on his tenor that was, because of the Texan's frequent use of this device, termed a "Texas honk." Also typical of Jacquet's saxophone playing are his patented wild shakes and squeals that he almost single-handedly made a part of the jazz tenor style, in turn influencing many a saxophonist in the rock-and-roll bands. The all-out jam that concludes this version of "Bugle Call Rag" finds Paul's zinging, ecstatic electric guitar and Jacquet's screaming, high-pitched tenor combining to convert this ragtime tune into an updated JATP exhibition full of exhilarating sonic booms and a crowd-pleasing, frenetic pace. Also significant here is the fact that JATP organizer Norman Granz broke the color line by writing into every contract that blacks and whites could attend the concerts together, just as Granz arranged for black Texan Illinois Jacquet to jam with Wisconsin's white Les Paul.

Backing up ten years to 1934, we find an early pairing of Wisconsin and Texan jazz artistry on recordings by the Adrian Rollini Orchestra. Two tunes, "Davenport Blues" and "Riverboat Shuffle," feature trumpeter Bunny Berigan and Texas trombonist Jack Teagarden of Vernon in something of a swing version of the dixieland style.[13] The first tune opens with Teagarden's smooth trombone sound, after which the various musicians of the group, including Benny Goodman on clarinet and the Rollini brothers, Adrian and Arthur, on bass and tenor sax, respectively, take their turns soloing. Berigan appears only briefly as a soloist, whereas Teagarden returns for a full-blown chorus, before the side ends with his opening theme statement plus a few variations that show off his inimitably tossed-off, lipped turns or appoggiaturas. On "Riverboat Shuffle," Berigan can be heard ably leading the ensemble, but here again Teagarden enjoys the lion's share of the soloing, and as he does so displays his virtuoso handling of his horn. A more impressive coupling of Berigan and Teagarden occurred five years later when they formed part of an All-Star Band that once again included Benny Goodman and Arthur Rollini. Here, on a piece entitled "Blue Lou," which is not really a blues but a very popular riff swing number written by black saxophonist Edgar Sampson, Berigan solos first with some of his spectacular high register work, after which Big T follows with one of his powerhouse breaks full of his robust but always relaxed swing.[14] Berigan then returns for a second solo with more of his skyrocketing high notes. Both of these soloists were certainly virtuosi on their instruments and influential on all subsequent jazz musicians who aspired to mastery of the trumpet and trombone. No matter what state they came from, each had learned the art of jazz and could "converse" in the same musical language that would become universally understood and admired.

In 1935 Berigan teamed up with another Texas-born jazzman, pianist Teddy Wilson of Austin, to record a tune entitled simply "Blues in E Flat."[15] This piece is a classic blues with fine extended improvisations, first by Red Norvo on vibes, then Bunny Berigan on trumpet, followed by Chu Berry on tenor, and finally Teddy Wilson on piano. Almost ten years before the JATP live recording, this studio performance is an example of a mixed black and white group creating together beautifully and movingly thirty years before the advent of racial integration. Berigan proves on this piece that he possessed a true feeling for the blues and could express it through his impeccable control in every register. Likewise, Teddy Wilson, although he rarely recorded the blues, demonstrates his deep identification with the form and its often somber state of mind, even as he exhibits his rather lighthearted piano artistry with its rippling runs and ringing tones. Both of these instrumentalists were better known for their renditions of pop songs, in Wilson's case when he worked with the Benny Goodman Trio and with singer Billie Holiday. Berigan's most famous recording came in 1937, with his stirring version of "I Can't Get Started," which featured both his technically secure trumpet playing and his romantic vocal treatment of the song's fetching lyrics. A 1936 film clip with Bunny singing and playing his trumpet on the tune "Until Today," with the Freddie Rich Orchestra, does not make the same impact as hearing his rendition of "I Can't Get Started," but it does furnish a close-up of the handsome young musician in action, only five years before his premature death at age thirty-three.[16] Teddy Wilson would live until 1986, recording widely, including a session with bebop giants Charlie Parker and Dizzy Gillespie in 1945. But the 1935 date, with Berigan and Wilson sharing solo time, stands as an early example of the superlative, elegant jazz of these two musicians, one from a Wisconsin farming community and the other Texas-born and Tuskegee University–trained.

On the 1937 recording of Berigan and his orchestra performing "I Can't Get Started," his star trombonist at the time was "the great Sonny Lee" of Huntsville, who "played both lead and jazz trombone."[17] Since this piece was a feature for the trumpeter-leader, Lee does not take a solo, but he would on two other tunes recorded by the Berigan orchestra in the same year. On "The Prisoner's Song," Berigan opens the tune by playing with a type of wa-wa mute, and later solos without the mute,

Jimmy Dorsey Orchestra from 1943. Sonny Lee is the last trombone player pictured on the far right. Reproduced from *The New Grove Dictionary of Jazz*, vol. 1, edited by Barry Kernfield (1988).

bending, ripping, and shaking his notes in a typical jazz style. As for Sonny Lee on trombone, his open solo shows that he had been listening to his fellow Texan, the amazing Big T.[18] Lee's entrance is assertive swing of the kind that Teagarden trademarked from the late 1920s on, with Lee romping and riding, just as Teagarden did, and echoing the latter's patented lip turns and some of his flexibility on what before Teagarden had seemed a difficult instrument to manipulate. Also in 1937, the Berigan orchestra recorded "Mahogany Hall Stomp," and again Lee takes a fine solo, but this time using a mute, which softens his sound, even though he still maintains his swing and shows off his considerable technical skill.[19] Both of Lee's solos attest to his being a real pro, and obviously for this reason he was spotlighted by the Wisconsin trumpeter-leader in what at the time was one of the more popular swing-era orchestras.

In 1936, before Sonny Lee joined the Berigan orchestra, he had been a member of the first band led by Wisconsin clarinetist Woody Herman. On a number entitled "Take It Easy," Lee plays an obbligato to Woody's singing of the pseudoblues lyrics, with nice lip turns and a mellow sound, and then takes a short break toward the end of the song.[20] A fuller example of Lee's blues playing is found on the tune entitled "I've Had the Blues So Long," which shows him working within a true blues groove. Here Herman again sings the lyrics and also takes up his clarinet for a few tasteful licks. On a piece entitled "Slappin' the Bass," Lee contributes a driving break on this up-tempo tune, showcasing more of his fine technical facility. Further exhibiting Lee's stylistic range is the flexible phrasing of his warm, extended mute solo on the tune "Nola," which also contains an example of Herman's lilting clarinet. Lee's most impressive outing comes on "Fan It," on which the trombonist reveals that he could approach the level of Teagarden's technical prowess, as Sonny trills, rips upward, leaps from low to high notes, and in general offers a swinging brand of thirties jazz. The jam at the end of this piece has Herman's clarinet wailing above and Lee blowing riffs below and also tailgating in the best Dixieland manner. As the featured trombonist in both the Berigan and Herman bands of the late 1930s, Sonny Lee participated in the most popular recordings of the star trumpeter and was a member of the first of many bands that the clarinetist would lead, bands in which, as we shall see, a number of other Texans would assume prominent roles.

In 1937 Herman's band included Houston-born alto saxophonist and arranger Dean Kincaide, but this Texan did not solo in any of the performances of that year and contributed more as an arranger than a soloist to the Wisconsin leader's rise as a big-band star. Herman's most famous number, entitled punningly "At the Woodchopper's Ball," was originally recorded in 1939 by the first of the leader's bands to be referred to as the Herd. Here once again a Texan had a central role on this premier recording of a tune that ultimately sold five million copies, "one of the biggest big band monster hits ever."[21] The trumpeter who solos using a wa-wa mute, employing hand effects to produce some excellent growls and syncopation, is Horace "Steady" Nelson, who was born in Jefferson, Texas, in 1913, the same birth year as that of Woody Herman. Like much of Herman's early material, "At the Woodchopper's Ball" was based on a blues pattern, and in fact Herman's outfit was known during this period as the Band That Plays the Blues.[22] By this date the Herman Herd was already a very swinging outfit, even before its more famous period at the end of the war in 1945. The roaring open trumpet solo on "Big Wig in the Wigwam" is not identified but could also be the work of Nelson. The same is true of "Dallas Blues," on which of course it would be wholly appropriate if the Texas trumpeter were the sideman who takes a solo that is as forceful as the one on "Big Wig." The soloist on "Big Wig" certainly sounds to my ear like Nelson, who has been credited with the trumpet solo on "Woodchopper's Ball." Another tune on which Nelson definitely performs is "Blue Prelude," from 1940, which served at the time as the band's theme song before it was replaced by "Blue Flame."[23] Once more Nelson plays a wa-wa response to the lyrics sung by Herman, with the trumpeter's sound and style reminiscent of Cootie Williams, who at the time was doing his more famous wa-wa treatments for the Duke Ellington Orchestra. In 1941 Nelson returned to Texas, where in Houston he had first played in clubs on South Main before joining up with Herman. Nelson later moved to California, where he performed on the radio shows of Garry Moore, Dinah Shore, and Jimmy Durante and also played with the bands of Jimmy Dorsey and Hal McIntyre.[24] But it was Nelson's brief stay with Woody Herman that placed him at the beginnings of the Herd tradition and involved him in the recording of some of the Herman unit's most vital blues numbers, "At the Woodchopper's Ball" and "Blue Flame."

Budd Johnson on the album jacket of his *Let's Swing* (Prestige
Swingville 2015, 1960). Used by permission of Fantasy Records.

In 1944 Woody Herman would for the first time record in the new
bebop-influenced style of his bands of the mid- to late 1940s, and on this
occasion too a Texan—in fact two Texans— formed part of the Herman
Herd that cut a tune entitled "Cherry." Soloing on tenor saxophone is Budd
Johnson, a black multi-reed musician from Dallas. Not soloing but present
in the saxophone section is Mexican American multi-reed musician Ernie
Caceres from Rockport, Texas. The inclusion of a black and a Mexican
American musician was another first for the band, with a later version of
the Herd briefly featuring black alto saxophonist Johnny Hodges and
Cuban trombonist Juan Tizol, both from the Ellington Orchestra. On
"Cherry," Woody's clarinet is in especially fine form on this rocking, bluesy
tune, but Budd Johnson, soloing on tenor, digs deep into his emotive bag
of Aeolus to let loose with tones and lines that were unusual for the
Herman band, being the first black jazz inflections heard on its recordings.
Joop Visser even concedes that Johnson's "happy synthesis of [the styles
of tenor saxophonists] Lester Young and Coleman Hawkins . . . steals the
show."[25] One other tune on which Budd Johnson performs admirably is

entitled "It Must Be Jelly ('Cause Jam Don't Shake Like That)." Although Herman and vocalist Frances Wayne sing the novelty lyrics for fun, Johnson on tenor isn't fooling around, as he once again digs in for some beautiful, serious jazz, filled with swooping phrases, bent notes, and a conversational style, followed by Herman's pure, penetrating tone on clarinet. Instrumentally, the contrasting sounds and approaches of the two musicians complement one another and make for a fully satisfying performance.

Next to "At the Woodchoppers' Ball," probably the most famous number Herman recorded was "Four Brothers," a composition and arrangement by Texas multi-reed musician and composer Jimmy Giuffre of Dallas. Giuffre's arrangement for three tenor saxophones and a baritone established an identifiable bebop-era sound for the Herman Herd, which continued to employ the same saxophone setup for several decades to come.[26] The first recording of "Four Brothers," made in December 1947, showcased the four brothers of the title, which refers to saxophonists Zoot Sims, Serge Chaloff (on baritone), Herbie Steward, and Stan Getz, who solo in turn and conclude the piece with cameo breaks. Giuffre was not a member of the Herd at the time of this recording but would appear as a tenor saxophonist in Herman's so-called Second Herd of 1948 and 1949. One tune recorded by the Second Herd in July 1949 is entitled "Not Really the Blues," a Johnny Mandel composition and arrangement of which it has been observed that the piece "happens to be one of the few jazz compositions with a totally apt title. It is the blues, but spread out over sixteen bars instead of the usual twelve."[27] One of the trumpets in the 1949 Herd was Shorty Rogers of Great Barrington, Massachusetts, and it was through the association of Giuffre and Rogers as alumni of the Herman band that they later worked together in Los Angeles, recording under the name of Shorty Rogers and His Giants. In 1955 Rogers and Giuffre recorded a stirring quintet version of "Not Really the Blues," with Giuffre soloing to wonderful effect on tenor, his funky, down-home style in full tilt, and Rogers swinging away with his typical nonstop trumpet lines.[28]

Woody Herman was responsible for training and promoting innumerable sidemen who went on to success on their own, and Jimmy Giuffre was but one more Texan who profited from working with the Wisconsin leader. In the mid-1950s, Giuffre would form his own pianoless trio, which brought him the widest recognition, both for his playing and his writing talents. In 1958 Giuffre and his trio, consisting at the time of Bob Brookmeyer on trombone and Ralph Peña on bass, performed at the Newport Jazz Festival. A film of the festival has captured the Giuffre 3 doing one of his more famous compositions, the folksy tune entitled "The Train and the River," written originally for his trio with Jim Hall on guitar.[29] Even though Giuffre achieved considerable fame through his own small units, his composition and arrangement of "Four Brothers" for the Herman band first established his name as an innovator in the field of postwar bebop and created for the Herman Herds' reed sections an identifiable sound and style.

Along with Giuffre and Rogers in Herman's Second Herd of 1948 was another Texan, bassist Harry Babasin of Dallas. Babasin participated in a performance on May 12 that produced the Second Herd's own version of Giuffre's "Four Brothers," but unfortunately this live recording from the Commodore Hotel in New York does not pick up the bassist's notes as fully as one could wish. Nonetheless, in the opening of Giuffre's tune, Babasin can be heard keeping time and also furnishing just the right notes for the

CD insert of *The Jimmy Giuffre 3* (Fresh Sound Records, FSCD-1026, 1992). Pictured left to right are Jim Hall (guitar), Ralph Peña (bass), and Jimmy Giuffre (baritone sax).

soloists. On Al Cohn's tune entitled "The Goof and I," Babasin cuts through more clearly, with his bass lines audible behind the sax soloists and between some of the section work, even though the thundering drummer frequently tends to drown him out. Babasin's bass is clearest during Woody Herman's brief solo, as again two men from distant states work well together to create some swinging big-band jazz.[30] Babasin would, like Giuffre, end up in Los Angeles, where in 1952 he arranged for and performed on a recording session with Charlie Parker and Chet Baker, and in 1953 he would form part of a historic recording that first combined jazz with the Brazilian bossa nova.[31]

The sidemen in Herman's Herds were aware of Charlie Parker and the bebop revolution at least five years before Babasin recorded with Parker and Baker in 1952. Not only did Giuffre compose his boppish "Four Brothers" in 1947, but in that same year Shorty Rogers arranged "I've Got News For You" for the Herman band, transcribing for the sax section—as part of his arrangement—the alto solo played by Parker on his 1947 recording of "Dark Shadows."[32] In 1948 the Second Herd performed the Rogers arrangement of "I've Got News For You" on two occasions, at the famed Hollywood Palladium on March 12 and at the Commodore Hotel in New York on May 12. Both Giuffre and Babasin can be heard on the recording from the May 12 live performance, with the former contributing to the sax section's reading of the Parker solo as transcribed by Rogers.[33] Babasin not only recorded with Parker in 1952 but earlier in 1947 he had joined with bebop pianist Dodo Marmarosa, on a session that even included a tune entitled "Bopmatism." The Herman Herds were among the first big bands to adopt the bebop dialect, and Herman's sidemen—Texans among them—learned their lessons early on and continued to reap the benefits of their time with the Wisconsin leader who was always open to an eclectic repertoire.[34]

The next Texan to form part of the Woody Herman organization was Gene Roland, also of Dallas. A fellow student with Jimmy Giuffre and Harry Babasin at North Texas State University in Denton, Roland is credited with the idea of arranging for a sax section of four tenors, which Giuffre modified in writing and arranging his "Four Brothers" for the Herman Herds' three tenors and a baritone sax. Roland was the first important arranger for the Stan Kenton Orchestra in the mid-1940s but also arranged for a number of other bands, including that of Woody Herman, whose staff he joined in 1957 as chief arranger. In 1958 Roland contributed seven of the twelve arrangements recorded by the Herman band for its album entitled *Woody Herman '58*. In speaking of his arrangement of "Blue Satin," Roland remarked that it was a "slow blues typically in the Woody Herman idiom," which reveals that the Texan was well aware of Herman's "language strongly influenced by Basie and Ellington," and in fact Roland's arrangement especially recalls the unrushed but pulsing, blues-rooted Kansas City swing of Count Basie's band.[35] In addition to the brass and reed sections, Roland's arrangement features Bill Harris's witty trombone and Don Michaels's climactic percussion. Again, of his original tune "Bar Fly Blues," Roland reported that it was written especially for Herman, "Not the title, but for his particular type of slow blues alto playing."[36] Alto was Herman's first instrument, rather than clarinet, and this piece by Roland serves as a showcase for the leader's fine saxophone solo, punctuated in Roland's arrangement by shaking, muted brass. The loping piano motif, which is something of a Texan trait, sets the relaxed blues mood, with trombonist Bill Harris supplying some sad, slithery phrases. The title of another Roland arrangement, "Wailin' in the Woodshed," plays on the similar title of an early recording from 1941, "Woodsheddin' with Woody," on which Texan Steady Nelson had formed part of the trumpet section, along with Wisconsin trumpeter Cappy Lewis of Brillion.[37]

How many Texans may have passed through the Herman big-band academy I am unable to say for certain but will mention the latest addition of which I am aware, trumpeter Dennis Dotson of Jacksonville. Although I have not heard Dotson's work with Herman from 1975, I do know and admire his performances on the 1990 recording of *Return to the Wide Open Spaces*, made with fellow Texans James Clay and David "Fathead" Newman.[38] The 1975 Herd was not Herman's last, since he continued to lead aggregations up to his death in 1987, but even so, Dotson represents a long line of Texans stretching from Sonny Lee in Herman's first group of 1936 through Steady Nelson, Dean Kincaide, Budd Johnson, Ernie Caceres, Jimmy Giuffre, and Harry Babasin in the 1940s to Gene Roland in the 1950s and on to the final Texas musician that I will now consider, black drummer Gus Johnson of Tyler, who teamed up with Herman in the 1960s.

The only recording by Woody Herman with a small group of himself, a piano, bass, and drums was made in 1962, and on this occasion Gus Johnson occupied the percussion seat. Budd and Gus Johnson (no relation) were two of the few blacks ever to record with the Herman Herds, but both were key players on the recordings on which they appeared.

Titled *The Woody Herman Quartet: Swing Low, Sweet Clarinet*, the 1962 album with Gus Johnson consists almost entirely of standard jazz tunes, from "Rose Room" and "Don't Be That Way" to two of clarinetist Artie Shaw's famous features, "Begin the Beguine" and "Summit Ridge Drive." The one more typical Herman piece is entitled "Pee Wee Blues," a tune written by clarinetist Pee Wee Russell and arranged by Herman's pianist, Nat Pierce. In speaking of the members of his quartet, Herman remarked that "the guys are the rhythm section that's been with me for quite a while and we work well together."[39] This is perhaps most evident on "Sweet Lorraine," which swings at any easy gait, with Johnson's unobtrusive snare-drum punctuations just enough to keep things perking along nicely. After the waltz-time theme statement on "Begin the Beguine," Johnson drives the group expertly with his steady timekeeping and his rim-shot backbeats in four-four; his drum roll before the closing section sets up a fine contrast for the return to the three-four theme. But it is Johnson's haunting rhythmic pattern on the tom-tom and his subtle cymbal work for "Pee Wee Blues" that are the high point of his presence on this album. But then his drumming on "Don't Be That Way" is also outstanding, as it is on "Summit Ridge Drive." All in all, Gus Johnson shows here why he was so successful as the percussionist for the Jay McShann Orchestra, the last of the great Kansas City big bands in the early 1940s, and for what was tagged the New Testament band of Count Basie in the early 1950s. Just as Woody Herman could make authentic jazz with white, black, and Hispanic musicians, Gus Johnson could contribute to any type of ensemble, and both men from states with little in common in terms of weather, history, or cultural heritage could unite to create jazz's harmonious, swinging, and always engaging sounds.

In addition to Bunny Berigan and Woody Herman with their big bands and combos, one other Wisconsin jazz musician who linked up with a Texan was bassist Buddy Clark of Kenosha. In 1956 Clark joined Jimmy Giuffre for a recording session with a sextet led by Lennie Niehaus, an alto saxophonist and composer who had made a name for himself by leading the sax section of the Stan Kenton Orchestra. In putting together his pianoless sextet, Niehaus brought together the special talents of the Wisconsin bassist in conjunction with drums and a front line of trumpet and alto, tenor, and baritone saxes, a rather unusual combination that proved refreshing in the best West Coast tradition. Clark reportedly toured Europe with a Giuffre unit in 1959, but I have thus far found no recordings for such a group.[40] Fortunately, the Niehaus Sextet session allows a listener to hear these musicians from Wisconsin and Texas work-ing as part of a superb ensemble, with the music on Niehaus's album marked by the clean lines and crisp execution of so much of the West Coast music of this period.[41]

Paired with drummer Shelly Manne, Clark propels the group with his bass on which he produces a round, full tone, and on the blues entitled "Elbow Room," he takes an extended solo marked by his warm sound and flowing lines. The pairing of Clark and Giuffre is particularly notable on the tune entitled "Three of a Kind," a type of jazz fugue in which at one point only string bass and baritone sax play together to achieve a rich tonal blend.[42] (This same effect would be achieved in 1957 when Giuffre, also on baritone, teamed up with bassist Ralph Peña on "Gotta Dance," Giuffre's own composition, performed by his trio for the album *The Jimmy Giuffre 3*. It may be that Giuffre was inspired by his work with the Wisconsin bassist to write for the baritone-bass combination in his driving "Gotta Dance.")[43] On "Fond Memories," the moving lines of the tenor, alto, and baritone saxophones, combined with those of the bass, make for an especially touching effect, with the baritone and bass adding much to the lush overall sound. On "Knee Deep," the bass and baritone are again hand in glove as they swing together with a marvelous sense of unity. This album's peculiar instrumentation and its particular personnel are a perfect emblem for the kind of harmony that jazz has always made possible by bringing together, as it so often does, musicians from different parts of the country and even the world, regardless of backgrounds or personal styles.

In listening to the jazz recordings discussed here, one cannot neces-sarily identify the players as either from Wisconsin or Texas. Perhaps with a musician like Jack Teagarden, whose trombone sound was so special to him and has been described as similar to a Texas drawl, one may recog-nize a regional intonation or technique. But in making jazz, musicians from these two regions of the country played the same notes, the same tunes, the same kinds of syncopated rhythms, and with the same or at least a sim-ilar type of swing feel. If Texans leaned more toward blue notes, this could be an identifying mark, as in the case of Budd Johnson of Dallas. Yet as we have seen, Woody Herman and his early unit was billed as the Band That Plays the Blues, and Joop Visser even asserts that Herman had "a blues feeling that is not usually found in white performers, except Jack Teagarden."[44]

What distinguishes these musicians is ultimately, I suggest, less consequential than what they share—a love of jazz that transcends regional boundaries and racial and cultural differences. Even if they created distinctive sounds on the same instruments, such sounds were not necessarily regional in nature but merely the result of different ways of approaching their horns, of holding them, of positioning the mouthpieces between their lips or in forming their embouchures. Without wishing to minimize the impact of differing backgrounds, I would emphasize the fact that in jazz any player can join with his fellows to produce happy or sad melodies and fast or slow rhythms that have appealed to listeners worldwide. Wisconsin and Texas, in this sense, are no different from Sweden or Japan, where jazz has also brought together musicians of differing races, religions, and geographical regions, who have yet found in such music a common meeting ground for relieving the sorrow of loss and for celebrating the joy of being alive.

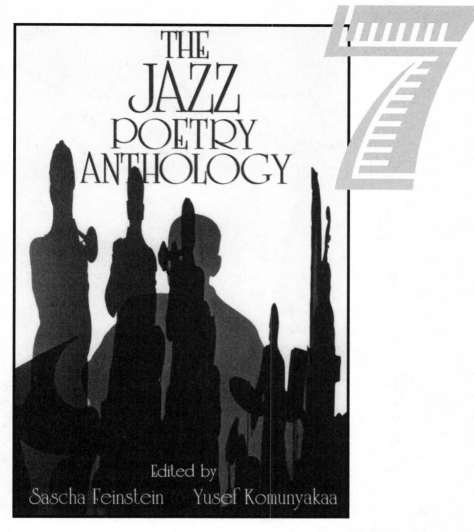

JAZZ IN LITERATURE

n 1923, the year of the first classic recordings of jazz by King Oliver and Louis Armstrong, American poet William Carlos Williams published a remarkable poem on the special qualities of this new American music. Originally appearing in his book *Spring and All* as simply poem 17, Williams's twenty lines in unrhymed couplets were later printed under the title "Shoot it Jimmy!" which derives from the sixteenth line of the poem. Spoken in a slang jargon by a musician of the day, the poem expresses attitudes already common to the performance of early jazz, and even in many respects characteristic of the music throughout its history. Most importantly, the speaker considers the art of jazz to be based not on a reading of sheet music, which he calls "a lot a cheese," but on the musician being given a "key" and let "loose" to play a music that "they can't copy."[1] Even by the seminal year of 1923, Williams understood that jazz is an art of improvisation and that the originality of a musician's performance depends not on his sticking to what someone else has written but rather on inventing his own melodic conception within a particular tonal center.

Over twenty years later, Williams heard the band of Bunk Johnson, a jazz trumpeter who was probably born in New Orleans in 1879 and who, as a result of having his horn smashed in 1932 and of losing his teeth soon thereafter, had apparently not played for eight years when he was rediscovered around 1940 working as a farm laborer. Fitted with a new set of teeth, Johnson began performing again in 1942, and in 1945 Williams heard him and his four-man unit in New York.[2] After listening to Johnson and his men, Williams was inspired to write another poem, this one entitled "Ol' Bunk's Band," which imitates in its sound and structure the jazz of Bunk's traditional Crescent City combo. In particular, the poet utilizes repeated three-word phrases (his title being one) in imitation of the short musical phrases known in jazz as riffs.[3] During the nearly quarter century between Williams's "Shoot it Jimmy!" and his "Ol' Bunk's Band" (both, it will be noted, three-word "riffs"), a number of other American poets and prose fictionists—both major and minor figures—would try their hands at imitating, celebrating, and attempting to understand the exhilarating music of jazz to which some of them and many who followed them responded with almost religious ardor.

In 1926 Hart Crane published *White Buildings*, his first collection of poems, which included his "For the Marriage of Faustus and Helen," whose second section offers some of the most perceptive lines ever written on jazz. Indeed, the very title of the poem proposes that jazz unites the intellectual and sensual, a farsighted view for the 1920s and even for decades to come. Like Williams, Crane recognized early on the significance of the new

PREVIOUS PAGE: Cover of *The Jazz Poetry Anthology*, edited by Sascha Feinstein & Yusef Komunyakaa (1991). Photograph, "Jazz Shadows," by William Claxton. Used by permission of Indiana University Press.

music and praised in paradoxical terms its "snarling hails of melody," its "rhythmic ellipses," its "new soothings, new amazements / That cornets introduce at every turn," its "deft catastrophes of drums," and the "reassuring way" of its "incunabula of the divine grotesque."[4] In the same period, poet Mina Loy also captured in paradoxical language the unique combination in jazz of what she calls the "brute-angels," asserting that "the seraph and the ass / in this unerring esperanto / of the earth / converse / of everlit delight."[5] Through her reference to Esperanto, Loy reveals her recognition of the universality of "cajoling jazz" that "blows with its tropic breath / among the echoes of the flesh / a synthesis / of racial caress."[6] Along with such poets as Williams, Crane, and Loy, and short story writers like Julio Cortázar and Eudora Welty, Texas poets and prose fictionists have also contributed to jazz literature their own insightful and moving commentaries, either as tributes to iconic master performers or as meditations on the meaning of the music and the cultures from which it arose.

Much jazz literature simply lists the names of musicians or the famous tunes they performed as a way of paying homage to them and their artistry.[7] But the poems and short stories can also depict the players as visionaries, even as godlike in their ability to create emotionally stirring and often technically skilled improvisations. One poem by John Sinclair on pianist-composer Thelonious Monk refers to his creating lines of "utter genius"; another poem by Kazuko Shiraishi christens tenor saxophonist John Coltrane a "saint"; a poem on Louis Armstrong by Melvin B. Tolson, who taught during the 1920s at Wiley College in Marshall, Texas, and whose speaker in his poem compares Armstrong to the angel Gabriel, declares that the latter knew that "[he'd] be the greatest trumpeter in the Universe, / if old Satchmo had never been born"; and still another poem on Armstrong by Fred Chappell even considers the trumpet star a savior ("I couldn't count how many times / You saved my life") and calls Satchmo's trumpet "the Tree of Life."[8] Such hagiography is common to jazz literature even when it acknowledges the ravages of alcohol or drug addiction in the lives of musicians like Charlie Parker, the extraordinary saxophonist of the bebop era. This is vividly true of Langston Hughes's "Trumpet Player," in which he criticizes jazz musicians for trading "moonlight" for a "spotlight," the "sea" for "a bar glass / Sucker size," yet he concludes the poem with these lines that approve the music's conversion of pain into art: "softly / As the tune comes from his throat / Trouble / Mellows to a golden note."[9]

One of the finest of all literary works on jazz, based in part on the life of Charlie "Bird" Parker, is Argentine Julio Cortázar's short story "El perseguidor" (translated as "The Pursuer"). Cortázar has managed in his fiction to reveal much about the inner life of the musician, the sense that only in the time that he is playing can he find the further dimension of Time that he seeks. The Parker-like protagonist tries to explain this idea to his imperious biographer by relating it to a ride on the metro: "because to ride the metro is like being put in a clock. The stations are minutes, dig, it's that time of yours, now's time; but I know there's another, and I've been thinking, thinking. . . ."[10] Typical of numerous characters in literary works on jazz, the protagonist is seen by his adherents as "some kind of angel come among men," and yet in Cortázar's story the near worship of the musician involves a profound misunderstanding of the artist, ironically even by his biographer.[11] Jazz followers, often referred to in literature as disciples, are capable, it seems, of betraying their idols by encouraging their weaknesses or criticizing them when they fail to perform as expected, that is, in the same style or at the same level as when they first achieved their fame. More frequently, perhaps, the jazz fan is forgiving of the artist's "sins." In the case of trumpeter Chet Baker, an elegiac poem by Miller Williams confesses that the jazzman's heroin addiction and his habit of taking advantage of his devotees—tendencies also present in the behavior of Charlie Parker—has left the poet deeply saddened, and yet he still loves Chet "for all the things he did with air."[12]

Another of the classic literary works on jazz is Eudora Welty's short story entitled "Powerhouse," a tribute to pianist-composer Fats Waller. Here, as in the Cortázar story, the artistry of the writer equals in many respects the artistry of the jazz musician who is the subject of the piece, which is only rarely true of writings on jazz.[13] Welty's prose can "swing" with the imaginative and rhythmic impact of jazz, as when she describes the pianist physically and reproduces his typical parodic renditions of sappy pop songs:

> His hands over the keys, he says sternly, "You-all ready? You-all ready to do some serious walking?" . . . Then, O Lord! . . . they are all down the first note like a waterfall.
>
> This note marks the end of any known discipline. Powerhouse seems to abandon them all—he himself seems lost—down in the song, yelling up like somebody in a whirlpool—not guiding them—

hailing them only. But he knows, really. He cries out, but he must know exactly. "Mercy! . . . What I say! . . . Yeah!" And then drifting, listening—"Where that skin beater?"—wanting drums, and starting up and pouring it out in the greatest delight and brutality. On the sweet pieces such a leer for everybody![14]

Like Crane and Loy, Welty understands the blend in jazz of a joyous spirit and an animal energy, an almost heavenly creativity rooted in the earthiness of everyday life. The tension achieved in jazz from these opposing forces surely accounts in large measure for the music's global appeal.

A short story by Donald Barthelme, who grew up in Houston, is perhaps not in the same class with the stories by Cortázar and Welty, but it does provide a humorous, discerning glimpse into the world of the jazz performance and what has been called the "cutting session," where musicians attempt to outdo one another technically and expressively. Barthelme's "The King of Jazz" is a telling commentary on the constant challenges faced by musicians who would vie for first place in the pantheon of their chosen instrument, or within the realm of a particularly demanding style like bebop.[15] Each king is inevitably dethroned by a newcomer who has learned the skills required and then developed them a step further than his predecessors. Such was the case of Texan Jack Teagarden, who arrived from the Southwest to unseat or upstage Miff Mole, the leading white trombonist of the mid- to late 1920s, and even to best, some claim, black trombonist Jimmy Harrison.

A sonnet on Jack Teagarden by English poet Peter McSloy alludes to the music making of the Texan but also depicts the man and his lifelong pleasure in tinkering with machines: "He gave of his solemn cheer / And played and sang his stately blues. We see / In photographs a smiling melancholy mask, / Dreaming of being a quiet engineer, / A lazy steady brakeman on the T&P."[16] Another poem, entitled "After Listening to Jack Teagarden . . . ," by James McKean, is less interesting than the poet's prose commentary on the relationship between writing poetry and performing jazz. After quoting from a famous article on legendary cornetist Bix Beiderbecke written in 1936 by Otis Ferguson for *The New Republic*, in which Ferguson refers to "Jack Teagarden's 'beautiful eight bar creation' in a recording Hoagy Carmichael made of his own 'Georgia,'" McKean observes that "Thus it is for poetry too—that form is absolutely necessary, either given by tradition or discovered organically in the first few lines, so that the clear, new voice can explore, revise, spin, and renew. At some point, the set figure is let go, memorized, and then reinvented enthusiastically."[17] Teagarden's improvisation, based on Carmichael's composition "Georgia," represents the creative process that begins with a thorough knowledge of the material of one's art and then develops from it one's own individual "voice," reinventing the original material in one's own image—a talent that for listeners of jazz elevates its creators to an almost sacred stature.

Another poem dedicated to a Texan is "Elegy for Kenny Dorham," by Joel "Yehuda" Wolk, who remembers the trumpeter's fleet lines of thirty-second notes, but also his "message / floated in the / church" at his last performance given in "The Old West Church, / Boston / . . . to raise / dialysis money."[18] The poem alludes to Dorham's death in 1972 from kidney disease, at the same time that it recalls, by its use of the word "message," the fact that Dorham was a founding member of the Jazz Messengers. Primarily, however, the poem mourns the passing of a man whose music communicated spiritually and will continue to do so, even though his "mouthpiece . . . hung itself up" as a sheriff hangs up his badge. Knowing that the recorded music of jazzmen like Dorham survives is a consolation to the bereaved. Many such poems on deceased jazz figures celebrate the enduring power of their music, its capacity to uplift and heal the heartaches of life even when ironically the musicians are dead, and were themselves often beaten down incurably both by discrimination and by substance abuse of their own bodies.

An earlier Texas trumpet player who appears in at least two works of literature is Oran "Hot Lips" Page of Dallas. Although there does not seem to be a poem devoted exclusively to Page himself, he is mentioned in a section of Hayden Carruth's "Paragraphs," which recreates a performance by an all-star lineup from 1944. Carruth evokes Page's trumpet tone by comparing it to "the torn edge / of reality."[19] Page also puts in a brief appearance in Jack Kerouac's classic Beat novel, *On the Road.* Sal Paradise, the novel's narrator, is recounting a mini-history of jazz, beginning, after Sousa marches and ragtime, with Louis Armstrong "blowing his beautiful top in the muds of New Orleans" and continuing with "swing, and Roy Eldridge, vigorous and virile, blasting the horn for everything it had in waves of power and logic and subtlety." Sal then comes to Charlie Parker, who is compared in Kerouac's *Mexico City Blues* to a "calm, beautiful, and

profound / . . . image of Buddha."[20] Sal first describes Parker "blowing
his taped-up alto among the logs," and then after having practiced on his
horn for hours (what in jazz is called "woodshedding"), the narrator
reports that Bird would seek out and watch "the old swinging Basie and
Benny Moten band that had Hot Lips Page and the rest"—the latter including Lester Young, "that gloomy, saintly goof in whom the history of jazz
was wrapped."[21]

Kerouac's reference to Parker's "taped-up alto" is paralleled in a short
story by Texas writer C. W. Smith, whose "The Plantation Club" contains
a description of the protagonist musician's "crappy axe," that is, in jazz
parlance, his pathetic saxophone. Smith's high school–age narrator goes
on to observe that this horn belonging to Stoogie, the protagonist, was

> one of the worst. The soft metal keys were always bending, which
> kept the pads from seating properly on their holes, and it was so out
> of tune with itself that Stoogie had to adjust each note with his ear
> and embouchure as he played. It was his tenth horn in as many
> years—he was broke so often that hocking them was his only resort;
> he could never keep one very long, though his metal Otto Link
> mouthpiece had been carried from one [horn] to the next.[22]

Not only does this passage parallel the one in Kerouac's novel, but the
truth behind the fiction has been documented historically by an episode
aired on public television in the *History Detectives* series. The daughter of
a jazz musician from Portland, Oregon, submitted to the television detectives her story about a saxophone that her father owned, which he said
had belonged to Charlie Parker. According to her father, he had bought
the horn from a pawn shop where Parker had hocked it, apparently to feed
his drug habit. When Parker did not buy back the saxophone, the Portland
musician did, with the pawn ticket that Parker had given him when he
could not believe that Bird would leave his horn in hock. Even without the
pawn ticket to go on, the History Detectives tracked down the pawn shop
and found that the story of Parker having left his horn there had been
handed down since the late 1940s. In the course of their detective work,
the investigators spoke with a dealer at the Portland Music Company, who
identified the instrument's date and model and declared that Parker would
have played such a saxophone. When one of the detectives remarked that

he thought Parker would have played a better horn, the dealer replied, "Well, it's not gold-plated and it's not the fanciest brand, but that kind of stuff really doesn't matter with somebody of Charlie Parker's skill. The saxophone is not nearly as important as the saxophone player. Saxophones are really like microphones, and he was singing through this thing, so he could have made any saxophone sound great."[23] In Smith's "The Plantation Club," the teenage narrator has purchased, with money saved and $200 from his parents, a Selmer Mark VI saxophone, which he says of himself "the worst player in town had," while "the best player [Stoogie] had a Brand X nickel-plated monster."[24] But even with his poor instrument, Stoogie improvised on Gershwin's "Summertime" with such "danger and despair" that the narrator "gawked while phrases blossomed from the bell of his horn," dancers in the black dive "warming up . . . waving and whooping 'Yaah!' as though his solo was the last-lap turn in an evangelical sermon."[25]

Limitations, whether social, physical, economic, or instrumental, cannot, it seems, deter the gifted and determined artist. This is in part the theme of "One of Three Musicians," a poem by Steve Jonas on Texas reedman Ornette Coleman. The poet describes the first time that he heard Coleman play in New York in 1967, which made him think of Picasso's painting, *Three Musicians*, in conjunction with the earliest form of jazz produced in New Orleans:

<blockquote>

neo-

classical in-

struments: cigarboxes w /

soft line strains drawn

across barrel staves, tin

cans thrown

(or kicked) in Congo Square

these "fakers"

with jaw bone percussions out of dead

horses & instruments from

the child's hand

They reproduce the spasms, the screams

the outbursts of dark religious ex-

orcisms.[26]
</blockquote>

A poem by Kenneth Rexroth, entitled "Written to Music," is subtitled "Eight for Ornette's Music" and contains the line "oh teacher of splendor," which neatly sums up the effect on the poet of Coleman's "free jazz."[27] The Texan also inspired a poem by John Taggart, his "Coming Forth by Day," subtitled "after a composition by Ornette Coleman." Taggart's piece, like a poem by Texan Gillian Conoley, is essentially a meditation on the jazzman's music, but whereas Taggart identifies the music of Coleman as the source of his poem, Conoley's "The One" refers to no specific musician, tune, or performance.[28] In all three poems by Rexroth, Taggart, and Conoley, jazz has moved the poets to create their own works of art, and this holds true for other media that treat of jazz, from painting and sculpture to dance and film. Operas and plays have also taken jazz as their subject matter, basing it either on the lives of particular musicians or the idea of the music as a symbol of such concepts as freedom, defiance, prejudice, or love.[29]

Most Texas poets who have written on jazz have focused their lines on such individual figures as Charlie Parker, Dizzy Gillespie, Billie Holiday, or Bill Evans. Only Vassar Miller of Houston went back to an earlier period and to a vocalist who is not so purely in the jazz idiom, singer Sophie Tucker. Miller's poem, "Dirge in Jazz Time," also contrasts with the poetry of her fellow Texans in that it is more formal in structure, rhymed and with the final line in each stanza repeated with only slight variation. Her title is somewhat paradoxical, since jazz is not often thought of as funereal, even though the origins of the music lie partly in the somber music that accompanied New Orleans funeral processions to the cemetery, only to be livened up on returning from the burial site. A sense of paradox is deepened with the refrain's reference to the singer as a "Red-hot Mama who is cold tonight," which Miller derived from Tucker's 1920s hit "Red-Hot Mama." The poet also alludes to another of Tucker's popular songs through the assertion that "One of these days you'll miss me," a line from Tucker's recording of "One of These Days," which she belted out with her quite powerful voice. The final stanza makes the singer's death all the more poignant when the poet calls for the "jazzmen" to "muffle their drums / And their saxophones she will hear no more / Where winter forever numbs, / Where no one can warm her whose heart burned bright, / Where Red-hot Mama is cold tonight."[30]

Another Houston poet, Lorenzo Thomas, wrote frequently on jazz, but one of his most acclaimed poems on this subject is "Historiography," which, once again, concerns the life and music of Charlie Parker. (Probably the earliest piece on Parker by a Texan was written in 1955 by Grover Lewis, at the time a student at then North Texas State University in Denton. This impressive essay, entitled "Dirge for Bird," is included in *Splendor in the Short Grass: The Grover Lewis Reader*.)[31] Lorenzo Thomas's poem on Parker contrasts the brilliance of his musical mind with the fact of his drug addiction, as a way of answering those who would concentrate on his being a "junkie" rather than on his "thinking and singing." Thomas concludes the poem with the claim that, according to his

> records, there was something
> More. There was space. Seeking. And mind
> Bringing African control on the corny times
> Of the tunes he would play. There was Space
>
> And the Sun and the Stars he saw in his head
> In the sky on the street and the ceilings
> Of nightclubs and Lounges as we sought to
> Actually lounge trapped in the dull asylum
>
> Of our own enslavements.[32]

A third Houston poet (originally from Commerce, Texas) is Susan Wood, who has written a poem on jazz singer Billie Holiday entitled "Strange Fruit," after her famous song of the same title. In the poem, Wood is remembering Holiday, or Lady Day, as tenor saxophonist Lester Young styled her, from 1956, when at age ten the poet first saw Billie on *The Tonight Show*. The singer appeared on the television show with her trademark "white gardenia in her hair," which, the poet says, filled with its sweet smell

> the living room in a gray house
> in Commerce, Texas, where I have already decided
> that I hate the South, that the sign in front of the courthouse—
> "The Blackest Land, The Whitest People"—is evil, that it isn't fair
> that the maid has to sit in the back seat.[33]

Somehow Wood knew all this even at ten, but she attributes to herself no "special virtue" and even confesses that she "didn't know anything" about

Holiday's "voice with the sound of brandy in it, even more behind / the beat than usual, the rasp already a wounded growl," yet she did know "enough not to forget it." The poet then recalls when Holiday first sang the song to an audience of "white, middle-class / folks with *The New Masses* stuffed in their back pockets"—the effect was electric, as her

> clear vowels[,] with no Baltimore in them, gathered strength
> until everyone in the room could see that black man dangling
> from the poplar tree, could smell the sudden smell
> of burning flesh, until that last word struck like a riding crop
> on a bare back. How the room went silent for a long time
> until someone clapped. And then everyone did.

The poem ends with a line from "Them There Eyes," a song Holiday sang with her Satchmo-inspired, innocent sensuality. In quoting the line, Wood comes full circle to say with the singer that she "fell in love with you the first time I looked at you." But the poem is more than a piece of fan adulation, since it summarizes Holiday's career, alludes to racism and lynch murder, and recalls Wood's own premature yet clairvoyant sense of right and wrong. As with the best literature on jazz, Wood's poem both celebrates the musician and her music and relates them to vital social and moral issues.

The most accessible sources for poetry written on jazz are *The Jazz Poetry Anthology* and *The Second Set*, edited by Sacha Feinstein and Yusef Komunyakaa. But curiously, no poem on Dizzy Gillespie appears in either of these two volumes, and after discovering that the earlier volume did not contain a poem on Gillespie, East Texas native Betty Adcock was moved to write her "Poem for Dizzy."[34] This is not just one more glorification of a jazz musician but probes the meaning of Dizzy's music and life and the lessons to be learned from both, suggesting at the same time some important differences between Gillespie and his contemporaries. Thinking of Dizzy's famous puffed cheeks and bent horn, the poet compares them to a South Wind–like cherub blowing a trumpet that is aimed heavenward, hinting once again at the spiritual dimension of jazz performance. In contrast, she refers to Miles Davis's "demon," his at times nasty, confrontational manner. In a similar vein, she infers that Gillespie, unlike Charlie Parker, was never tempted by drugs and as a result outlived such contemporaries as Davis, Parker, Coltrane, and Monk. The lesson to be taken from such contrasts is that Dizzy knew how to survive, with the poet claiming, "This too was real jazz." With respect to Dizzy's nickname, which he acquired at least in part from his clowning around, the poet suggests, in spite of his zany antics, that when it came to his art, he was "serious as sunrise" and ignored those who would criticize him as a buffoon, who "scoffed / or bristled at [his] little stageside dance." The poet also provides a personal anecdote about seeing Gillespie wandering alone taking photographs, and reveals how she learned from his saxophonist, James Moody, that this was his habit wherever he went. For the poet, this furnishes further insight into Dizzy's personality, a side that most of his listeners probably never suspected, "more private maybe / than anybody knew." In total, the poem reveals the admirable qualities of the trumpeter that gave his music, from the poet's point of view, more soul than that of any of his cohorts and instructed us in hope and "oldest love."

San Antonio poet Rosemary Catacalos has also written about a jazz life that serves as a learning opportunity. In her poem "The Lesson in 'A Waltz for Debby,'" Catacalos suggests that various events of the day—a woman in Beirut reacting to gunfire by pulling "her apron over her head" and wringing "the air in entreaty"; Mayan Indians in Guatemala being "hung in trees with their wrists slit and left / to die slowly, turning like obscene ornaments / or jungle birds"; and "six whales / rising and falling on the water: the usual and regular breathing of God"—all have "everything to do with how" pianist Bill Evans wrote his famous jazz waltz for three-year-old Debby.[35] Like Susan Wood and Betty Adcock, Catacalos finds wide-ranging connections between jazz and the world at large, with Wood and Catacalos especially focusing on racism. But whereas Wood goes back to her own childhood for examples of painful or difficult revelations, Catacalos observes her three-year-old nieces balancing on a Buckminster Fuller geodesic dome and realizes that one of them keeps inside her the pain she feels from having an uncle who is a missing person. The poet then relates the weight of this hidden pain to the fact that "her swing / would not fly, though she leaned with all her might / and crazily against gravity," thinking that "all the waltzes / in the world wouldn't save her from learning this." But ultimately Catacalos contrasts such a painful lesson of life's impossibilities with Evans's creation of "clear notes phrased with possibility. / And since jazz musicians mostly work nights," the poet discovers that Evans was "always finding [his] way in the dark." Even though Evans knew that Debby would one day learn that life does not "always come in gentle measures, the swoop and / sweep of a good dream doing what comes naturally," he nevertheless "went ahead" and wrote the waltz that contains those "gentle measures" and the "swoop and sweep" of that innocent dream.

One final poet to consider is Harryette Mullen, who grew up in Fort Worth and has written a number of jazz-related poems. In her "Playing the Invisible Saxophone *en el combo de las estrellas*," Mullen refers neither to specific jazz musicians nor to any particular jazz composition or perform-ance, but rather asserts that in the future she will "write a real perform-ance poem" that will be "a jazzy snazzy poem extravaganza, with pizzazz." She continues in black dialect to announce that "Poem be going solo, / Flying high on improbable improvisational innovation. / Poem be blowing hard!"[36] As in much of her work, Mullen plays with the language, employs a colloquial pun ("a poem that raises cane"), creates anagrams (here the closest are "musician magician" and "magical musical"), alliterates ("a wordsong that moves folks' minds"), and generates internal assonance ("sparkled with star presence"), all in order, as she says, that "each sound be a musical note / that flies off the page like some crazy blackbird." Also typical of her work is the use of Spanish, which she learned in Texas—here the title phrase, which also ends the poem: "en el combo de las estrellas." Musical imagery and allusion predominate in Mullen's long poem of 320 quatrains, *Muse & Drudge* (1995), which she has called "a crossroad where Sappho meets the blues lyric."[37] In common with many poets drawn to jazz, Mullen attempts to reproduce what she calls this "kinetically ener-getic" music in her own writing, seeking to recreate its rhythm "like rain into earth," a rhythm that on being heard, read, and felt by listeners and readers "gets em up dancing to their own heartbeats."

That jazz is a wordless universal language understood across borders and cultures is confirmed by the worldwide response of writers who have not only paid tribute to the music but have striven to imitate or emulate it in their own writings, and even to glorify its creators as more than artists. Jazz societies in countless countries devote themselves to the most serious study of the music and its performers, no less than literary critics analyze and assess the performances of poets and prose fictionists, some of whom almost from the beginnings of jazz have created writings based on or relat-ed to the music and its makers. Perhaps as much as any literature of the twentieth century, jazz has spoken clearly and meaningfully to its listeners, and especially to writers, who have heard in its notes a message that in many ways transcends the written word and yet has moved authors in every genre to aspire to the music's capacity for communicating on the highest and deepest human levels through mechanical skill, aural invention, and emotional and intellectual expression.

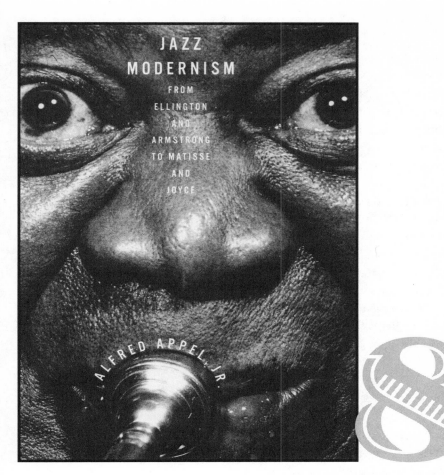

THE ALCHEMY OF JAZZ

Given the fascination of many modes of modernism with essence and its presence, jazz has to be read as a mode of modernist art, in fact a paragon of sorts.

—Frederick Garber, *"Fabulating Jazz"*

According to Jelly Roll Morton, the great Louisiana-born jazz composer and pianist, it was in 1902 that he composed his seminal "King Porter Stomp," a tune recorded by almost every big band of the swing era.[1] One hundred years later, in 2002, any number of CD reissues of Morton's own recordings were available, including a five-CD boxed set issued that year from JSP Records of London. Not only can Morton's own recorded jazz be found in CD bins, but jazz of every imaginable type is being issued or reissued almost daily, which evinces, for any needing such proof, the staying power of this American music. Further evidence of the lasting appeal of jazz is attested by the appearance in 2002 of countless articles, books, exhibits, and documentaries on this music and the lives of its artists. Two such books published in this year were Alfred Appel Jr.'s *Jazz Modernism from Ellington and Armstrong to Matisse and Joyce* and a reissue of Studs Terkel's *Giants of Jazz*, which first appeared in 1957 and was revised in 1975.[2] Although these two volumes are basically forty-five years apart in their conceptions, and although much has been written and discovered about jazz since the original printing of Terkel's book, both of these studies have much in common when it comes to their treatment of key figures in the history of jazz. Both texts are valuable guides for the serious jazz fan as well as for those readers seeking a reliable introduction to the principal contributions the music has made to American and even world culture.

What may surprise some jazz aficionados is the fact that both Appel and Terkel focus special attention on the music of Fats Waller, and in Appel's case also on Waller's satirical commentaries in the lyrics he sang. Some jazz purists have long denigrated Waller as having pandered to commercial taste and having demeaned himself and jazz through his mixing of an undeniable pianistic virtuosity with a clownish comedy routine. But Appel especially finds that this view misses the profound modernist achievement of Waller's refashioning of Tin Pan(dering) Alley tunes into ironic, witty, knowing asides on the content of the pop songs that he was basically assigned to record by studio executives. (My play on Tin Pan Alley is typical of what Appel does throughout his punning text, his own wordplay often based on Waller's witty double entendres.) Appel also applies this same "reading" to Louis Armstrong's recasting of popular songs and thereby reveals that both Waller and Armstrong were alchemical masters of the modernist technique made famous by Picasso and Joyce and other artists and writers of the first decades of the twentieth century. Art in the hands of such modernists converted, according to Appel, trash into treasure, base metals, as it were, into gold.[3]

What again may surprise jazz cognoscenti is that Appel includes in his revaluation of jazz as a modernist art the vocal and instrumental performances of Texan Jack Teagarden. In reconsidering Big T's recordings in the 1940s as the only white member of the Louis Armstrong All-Stars, which was "the first black band to feature a white musician" (Teagarden had made a studio recording with Armstrong in 1929), Appel hears in the work of this "finest white blues singer" and revolutionary trombonist an ability through "the pressing earnestness of his light baritone voice [to turn] banalities—'don't save your kisses / pass them around'—into a *carpe diem* philosophy, almost; . . . [to make] its unvarnished lyrics ring true."[4] In discussing Teagarden's recording of "St. James Infirmary" from a 1947 concert with the Armstrong All-Stars, Appel notes that the singer-trombonist "completes the blues with his inimitable laconic soulfulness—Afro-Cowhand, it could be labeled to attract more educators to the idea of jazz multiculturism."[5] As for Teagarden's trombone solo following his vocal, Appel observes that it "is aleatory music, modernism by definition, though to him it was a proven crowd-pleasing vaudeville trick: using a water glass in place of the trombone's chamber and flared bell, which produced an ethereal, plaintive sound—and here, in the infirmary, some rasping, ascending and descending buzzes, the anguished inner voice of a mourner."[6] Appel contrasts Teagarden's more straightforward interpolation of "I'll let the congregation join in," during his 1956 singing of "Aung Hagar's Children's Blues," with the practice of Armstrong and Waller, who "would have played it for laughs."[7] Mainly the Texan from Vernon serves to illustrate the primary thesis of Appel's book, since the author asserts that "Teagarden the singer epitomizes multicultural jazz music and the modernist impulse to turn dross to brass."[8]

Jazz Modernism makes its point repeatedly through Appel's comparisons and contrasts between recorded performances of jazz and modernist artworks, such as Picasso's 1912 *Guitar, Sheet Music, and Glass*, Matisse's *Jazz* of 1947 (which includes a cutout entitled *The Cowboy*), and Texan Robert Rauschenberg's *Monk*. Included among the musical examples are the compositions of Duke Ellington and the jazz singing of Billie Holiday as accompanied by tenorist Lester Young. Mostly, Appel selects musical examples with wordplay, "Tom foolery," and in the case of the duo of Louis Armstrong and Texas reedman Budd Johnson singing "Sweet Sue, Just

You," what Appel terms "charming nonsense," even though critic Dan Morgenstern has revealed that Johnson's chorus is actually his scatting of the lyrics in pig latin.[9] Curiously, Appel rejects Rauschenberg's *Monk* from 1955, which would seemingly be a perfect fit for his view that jazz and modern art are fellow travelers, especially since this collage piece incorporates a record label from a long-play recording of Thelonious Monk's famous "Round about Midnight." But Appel finds that the Texan's artwork is not "jazz modernism because it doesn't swing or sing—that is, its collage doesn't make verbal sense, one of the considerable achievements of the celebrated 1912–1913 collages of Picasso, Braque, Sonia Delaunay, and the infinitely legible Carlo Carrà. . . . Rauschenberg's tangled if not agonized abstract expressionist impasto pigments at the top of *Monk* are truly off-key. "[10] This estimate of Rauschenberg's art reflects Appel's preference for more mainstream jazz and accounts for his apparent disdain for the Free and New Wave schools of jazz that began to appear beginning in the 1960s and that, obviously for Appel, were lacking in swing.

On the other hand, Appel finds the work of Piet Mondrian, particularly his *Broadway Boogie Woogie* of 1942–1943 and *Victory Boogie Woogie* of 1942–1944, fully illustrative of his jazz modernism theme, in part because these works were created while the painter was listening in New York to recordings of boogie-woogie piano. Among the boogie recordings that Appel relates to Mondrian's artwork are pianist Pete Johnson's 1938 "Roll 'em Pete," with Texas trumpeter Oran "Hot Lips" Page, and Johnson's 1940 "Boo-Woo," with Texas trumpeter Harry James. The critic remarks that these two recordings were in the artist's own collection and that in *Broadway Boogie Woogie*

> Mondrian's basic geometry is boogie-woogie for the nonce, the left hand's "vertical" bass line ostinato (propulsive repeated figures) playing against the right hand's "horizontal" dotted eighth or sixteenth notes, heavy chords, simple riffs, tremolos, and choruses of percussive single notes, spaced variously, positing a stop-and-go-traffic neon-light time overview of broadway and times square. Synesthesia rules, and the painting swings.[11]

If Mondrian's art "swings," this is surely owing in part to the source of its inspiration, since in fact the two boogie recordings in his collection are outstanding representatives of the style, and the participation of the two Texas trumpeters is largely the reason why.

In addition to commentaries on modernist paintings, Appel also incorporates modernist literary works into his analyses of jazz, with James Joyce's *Ulysses* figuring prominently in Appel's attempt to link jazz and modernism. Appel partly criticizes the novel's "obscurantism" by way of contrast with jazz when he writes that "the brass of Ellington and Teagarden is of course accessible and even *Ulysses* is not beyond rescue."[12] He later continues in this vein when he declares that "'Rhythm saved the world,' sings Armstrong, and Joyce is readily comprehensible when he's got rhythm, as he does in the sociopolitical parodies of 'Cyclops,' comic invention and patter of 'Circe,' and rolling lyricism of 'Penelope,' the Molly Bloom chapter."[13] Also of significance for Appel in connecting jazz and modernism is Eudora Welty's modernist short story "Powerhouse," which was in fact based on a performance by Fats Waller that the Southern writer attended about 1939 in her hometown of Jackson, Mississippi. Appel rightly proclaims that Welty's is "probably the best story about jazz," and he accounts for its "great power and originality" on the basis of the author's "conflation of church and state—the state of a jazz musician who formulates the author's extraordinary sense of the tone and pace of a sanctified church meeting and the closed-off Negro world of 'juju,' of fear and deathly superstition."[14] The critic then brings Welty's art to bear analogically on Waller and Armstrong who, "if music-making is an act of faith, . . . are bishops in the church of lost songs, where it is truly Christian to save a dog tune."[15]

In the case of Studs Terkel's *Giants of Jazz*, the prose of this book is not as jazzy as Appel's, and neither does Terkel employ a comparative approach that ranges, as Appel's does, from Waller's takeoffs on "My Window Faces the South" and Ellington's "music as a healing, multicultural balm" to painting, baseball ("Harry James, who recorded 'Dodgers Fan Dance' [1941], was said to care as much about a band recruit's baseball skills as his musicianship"), Walker Evans photographs, Brancusi sculpture, and Calder wire "sketches" of Josephine Baker.[16] Yet Terkel's writing style does serve to inspire the reader to listen to the music, which clearly is the principal aim of both these books. Terkel's prose is lucid rather than witty and punning, and through its clarity it is in fact so inspirational—in recounting the lives of lowly musicians who rose on the wings

Jacket cover of *Giants of Jazz*, by Studs Terkel (2002).

of jazz to become King, Count, Duke, and legendary Bix and Bird—that his book can serve as an ideal introduction for the young reader and a refresher course for the jaded know-it-all. Terkel was and is a populist, and his *Giants of Jazz* is a popularizing narrative of the lives of thirteen musicians and their music.

Terkel begins with one of my own personal favorites, Joe "King" Oliver, and ends with John Coltrane. In each case Terkel emphasizes the difficulties the musicians faced in their careers, including poverty, prejudice, competition with other musicians, parental objections to the playing of such music, and drinking or drug addiction. An instance of parental objection is provided by Fats Waller's father, a minister who opposed his son's dropping out of school to perform "the devil's tunes."[17] Although Fats was a good student at De Witt Clinton High School, his math teacher asked him why "a very bright boy" like himself could not comprehend "simple algebra."[18] Terkel reports that Fats always had a clever response to any question: "maybe it's because my head's all filled with music. An' it ain't got any room left for all those x's an' y's an' q's."[19] As both Terkel and Appel assert, with Waller music and humor always went hand in hand, and Terkel's description of Fats's "tongue-in-cheek versions of pop songs" is right on: what made his performances "click was his 'happy frog' kidding of the drippy lyrics."[20]

Whereas Appel's book offers the special feature of 127 full-color reproductions of paintings, photographs, record labels, and sculptures, the Terkel book furnishes readers with tasteful, revealing line drawings by Robert Galster. Terkel's artist has faithfully captured the recognizable appearance and even something of the inner spirit of the writer's thirteen jazz musicians: Oliver, Armstrong, Bessie Smith, Beiderbecke, Waller, Ellington, Goodman, Basie, Woody Herman, Gillespie, Parker, and Coltrane. The Galster drawings were included in the 1957 edition of *Giants of Jazz* but not the 1975 revision of Terkel's book. It was good to have such sketches restored in the 2002 edition.

Necessarily, the first printing of *Giants of Jazz* did not include a chapter on John Coltrane and did not mention other figures who would come to prominence only after 1957. Aside from not containing the Galster sketches, the 1975 revised version of *Giants of Jazz* and the 2002 edition differ only in that the latter drops a sample list of New Music, which included recordings by Thelonious Monk, Miles Davis, Eric Dolphy, Cecil Taylor, and Fort Worth native Ornette Coleman. In Terkel's chapter on Coltrane, he does note that 'Trane "was listening to younger musicians like Ornette Coleman and Cecil Taylor, people who were using many of the styles that fascinated him."[21] In his *Jazz Modernism*, Alfred Appel does not mention Coleman at all, perhaps because Appel felt that, as he observes of Coltrane and Dolphy, Ornette, with his so-called Free Jazz, has "eschewed the salient characteristics of 1920–1950 classic jazz: accessibility; humor; a capacity for joy; the Great [white] American Songbook, the backbone of jazz multiculturalism . . . ; and the goals and ideals of racial integration."[22] On the contrary, Coleman definitely does exhibit a sense of humor and a "capacity for joy," and has at times improvised on tunes from the Great American Songbook, so that in this regard the Texan too is very much a jazz modernist.

For his part, Studs Terkel believes, as the title of his final chapter has it, that "jazz is the music of many" and that "its language is universal. . . .

It speaks in the tongue of joy and freedom."[23] Both Terkel and Appel make this point vividly and for this reason alone both of their books are valuable reflections on an American music that continues to inspire artists in every field—among others, television series, film, dance, drama, poetry, and detective novels—just as it goes on moving listeners around the world and in every walk of life.

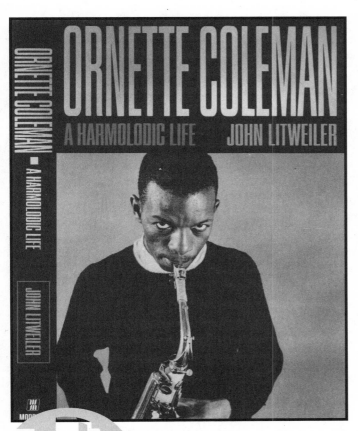

ORNETTE COLEMAN'S HARMOLODIC LIFE

"Texas Jazz—Myth or Reality?" was the title of an August 1993 symposium held in Houston, during which the *Houston Chronicle*'s Rick Mitchell observed that a Texan is listed on almost every page of Leonard Feather's 1960 *Encyclopedia of Jazz*.[1] The jury still seems out on the question posed by the symposium title, but the photographs of Texas jazz musicians projected on a screen by Dallas archivist Allison C. Tucker left no doubt that countless native Texans have played a part in many of the major developments in America's most original music. And according to John Litweiler's biography, *Ornette Coleman: A Harmolodic Life*, this Fort Worth-born multi-instrumentalist, composer, and bandleader is one of "four artists whose music and presence" have marked "major turning points in the course of jazz history."[2] The other three are legendary Buddy Bolden, Louis "Satchmo" Armstrong, and Charlie "Bird" Parker.

After the jazz eras denominated Hot, Swing, and Bebop, Ornette Coleman heralded another age with his 1959 albums *Change of the Century* and *The Shape of Jazz to Come*, which were comparable in their impact on the jazz world to the revolutionary recordings by Armstrong's Hot Five and Hot Seven in 1926–1927 and the first Dizzy Gillespie-Charlie Parker masterpieces of 1945. The Free Jazz era ushered in by Coleman derives its name in part from his 1960 album of the same title, *Free Jazz*; earlier, in 1959, on his tune entitled "Free," Coleman played his famous white-plastic alto saxophone in a solo that Litweiler describes as "shattering in its power." He adds that the solo on "Free" "was a particularly remarkable achievement—clearly, 'free form' meant, not 'free from form,' but 'free to create form' and remains true of the best post-Coleman musicians right up to the present."[3]

John Litweiler's biography is an excellent and sympathetic study of the founder of the Free Jazz movement, who would be commissioned by the French government to compose a work entitled *The Country That Gave the Freedom Symbol to America*, which was performed in 1989 at the bicentennial of the French Revolution. But even before Coleman received official recognition in Europe, he had already been elected to the *Down Beat* Hall of Fame in 1969 and the magazine's readers had voted him in 1987 "Jazz Musician of the Year." Although Coleman, who was born in 1930, is still active at sixty-three and apparently full of ambitious, revolutionary projects, it is fitting that in 1992 Litweiler paid such high tribute to one of the geniuses of jazz, providing for the public story of—in pianist Herbie Hancock's words—"a man of great conviction, a pioneer always moving forward down the path he has chosen, a can opener who opens all of us up as musicians. I could not play what I play had it not been for Ornette Coleman."[4]

Making extensive use of interviews with relatives, fellow musicians, and jazz fans, as well as commentaries by such astute critics as T. E. Martin, Max Harrison, Whitney Balliett, Martin Williams, and Dan

PREVIOUS PAGE: Ornette Coleman on the dust jacket of *Ornette Coleman: A Harmolodic Life,* by John Litweiler (1992). Used by permission of HarperCollins Publishers.

Morgenstern, along with Litweiler's own insightful analyses of Coleman's performances, the biographer has woven together a thoroughly readable account of the man and his music. The book focuses primarily on the highlights of Coleman's struggles and triumphs, revealing in the process why he has been alternately vilified as a fraud and lauded as a generous, living saint. Litweiler makes clear throughout the biography that Coleman's music is a mixture of "thwarted cadences and crushed emotions," of an "optimistic playing" and "creative flow" of ideas "truly beautiful to hear."[5]

Ornette Coleman's career began while he was a student in the segregated schools of Fort Worth in the mid-1940s, when he took up the saxophone on his own at age fourteen and became a self-taught musician. In the view of jazz historian Gunther Schuller, it was "precisely because Mr. Coleman was not 'handicapped' by conventional music education that he has been able to make his unique contribution to contemporary music."[6] There were early portents of musical genius, as when Ornette "misinterpreted" a standard scale while playing in a church band and was told that he had been "playing the instrument wrong for two years" and that he would "never be a saxophone player."[7] At I. M. Terrell, the city's black high school, Ornette was kicked out of the band "for indulging in some improvising in the midst of John Philip Sousa's 'Washington Post March.'"[8] But fortunately Coleman persisted, even though he would encounter even more discouraging critics, like the patrons of a Baton Rouge dance hall, where he was punched in the stomach and almost beaten to death because he "interjected some of his modern ideas" into the blues tenor solo he played while touring with a minstrel show.[9]

As it turned out, Terrell High School had been a much safer venue, and one where Coleman could share his vision with other talented young musicians, two of whom later figured prominently in Ornette's internationally acclaimed jazz ensembles. Trumpeter Charles Moffett ultimately switched to drums and toured Europe in 1965 with the Coleman Trio, and tenor saxophonist Dewey Redman appeared with the Coleman Quartet at the historically important Paris Concert of 1969. Another schoolmate at Terrell was woodwind player Prince Lasha, who emulated a Fort Worth tenorist named Red Connors, considered by Lasha to be "the greatest inspiration in the South-West."[10] Connors, who Coleman has said was better than legendary swing tenor man Lester Young, encouraged these young musicians and impressed on Ornette "the importance of reading music fluently."[11] In Fort Worth, fellow musicians congregated at the Coleman house to practice "because their own families objected to their playing in their own homes."[12] What began in Fort Worth continued elsewhere, as throughout Coleman's career his home—later his Artists House in New York—has provided a gathering place for his sidemen, who have often even lived with him.

In Fort Worth, the young musicians not only practiced at Coleman's house and elsewhere, but they received their fuller education playing with local bands in the city's clubs and nightspots. Clarinetist John Carter, another of Ornette's schoolmates, recalled that by the mid-1940s, with older men serving in the armed forces, "high school-age boys could go out and get work at what would ordinarily be a man's job."[13] Like many of his fellow musicians, Coleman performed in rhythm-and-blues bands, and he has said of himself that at the time he was a "honker," like Texas tenorist Illinois Jacquet.[14] His rhythm and blues experience would show up later in his blues entitled "Tears Inside," where Coleman plays in a style Litweiler refers to as his "strained sound, bent or splintered notes, and sometimes brutal attack."[15] The result of Ornette's early on-the-job training was not only his own "harmolodics," but what T. E. Martin calls a "rhythmic intuition unrivalled in the new wave and equaled by few other jazzmen."[16]

For Coleman there was also the vital influence that came from his work with church groups. In speaking of his 1973 trip to Joujouka, Morocco, to listen and play at the annual Bou Jeloud festival of Master Musicians, Coleman recalled that

> In Texas when I used to have to play for a country evangelist, healing people, doing things. . . . We'd get there and the piano would be in G. H— there'd be no such a thing as a key. . . . Those things [people being healed] would happen. So I had that experience myself, when I was playing for evangelists or in church, that particular thing we're talking about—I think that's more in church music. What I mean by church music, music that is totally created for an emotional experience.[17]

Coleman goes on to comment on the "meaning of the music at Joujouka," but it is implied by his biographer that Coleman's remarks also apply to the jazzman's own work:

It's a human music. It's about life conditions, not about losing your woman and, you know, baby will you please come back, and you know, I can't live without you in the bed. It's not that. It's much deeper music.

There is a music that has the quality to preserve life.

The musicians there [at Joujouka] I'd heard had cured a white fellow of cancer with their music. I believe it.[18]

Later Litweiler quotes a longtime admirer of Coleman, his business manager John Snyder, who touches on this same basic issue:

[Ornette] believes in the "healing" power of music and that there are as many ways of making music as there are people. He objects to the idea that there are mutually exclusive ways of going about it (e.g., the "jazz" and "classical" traditions, to name two). This objection manifests itself in his "harmolodic" theory, which is his structure for people to express their emotions and themselves through music.[19]

After the success of his 1959 recordings, made in Los Angeles with his quartet of Don Cherry on pocket trumpet, Charlie Haden on string bass, and Billy Higgins on drums, Coleman moved to New York and worked with a variety of groups, many of which included at least one of these three original quartet members. At the same time, Coleman began to associate with "Third Stream" composers like Gunther Schuller, John Lewis, and fellow Texan Jimmy Giuffre, who all blended "jazz" and "classical" traditions in their music. Coleman himself did a bit of jazz-classical crossover in 1965, when he arrived unannounced in London and proposed a concert at Fairfield Hall. He was enthusiastically received by the local modern jazz community, but because of a quota system, he had to be classified as a "concert artist" before he could perform. With two weeks' notice, Coleman composed *Forms and Sounds* for woodwind quintet and then sent for his bassist, David Izenson, and his drummer, Charles Moffett, to join him for the concert. Litweiler notes, "It was the first time an African-American musician, playing his own music, received the 'concert artist' classification, and Ornette financed the concert himself" (as he has often done throughout his career, which was true as well of avant-garde New England composer Charles Ives).[20]

In 1968, after Coleman had earned two Guggenheim fellowships for composition, written music for films, and had his *Inventions of Symphonic Poems* performed at UCLA (conducted by former schoolmate John Carter), the same British musicians union and the Labour Ministry that had frustrated and inspired him three years earlier declared Coleman's achievements irrelevant, and so he had to compose *Emotion Modulation* in order to qualify again as a "concert artist." Coleman's second London concert has been described concisely by Barry McRae, author of *Ornette Coleman*, which was published in 1988 by Apollo Press: "In order to get a work permit, he had spent many hours convincing the authorities that he was not a jazz musician. In the Albert Hall, he spent little more than two [hours] proving he was one of the greatest."[21]

At times during his long and fertile career, Louis Armstrong was criticized for avoiding political and racial concerns. Reportedly, Satchmo once responded by asking what good he would be to his people if, as a trumpet player, he got his teeth knocked out in a Civil Rights march. Though much of Ornette Coleman's most important music was created during the 1960s, when Black Power groups were active in the major cities where he performed, Coleman maintained that music was his medium for changing or "healing" people and therefore he avoided political activism. In 1960 he was in Chicago when the Black Muslims were holding their annual convention and he commented that "I could hardly play for all the hate around me."[22]

Despite the jealousy and even hatred that his music sometimes aroused in listeners, Coleman remained throughout that violent period a gentle man of peace, which is exemplified by his tune of that title from *The Shape of Jazz to Come*. At the same time that Coleman is an essentially serene, self-controlled person, in his music he is daring, witty, and humorous, as can be seen in his piece entitled "Congeniality" from that same 1959 album. But most often Coleman's music is characterized by a piercing blues cry, "a frenzy of terror with lashing trills and insane double-time phrases," and a loneliness typified by his classic "Lonely Woman."[23] Some prominent jazz musicians at first declared that Coleman was playing out of tune and did not know the chord changes, and Ornette seemed to respond indirectly when he remarked, "I have never in my life seen anyone explain how and what I'm doing in music. But everybody knows that it's something that hasn't happened before."[24] Bobby Bradford, a Dallas trumpeter who played on Coleman's 1971 *Science Fiction* album, once observed, "I think you'll find an urgency and dead seriousness in Ornette's music that said things weren't going to be about Jim Crow or a resigned black man or West Coast cool any longer."[25]

Jamaaladeen Tacuma, the electric bassist in Coleman's Prime Time band, offered a brief definition that explains something of the Coleman harmolodic approach: "Basically what we do is compositional improvising in which each person acts like a soloist. We work from a melody in a tonal point, and anything that you play has to be equal to the melody or better."[26] As for the term "harmolodics," Litweiler suggests that as early as the 1950s, when Coleman formed his first groups, he may have coined the word in order to combine harmony and melody as the focus for his music. The biographer bases this view on Ornette's own assertion that he had always called what he was doing by this name: "But I never started using [harmolodics] as much as I did say in the last five years . . . probably because I was always interested in trying to get to the place where I could be secure and successful in what I was doing, and I didn't want to appear as if I was trying to be an intellect or something, just to have a chance to play music."[27]

By the mid-1960s, it was evident that Coleman had reached his goal. By then, Litweiler writes, "Ornette's inspiration was international," and by the 1970s "the main lines of jazz development . . . continued to descend from Ornette's innovations of the late 1950s," with his music attracting "players from all nationalities."[28] To its credit, Fort Worth recognized the achievement of its native son and proclaimed September 29, 1983, Ornette Coleman Day, and the mayor presented the musician with a key to the city. The occasion was the opening of the Caravan of Dreams, which premiered Ornette's *Prime Design*, dedicated to Buckminster Fuller, the creator of the geodesic dome, one of which sits atop the Caravan building. Meanwhile, many of the ex-members of Coleman's groups had gone on to establish themselves as "graduates" of Ornette's "school" of Free Jazz. Litweiler even sees this revolutionary figure as a "benign parent" who today "can survey a large, active jazz scene that he fathered through his persistence and dedication."[29] Whether the music that Coleman has produced is "Texas jazz," it does—in such a piece as his "Ramblin'"—evoke for some listeners, like T. E. Martin,

> the western emptiness across which men (the horns) move with their mixture of bravado and loneliness. . . . The prairie sound is kept well

to the fore and given psychological complexity, hence its life, by the use of short stabbing phrases that fall into a compulsive swing. The whole is straightforward, though individual, and one can see little difficulty in sensing the man's inevitable understanding.[30]

On a more visceral level, as John Tynan of *Down Beat* magazine wrote on first hearing Ornette Coleman's 1958 debut recording, *Something Else!* the music "raises goose bumps."[31] And that's a response that Ornette Coleman's harmolodics can still elicit.

A JAZZ MASTER'S DIAMOND JUBILEE

onsidered an archetypal iconoclast, who in the late 1950s followed yet departed dramatically from the bebop movement of the 1940s, Ornette Coleman remains a mild-mannered one-man band, a composer of sounds that range from the humorous and witty to the poignant and profound. He speaks softly but packs a mean alto sax that can erupt with a cornucopia of raucous, erotic, and sensitive pitches. To date he has to his credit over forty recordings for jazz trio, quartet, double quartet, string quartet, woodwind quintet, symphony orchestra, and movie sound track, and he has even designed and made his own apparel.

Although Coleman hails from Fort Worth, he has not lived in Texas for over forty years and had not performed in Austin for well over two decades when he returned on November 14, 2004, for a long-awaited appearance at the University of Texas Performing Arts Center. On March 9, 2005, Coleman turned seventy-five, but he continues to create some of the most avant-garde music in the world—music that would seem to belie his provincial beginnings, music that confounded his critics from the start of his career and still amazes with each new permutation of his famous harmolodic theory. How he manages to do so after all these years remains, perhaps, the central mystery surrounding this unassuming, peace-loving, wholly humane musician.

Coleman's quartet for his November 2004 Austin engagement consisted of his son Denardo on drums and two string basses played by Tony Falanga and Greg Cohen, the latest of his instrumental configurations. Coleman's first group was his 1958 quintet, which evolved the next year into his classic quartet with Don Cherry on pocket trumpet, Charlie Haden on bass, and Billy Higgins on drums. Over the next forty-five years, there would be any number of combinations of "Coleman groups," including his Prime Time, which has featured percussion and stringed instruments of various types. Coleman himself has recorded on alto sax, tenor sax, trumpet, and violin, but his plastic alto has always been his primary, trademark outlet for expressing his keening, piercing, tender, and endlessly surprising notes and phrases. Standing or sitting on a stool during his Austin appearance, he played without any attempt at showmanship or crowd-pleasing antics—in performance Ornette Coleman is a totally serious artist.

Throughout the Austin concert he sported a hat somewhat reminiscent of the porkpie worn by the great tenor saxophonist Lester Young, and was dressed to the nines in a pale blue suit, a striped shirt, and a purple tie. On meeting him backstage afterward, I was struck by how short he was in contrast to my image of him—from photographs and even live on stage—as a tall, imposing figure. It was symbolically satisfying to discover that he was in fact a giant not in height but simply in the stature of his art.

At one point in the performance, Coleman's white plastic sax fell to the floor from its stand. As he reached for it he almost knocked over his trumpet. It appeared a tense moment for the audience, but Coleman calmly rearranged his horns, changed the reed on his sax, and continued with

PREVIOUS PAGE: Jay Trachtenberg (left), producer of KUT radio's "Jazz, Etc.," and Ornette Coleman, following the performance by the Coleman Quartet at the Performing Arts Center, University of Texas at Austin, November 2004. Used by permission of Casey Monahan.

the tune in progress, not even retuning the instrument but obviously adjusting the notes by his impeccable ear. This demonstrated what comes through on his recordings: he not only hears sounds peculiar to himself but he can play them on any instrument he happens to pick up.

Early in his career, Coleman was accused of being a fake, of being unable to play his horn properly. But looking back it is clear that from the first he had mastered his instrument for his own purposes. Today his mastery is perhaps even greater, as he begins and ends any piece flawlessly, leaping to high, affective notes that are perfectly attuned and penetrating in their emotive power. Even if his sound is not the smoothly flowing, scalar- and chordal-based aerobatics of bebop genius Charlie "Bird" Parker, Coleman's wide-ranging sound production is completely appropriate to his equally intellectual approach. If he does not swing in the same way that Bird did, Coleman can certainly create that sine qua non of jazz, even on such a seemingly unlikely selection as "What a Friend We Have in Jesus," which is included on his 1996 CD *Sound Museum*. (To my disappointment, the quartet that had recorded this notable album was not the group that would appear in Austin. That special Coleman aggregate featured the incredible female pianist Geri Allen as well as bassist Charnett Moffett, son of drummer Charles Moffett, Coleman's fellow Fort Worthian and a crucial member of the leader's well-traveled trio of the mid-1960s.)

The title "Sound Museum" should not suggest to readers that either in 1996 or in 2004 did Coleman resort to dated material, since the tunes recorded or performed in person are all vitally alive. "City Living," for example, evokes a sense of rush-hour traffic, of the tension and stress but also the stimulation of the urban experience, and therefore is still very much a contemporary fact of life. "Monsieur Allard" is a catchy number that shows off the dexterity of all four members of the quartet, and "What Reason" is a touching tune that features the prodigious talent of Charnett Moffett (whose first name is a combination of his father's and Coleman's first names). Both of these pieces on the CD that I purchased after the concert were entirely new to me. At the time of Coleman's Austin appearance I was told that all the material to be performed was new, but even though this turned out not to be true, Coleman did not repeat any of his early masterworks, such as his now frequently covered "Lonely Woman" or "Peace," or one of my personal favorites, "Congeniality," all from his pace-setting 1959 album *The Shape of Jazz to Come*. "Women of the Veil" from *Sound Museum* was on the Austin program, but at a slower tempo than on the

CD and with extended solo space for Coleman's sax, which made it more meaningful than the recorded rendition. Even if the tunes on the Austin program were not new, Coleman has not been resting on his laurels. He goes on writing and playing with impressive energy, drive, and technical facility. And always he manifests his harmolodic theory of harmony and melody liberated from clef and key—*o jubilate*!

Although Coleman has composed a number of tunes that allude to bebop (such as his 1959 "Bird Food," his 1960 "The Legend of Bebop," his 1978 "Word for Bird," and his 1983 "Harmolodic Bebop"), he has never really depended on the repertoire of his predecessors. He did record in 1960 his own version of "Embraceable You," the Gershwin tune that Parker interpreted in his definitive bebop style of 1947. But Coleman's version of this standard could not be more different, with the Gershwin melody and chords hardly recognizable, whereas Parker keeps them constantly in mind. Coleman remarked of his version that his group (he being the only soloist) "played [it] the way standards are played and with as much spontaneity as we could."[1] Essentially this piece as performed by Coleman is virtually his own, just as every piece on every one of his recordings was composed and arranged by him, with exceptions like the Gershwin tune, the hymn noted above, and a piece on his 1995 CD *Tone Dialing* that he based on a Bach prelude. If Coleman took his cue from bebop, he went with it in his own spontaneous directions, even as he asserts that "Bird would have understood. He would have approved our aspiring to something beyond what we inherited."[2] Certainly Coleman has made a different kind of jazz, and he has also created in his 1972 *Skies of America* the kind of symphonic work that Bird probably yearned to write himself.

In Argentine novelist Julio Cortázar's short story "The Pursuer," based in part on the life of Charlie Parker, the biographer-narrator reports that Bird incorporated into his jazz solos a song by Connecticut composer Charles Ives, apparently his piece entitled "The Cage."[3] That Parker knew any works by Ives can be doubted, and that Coleman knew Ives's highly idiosyncratic music, at least in 1972 when he composed his *Skies of America*, is also unlikely. And yet Coleman's composition is indubitably related in sound and spirit to such experimental works by Ives as his *Three Places in New England* and his *Fourth Symphony*, especially in Coleman's section of *Skies of America* entitled "The New Anthem." In seven of the twenty-one sections of *Skies of America*, the saxophonist solos against the symphony orchestra, in particular and significantly on the ones entitled

"The Artist in America," "Foreigner in a Free Land," "Silver-Screen," "Poetry," "Love-Life," and "Jam Session." He also solos on "The Men Who Live in the White House," which seems to move from sinister in the ensemble section to jingoistic and perhaps demagogic in Coleman's solo passages. It is also significant that this man of peace does not solo on "The Military." Although it would be difficult to say that Coleman is an openly political artist, he certainly understands America as a land affected by a tendency to jingoism—as well as its many other aggressive leanings and movements. He has revealed as much in his remarks on his musical composition: "The skies of America have had more changes to occur under them in this century than any other country: assassinations, political wars, gangster wars, racial wars, space races, women's rights, sex, drugs and the death of God."[4]

Like Charles Ives and Walt Whitman before him, Ornette Coleman has heard America singing, fighting, loving, and longing, and his music reflects this larger, deeper, rather than merely political, picture of the nation and its peoples. The title of his 1978 CD says it all: Coleman's music is *In All Languages* and has reached around the world in its appeal. In Amsterdam a repertory group led by trumpeter Eric Boeren recorded a 1997 CD entitled *Cross Breeding*, the title tune one of seven Coleman compositions, including his "Free Jazz," which are interpreted by the Dutch musicians. The composer has himself performed with diverse groups and individuals, from guitarists Jerry García of the Grateful Dead and Pat Metheny to Moroccan Master Musicians of Joujouka. Coleman has also played his saxophone on the sound track for the film of *Naked Lunch* and has accompanied singer-songwriters Joe Henry and Lou Reed. Like many other jazz musicians, Coleman has resisted being limited by the term "jazz," as he attempts to encompass all forms of music and all peoples. His Latin-tinged tunes like "P.P. (Picolo Pesos)" on *Sound Museum* and "Guadalupe" on *Tone Dialing* are typical of his work and reflect his Texas upbringing with its spirited Hispanic overtones. His acknowledgments on *Tone Dialing* take up an entire page of the CD insert and end with his appeal for acceptance of his "sincere appreciation for [the] help" of any whose names he might have "inadvertently left off the list." Gratitude is but one of Coleman's many laudable qualities as man and artist.

The rather down-home yet advanced "Tone Dialing" was one of the most engaging tunes performed at the Austin concert, as was "If I Knew as Much About You (As You Know About Me)." The former opened with the dual basses setting a somber mood that prepared well for Coleman's passionate but delicate outpouring in the upper register. The titles of these and other selections are representative of Coleman's preoccupations in his music, in particular such titles as "Search for Life," "Sound Is Everywhere," "When Will I See You Again," and "Family Reunion." The last of these could be a theme song for a TV series, and the penultimate summons up a lovely, romantic melody that, set to words, could easily become a hit recording. "Local Instinct" is an updated version of Coleman's revolutionary *Free Jazz* of 1960, as forty-five years later he is still creating his extraordinary sounds, whereas almost all the avant-garde has departed the scene, including his own Don Cherry and Ed Blackwell, to whom he has dedicated *Sound Museum*.

Who would ever have imagined such a turn of events? Surely not his early detractors, who wrote him off as a flash-in-the-pan charlatan. But Coleman is a survivor in every sense of the word. He has endured ridicule and rejection and even a brutal physical attack by clients in a New Orleans bar who objected to his unorthodox style of jazz. Through it all he has remained true to his vision that the world "needs music that fills the heart with love and joy and the mind with joy whatever the style." As he goes on to say, "It's a very sad affair when one must put any music above another to fulfill a social position for wealth or personal ego."[5] In no way has Ornette Coleman been an egoist; rather, he has brought love and joy to the hearts and minds of inhabitants around the globe, from Texas to New York, from Africa to Sweden, from the Netherlands to Japan. His has truly been a generous gift, one to be celebrated every anniversary of this innovative Texan's birth.

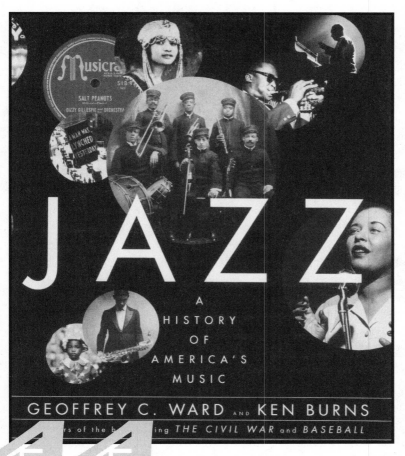

JAZZ

A HISTORY OF AMERICA'S MUSIC

GEOFFREY C. WARD AND KEN BURNS

rs of the b   ing *THE CIVIL WAR* and *BASEBALL*

A TEXAS TAKE ON KEN BURNS'S *JAZZ*

After having watched the ten PBS television episodes of *Jazz*, filmmaker Ken Burns and scriptwriter Geoffrey C. Ward's historical survey of America's "proudly mongrel music," I was asked by my indulgent, long-suffering Chilean wife whether, with the end of the series, I would experience withdrawal symptoms.[1] She knew that I had looked forward to each new episode, despite the damning advance reviews. For her part, she frequently dozed off, even though she found the visual imagery fascinating and enjoyed the commentaries of critic Gary Giddins, historian Gerald Early, and trumpeter Wynton Marsalis. But jazz music, except for a few items in my own record collection, such as King Oliver's "Edna," Bessie Smith's "Back Water Blues," Charles Mingus's "Oh Lord Don't Let Them Drop That Atomic Bomb on Me," and Fats Waller's "Your Feet's Too Big," is simply something she can—as I cannot—live without.

For me the most revelatory moment in the Burns series was the recollection by a white student at the University of Texas of having heard Louis Armstrong for the first time in 1931 at Austin's Driskill Hotel. Charles Black immediately recognized the African American as a genius and was forced to change his views about race. In later years, Black would serve on the legal team that brought before the Supreme Court the landmark case of *Brown v. Board of Education*.

From its beginnings, jazz has had such a mind-altering effect, and the Burns PBS series will undoubtedly change the thinking of many and will help the music make innumerable converts for years to come. Critical reaction to the film, however, has focused primarily on what the series does not include: the period from 1960 to the present is said to be unforgivably slighted, while Armstrong and Duke Ellington receive far too much attention. This has been the consistent complaint lodged by those who would champion fusion jazz, a figure like Anthony Braxton, or any number of splinter groups and avant-garde tendencies that appeared in the wake of Texan Ornette Coleman's Free Jazz movement, which can be dated from Coleman's 1959 album *The Shape of Jazz to Come* and his 1960 album *Free Jazz*. Coleman himself probably receives more time and attention than any other Texas musician spotlighted in the series, with pianist Teddy Wilson of Austin and electric guitarist Charlie Christian of Bonham tied for second, and trombonist Jack Teagarden of Vernon a distant third. And while it is entirely fitting that Burns has devoted considerable footage to Coleman, given his revolutionary contribution to the development of jazz, it is perhaps disappointing that the series does not reveal the role played in the music by so many other Texans. But this is just a minor, biased regret, since the series has for the first time rendered the much-needed service of highlighting the careers of the major figures in jazz, while setting them in the context of U.S. social history.

Texans Teddy Wilson, Charlie Christian, and Jack Teagarden all figured significantly in the social impact of jazz, and this aspect of the music
is effectively chronicled in the Burns series. Beginning in 1935, Wilson
was a member of the Benny Goodman small groups that first integrated
public jazz performances, and in 1939 Christian joined the Goodman
organization as a key member of the clarinetist-bandleader's Sextet. The
Burns PBS series briefly traces the careers of both these Texas sidemen
and their importance to U.S. racial history as well as their roles in developing the art of jazz during the swing era. The film series also acknowledges the vital part played by Wilson in the recording career of Billie
Holiday, the finest of all jazz singers. Christian's signal involvement in the
incipient bebop movement during 1940 and 1941 is recounted through his
participation in late-night jam sessions at Minton's Playhouse in New
York City. As members of Goodman small groups, both Wilson and
Christian enjoyed high visibility, were recorded extensively, and affected
profoundly the evolution of jazz and the history of U.S. race relations.

As for trombonist Jack Teagarden, he had been among the first jazz
musicians to record as part of a racially mixed ensemble, having done so
with Louis Armstrong in 1929. The Burns series briefly recaps an episode
in a later period of Teagarden's career, depicting him through a film clip
that shows the trombonist singing with Armstrong during the 1940s when
the Texan was a member of the trumpeter's All-Stars. At one point when
he was with the Armstrong group, Teagarden was not allowed to perform
in public with the rest of the trumpeter's all-black ensemble when it visited Armstrong's hometown of New Orleans. Armstrong protested by
refusing to play the scheduled concert without his white trombonist-
singer. In addition, Armstrong stipulated in his will that after his death he
was not to be buried in the city where he was born and raised. Armstrong
not only recognized the injustice of separating the races, but by hiring
Teagarden, he testified to the Texan's central position in the development
of the trombone in jazz history.

Another Texas trombonist, Tyree Glenn of Corsicana, formed part of
Armstrong's last All-Stars group during the mid-1960s and recorded with
the trumpeter-singer on his still-popular "What a Wonderful World." As
both trombonist and vibraphonist, Glenn recorded with the Cab Calloway
and Duke Ellington orchestras between 1940 and 1952. Although Glenn
does not figure in the Burns series, he, like many other Texas jazzmen, was
a versatile multi-instrumentalist who brought his own distinctive voice to

a number of prominent jazz organizations. While it is possible to find in every jazz entity representatives of various parts of the country, it is hard to find a single unit that did not include a Texan among its sidemen. From the Casa Loma to the Glenn Miller bands, from the Fletcher Henderson to the Stan Kenton orchestras, one or more Texans took part in important recording sessions by these and so many other outstanding outfits. Obviously, I am stressing but one regional side to the jazz pantheon, but to paraphrase jazz critic Glenn Coulter, simply to list the names of Texans among the leading musicians in jazz gives me, as a native listener, a deeply abiding pleasure.[2]

My incorrigible Texas chauvinism was brought out most fully by the short segment (too short for me) on Count Basie. This installment of the series begins by focusing on John Hammond, the controversial promoter responsible for having Benny Goodman recruit Charlie Christian for his Sextet. Hammond had grown increasingly impatient with the predictable formulae of the popular swing-era orchestras, and then in 1936 he discovered, via a late-night radio broadcast, the refreshing Kansas City riff style of the Count Basie band, which included at the time some half-dozen Texans. Rehearing the opening strains of Basie's 1938 "Jumpin' at the Woodside" sent chills down my spine, the only work over the ten nights to do so. Even as the voice-over interfered with this stirring performance, I could still feel the old Texas pride surging up when Denton native Herschel Evans came riding out at the end of the piece with what critic Gunther Schuller has described as his "notable, nagging, nastily squealy clarinet."[3] Lamentably, Schuller, author of the classic studies *Early Jazz* and *The Swing Era*, was not included among the interviewed commentators, although he is credited in the list of consultants.

Aside from the absence of an authority like Gunther Schuller, the limited exposure of the Basie band, and the exclusion of any number of lesser but integral units and individual figures, *Jazz* is a worthy production that tells the story of this world-class music as well as any film or book could have. (Not incidentally, the volume entitled *Jazz: A History of America's Music*, by Geoffrey C. Ward and Ken Burns, published by Alfred A. Knopf in conjunction with the film series, is equally engaging and goes into more depth through commentaries from musicians, critics, and other observers not included in the series, such as novelist Elizabeth Hardwick and biographer Helen Oakley.) As Casey Monahan of the Texas Music

Office recently concluded, the whole history of this music is a messy business, which is certainly evident from the bitter partisan exchanges in the 1940s among the "moldy figs" of traditional jazz, the conservative adherents of swing, and the "dizzy" advocates of the new bebop. Every listener has his or her favorite period, group, or soloist, but as the Burns series rightly indicates, the history of jazz is most beholden to Louis Armstrong, Duke Ellington, and Charlie Parker for much of its artistry and its most memorable sounds. Among Texans, Ornette Coleman of Fort Worth comes closest to these three men in terms of having made a monumental impact on the music, from having given to it a direction that in some ways has dominated jazz from 1959 to the present day.

Yet other Texans have also played significant roles in the creation of jazz, and this, too, is apparent from the Burns film series, even if it is not overtly acknowledged through captions identifying the individual performers. It would have been good had the series provided titles of tunes and the performing ensembles as they were being presented. Although all performers are listed at the end of each episode, the credits are in such small type and scroll past so quickly that it will be difficult for most viewer-listeners to know which came when. Even if newcomers to jazz rewind their videos, they will probably not be able to put the names of songs and groups together with their appearance in a particular sequence.

As with Herschel Evans and his important role as a soloist in the Count Basie band of the late 1930s, other seminal Texans perform anonymously during the episodes of *Jazz*. While no recording of Scott Joplin's ragtime is included in the series, the sheet music of his classic "Maple Leaf Rag" is projected on the screen as the Texarkana product is cited as the most prominent ragtime composer. Boogie-woogie prodigy Hersal Thomas of Houston is not mentioned, and neither is multi-reed man Budd Johnson of Dallas, who figured so considerably in the success of the Earl Hines Orchestra, led the first bebop recording session, and recorded with many well-known groups, including those of Count Basie, Woody Herman, and Dizzy Gillespie. One rather obscure but crucial Texas jazzman who can be heard playing at length in the film is trumpeter Carl "Tatti" Smith of Marshall. In reproducing the classic 1936 recording of George Gershwin's "Oh! Lady Be Good" with a Basie small group featuring tenorist Lester Young, the unlikely but remarkable Carl Smith is actually the soloist who is heard throughout the voice-over discussion of Young and his central position as one of the three premier saxophonists in jazz, along with tenorist Coleman Hawkins and altoist Charlie Parker. Ironically, Carl Smith made the influential 1936 date only as a substitute for Oran "Hot Lips" Page, the amazing blues trumpeter from Dallas, who goes unmentioned in the film but is discussed in the book version of *Jazz*.

The lineup of great Texas trumpeters is just one side of the equation, for Texas tenor saxophonists are another facet of the underrepresented role of Texas musicians in the film series. But to continue with the trumpeters (another of my personal biases), Harry James of Beaumont is mentioned and probably appears pictured in the trumpet section of the Benny Goodman Orchestra, although there seems to be no excerpts from his spectacular, swaggering solos. Another vital trumpeter, Kenny Dorham of Post Oak, is not heard from or even named, even though he should have been noted as a founding member of the Jazz Messengers when the script ticked off a number of instrumentalists who were members of that Art Blakey-Horace Silver aggregation. Neither is Dorham referred to in connection with Charlie Parker, in whose quintet he played from 1948 to 1950. But again, oversights (if they can be called such) are inevitable in a history that includes so many minor or near-great performers of jazz. But it should be noted that on the CD sampler issued in conjunction with the film series (along with CDs devoted to outstanding individual artists, including Ornette Coleman), Kenny Dorham is represented on the selection by the Jazz Messengers entitled "Doodlin'" from 1954.[4]

It would be possible to go on listing dozens of Texans who helped make jazz America's only original art form. Indeed, Texans were present in every new movement in jazz history, from ragtime, blues, and boogie-woogie through swing, bebop, hard bop, and free, or what Ornette Coleman has called his harmolodics. Pianist Red Garland of Dallas formed part of the first important Miles Davis Quintet, which included tenorist John Coltrane. Bassist Gene Ramey of Austin and drummer Gus Johnson of Tyler made up the rhythm section, along with pianist-leader Jay McShann, of McShann's 1940s orchestra, the last in the great line of Kansas City bands, which first brought Charlie Parker to prominence. Three Texans, saxophonists Booker Ervin of Denison and John Handy of Dallas and trumpeter Richard "Notes" Williams of Galveston, collaborated with Charles Mingus in the creation of his gospel-derived, blues-based hard bop of the 1950s. Four Texans who attended North Texas State

Teachers College in the early 1940s, Jimmy Giuffre, Harry Babasin, Gene Roland, and Herb Ellis, were all members of leading ensembles of the period. Giuffre, Babasin, and Roland were particularly active in California during the rise of West Coast jazz, recording with such figures as Shorty Rogers, Bud Shank, and Stan Kenton and helping put Third Stream, Brazilian-influenced, and other music modes on the jazz map. To recall even these few figures is to leave out sidemen in almost every name and also-ran band of every decade.

Just as there could well be another ten episodes of *Jazz* that would provide television time for more of the outstanding exponents of this music, so too could there be ten episodes dedicated entirely to Texans in jazz. Once again, the contributions of Texas musicians alone extend throughout the entire history of the music. These include such a band as San Antonio's Boots and His Buddies of the 1930s, which, unlike other jazz groups or individual artists from Texas, never left the state for fame in Kansas City, New York, Chicago, or Los Angeles. In Austin in 1930 a cornet player by the name of Tom Howell, who played with Fred Gardner's Texas University Troubadours, sounded so much like the legendary Bix Beiderbecke that it is uncanny. Howell is just one of the countless Texans who go unnamed in Ken Burns's *Jazz*. One hopes that the time will come—and is in fact not far off—for a television series based on Texans in jazz history. Surely the Burns series will spawn other documentaries on this enlivening, mind-bending, freedom-loving music, and they could do no better than to start with the state that has lent so many styles, sidemen, and solos to one of America's most sublime stories.

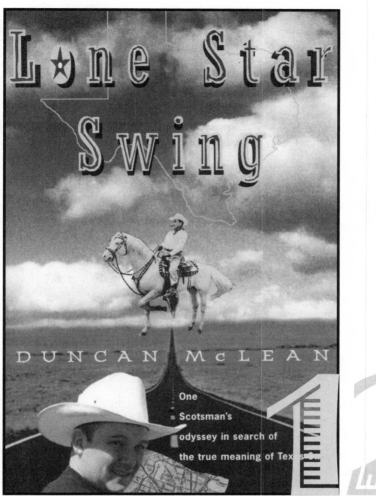

SWINGING THROUGH TEXAS
ON A SCOTTISH AIR

n the chapter "What Makes Bob Holler?" of Duncan McLean's *Lone Star Swing*, the vivid account of his 1990s trip through Texas, this Scottish writer describes his visit to Angelo's Barbecue on White Settlement Road in Fort Worth, the cowtown where, according to tradition, Bob Wills and the Light Crust Doughboys kicked off a music movement now known around the world as western swing. McLean captures perfectly the rank atmosphere at Angelo's: "The whole place swam in a reek of hickory smoke: the walls were smoked brown, so was the ceiling, the tables, the window. The stuffed moosehead by the door was smoky, so was the stuffed bear; the servers behind the counter looked half-kippered too."[1] Later the writer visits the Harry Ransom Humanities Research Center at the University of Texas at Austin and again he pins the tail on the donkey: "This is the place where the manuscripts of such folk as Dylan Thomas, Anne Sexton, D. H. Lawrence . . . reside. I never made it beyond the lobby. There I found display cases of *really* interesting stuff. Who needs the manuscript of *Women in Love* when you can look at the author's New Mexican bead moccasins? . . . Like many writers' chequebooks, Sexton's was worth far more money after her death than it was ever able to command during her life."[2] I was born in Fort Worth and have eaten at Angelo's a number of times (the latest shortly before I read McLean's book), and for over eighteen years I worked at the Harry Ransom Center. McLean showed me the places I know well, and his depictions are dead-on.

In recounting his quest for the spirit of Bob Wills and western swing, McLean has created a book that anyone interested in Texas should read. Often witty and ironic, the Scotsman sees into Texas culture as few of the state's natives or inhabitants can or have ever dared to. McLean's understanding and insight are owing, it would seem, to his having arrived in Texas with a memory packed with the words, phrases, place-names, accents, attitudes, longings, and contradictions of its once most popular music. Traveling light, he carries with him little more than a collection of transcription tapes of western swing that he plays in his rented Chevy as he cruises from East Texas (reporting at Spanish-moss-festooned Swanson's Landing that he first came across its name "in the sleeve notes of a Leadbelly LP") to Wichita Falls (where he encounters the heaviest auto traffic he has ever experienced—having only learned to drive a car in order to make his Texas trek), to El Paso (where the Border Patrol stops and hassles him for having no immigration papers), to "Hotter Than Hell" Presidio (where he eats a famous Sunflower Onion), and to Turkey (where

PREVIOUS PAGE: Cover of *Lone Star Swing: One Scotsman's Odyssey in Search of the True Meaning of Texas Swing* by Duncan McLean. Copyright © 1997 by Duncan McLean. Used by permission of W. W. Norton & Company, Inc.

he attends the annual Bob Wills Memorial Weekend and walks through the debris littering the rundown house where Wills first lived and learned to play breakdown fiddle).[3] Finally, he visits the all but ghost town in Texas that bears McLean's own name (where he views the Devil's Rope Museum and reads what he calls a kind of poetry made out of barbed-wire brands, my favorite being "Brinkenhoff Sabre 1883"). Between seeking a spirit and finding a ghost town, McLean manages to evoke much of who and what we Texans are.

The musicians who had first played western swing in the 1930s and were still alive at the time of McLean's writing are the principal subjects of his book. By way of these old-timers, he hopes to track down the real Bob Wills and the true meaning of his music. Several of the musicians who worked with Wills disabuse McLean of any notion he might have had that Bob could play jazz: "Breakdowns, maybe, but not jazz. Bob Wills was a two-fingered fiddler."[4] McLean's frustrating attempts to meet and interview two legendary musicians, Adolph Hofner and Floyd Tillman, are retold in the form of telephone conversations with each. A sideman with the Hofner brothers in 1933 and one of the earliest electric guitarists recorded on that instrument, Tillman cannot understand McLean (he hears "Lone Star *swig*" and thinks the Scotsman is writing a book about beer); assuming that McLean is calling from Scotland, he says that his house is too small and McLean wouldn't want to see it. When Tillman tries to take down the Scotsman's address, he can't get the spelling right of street, town, or county; and just when McLean is on the verge of having Tillman talk about his music, the phone card runs out of time.

In the chapter entitled "Still Waters Run the Deepest," McLean comes to a sudden revelation that Arch Montgomery, his host in Turkey, had played with Bob Wills. When he realizes this, he questions the musician's wife, "'How come you never mentioned that Arch played with Bob Wills?' June laughed. 'You never asked.'"[5] When it is time to leave this couple, McLean, after having joined in on "Twin Guitar Special" with Arch, observes,

> Their hospitality and kindness were not atypical of the Texans who'd helped me along the way, but it was given with such generosity and warmth that I'd certainly come to love them in only three days. . . . Another part of it was the knowledge that I was sitting just along the settee playing western swing with a man who'd sat just along the settee from Bob Wills nearly seventy years earlier, playing exactly the

same kind of music. I'd come to Texas in search of the roots of the music I loved, and here they were, withered a little maybe, but still alive and still picking.[6]

McLean's descriptions of western swing bring this music to life and moved even a resistant mule like myself to listen again to the Texas sounds this Scotsman celebrates. His definition of western swing, which he says "was a name given retrospectively to a music that was played over a huge geographical area by hundreds of musicians, all of whom put their pinch of spice into the great chili pot," emphasizes not the "talents of individuals" but the music's diversity.[7] He writes that "the crucial, exciting point of this great music" is that "it is as diverse, as varied, as ever-changing, and as rich in contradictions and surprising juxtapositions, as the country that spawned it."[8]

While I can accept and applaud the Scotsman's passion for the music and its heterogeneous sources, I can also disagree with certain of McLean's assertions, and even some of the musicians that he interviewed tend to do the same. When he asks electric guitarist Eldon Shamblin (who joined Bob Wills in 1937) whether he didn't think, despite the assortment of music the Texas Playboys performed, that the Wills group was "basically a jazz band," Shamblin replies, "Basically a dance band, I would say."[9] McLean suggests that "Wills' CDs should be filed next to Cootie Williams [Duke Ellington's great trumpeter], not Hank Williams."[10] Perhaps, but regardless of any minor disagreements, I find that ultimately McLean calls attention to the most important fact about this music: "Western Swing has always defined itself, not on the basis of any spurious notions of musical purity, but rather on its all-inclusiveness, its willingness to accept anything and everything that its many practitioners wanted to throw into the melting pot."[11] The Scotsman again alludes to western swing's openness to all styles and influences—from country and hillbilly to *conjunto* and *orquesta*, from folk and blues to Dixieland and big-band jazz—when he comments: "Music has become something to separate people, to build walls between them. I love the old stuff that brought people together, that knocked down walls."[12]

McLean came to Texas to discover the makers of a music that delighted him more than any other. He explains that, even though he did not want to leave his home on Orkney Island, he had to take a trip outside Scotland in order to receive the money that he had won for a collection of his prose fiction. Since the thing that he liked to do most was listen to western swing, he decided that he would spend the prize money traveling to Texas to hear the music live. The first example he comes across is in a Fort Worth nursing home where at first he is put off by the inability of the group of visiting musicians to tune their instruments. Eventually the elderly men, led by Roy Lee Brown (brother of Milton Brown, who is credited with establishing the classic style of western swing), are "so remarkably in tune" that McLean sits back, marvels, and enjoys the set, "as varied as any Western Swing aficionado could desire."[13] Later at the Noble Bean Coffee Shop in Fort Worth, he hears Buddy Ray, the fiddler who was "tearing up the small jazz venues of Fort Worth again, just as he had . . . forty or more years before."[14] McLean interviews Ray, who reveals of the famous Bob Wills "ah-ha": "You knew you were doing something right if Bob started yelling!"[15] At Canyon Lake, McLean interviews Walt Kleypas, whose piano playing on a 1950 recording of *12th Street Rag* the Scotsman describes as "two rock-steady, lightning-quick choruses, restating the melody and throwing in a few maverick licks and flicks for good measure."[16] One of the most touching moments in this account is when McLean reveals that Walt and his wife Lucille have been married for sixty years, and as they keep telling him, they are "still in love."[17]

Fortunately for Texas, the Somerset Maugham Award of the British Society of Authors went to a Scotsman who values this state's musical heritage. Like Jean Boyd's *The Jazz of the Southwest: An Oral History of Western Swing*, published in 1998 by the University of Texas Press, McLean's *Lone Star Swing* preserves through interviews the comments and reminiscences of western swing musicians, and in this respect both books have made a lasting contribution to regional history. Roy Lee Brown, Buddy Ray, and Walt Kleypas are only three of the musicians McLean heard in person and describes with understanding and appreciation. He also introduces his readers to John Moen of Wichita Falls, who had generously sent to him in Scotland copies of his complete collection of western swing tapes; a lady barber in Whitney (hometown of Wills's star singer, Tommy Duncan), who tells the Scotsman that she hates "all that redneck music";[18] and, as noted earlier, eighty-five-year-old Arch Montgomery, with whom McLean played such tunes as "Get Along Home, Cindy," "Trouble in Mind," and "Sally Gooden" and who came "as close as anyone was ever likely to get to a personification of where Western Swing sprung from, and what it had sounded like in its earliest days."[19]

After his session with Arch Montgomery, McLean declares: "This was what my whole trip was about: the joy of good music."[20] It is his own joy in western swing and its musicians that McLean's book conveys with an infectious enthusiasm that entertains, even as it shamed me into reconsideration of the distinctive achievement of this democratic music that I grew up with but had largely ignored.

The Complete Recordings of the
Father of Western Swing
MILTON BROWN
and the
Musical Brownies
1932 - 1937

120 Tracks, Newly Remastered on Five CDs

Produced By Special Arrangement With Roy Lee Brown

THE BIRTH OF WESTERN SWING

The swing era in jazz history has been dated, somewhat arbitrarily, from 1930 to 1945, even though the
characteristics of the movement—a smoother 4/4
time, a rhythm section with string bass rather than brass
tuba, and an emphasis on arrangements and dramatic solos,
among other prominent features—marked much of the
music prior to and after those two years in which the
Depression commenced and World War Two came to an end.
Swing practitioners like pianist Fats Waller and Texas trombonist Jack Teagarden were certainly exhibiting elements of
the "new" style when, in New York in 1929, they recorded
"Ridin' But Walkin'" and "Won't You Get Up Off It, Please,"
which Richard B. Hadlock describes as "bristling with wonderful solos" and "among the most notable records of 1929."
He goes on to say that "perhaps the finest moment of all is
Teagarden's solo on 'Ridin',' backed by Waller's thoughtful
counterpoint."[1] Waller's piano style has been designated as
"stride," and his influence extended not only to Count Basie,
one of the masters of the swing era, but to Thelonious Monk,

one of the geniuses of the Bebop Revolution of the mid- to late 1940s. Waller and Teagarden recorded again in 1931 before the pianist formed, in 1934, his group known as Fats Waller and His Rhythm, which recorded so many swinging, fun-filled sides, including in 1936 "Us on a Bus," with Waller's closing ad-lib lines that in a way sum up the entire period: "All out, Swing City."[2]

The influence of Fats Waller may have reached Texas during the same year that the pianist and His Rhythm first began to record. Although biographer Cary Ginell claims that the "closest comparison" between vocalist Milton Brown and "a singer from that era would be big band vocalist/entertainer Cab Calloway," there is an infectious quality to this Texan's singing, and to the western swing of his Musical Brownies, that suggests that the Texas combo was well aware of Waller and His Rhythm.[3] Ginell does note that Brown's hollering in his songs serves "as jazz exclamation marks (similar to those used by Fats Waller)."[4] However, Brown actually recorded with his group earlier than Waller did with his, if only by about six weeks. In any event, the two groups share certain similarities in the vocal styles of their leaders and in the easy swing and enthusiastic drive of their sidemen. While Brown and the Brownies are closer in some respects to a dixieland tradition, they, like Waller and his men, depended on Tin Pan Alley songs for much of their repertoire. Just as a sense of fun and good humor permeates the recordings of Waller and His Rhythm, so too do those same qualities pervade the sides cut by Brown and his aggregation. Beyond these possible connections, Brown and his six-piece western band purveyed an entirely different type of jazz, one that had received little attention in histories of the music before Jean A. Boyd made a case in 1998 for western swing as "The Jazz of the Southwest."[5] Previously, Gunther Schuller had briefly discussed western swing guitarists Leon McAuliffe, Muryel "Zeke" Campbell, and Bob Dunn as predecessors of Texas guitarist Charlie Christian, but Brown and the Musical Brownies (apart from Dunn) receive only passing mention in a footnote in Schuller's *The Swing Era*.[6] Yet it does seem undeniable that Brown, with his sextet of string players and piano, did create a kind of improvised swing as inventive and captivating in its way as that of Waller

PREVIOUS PAGE: Front side of 5-CD box set of *The Complete Recordings of the Father of Western Swing: Milton Brown and the Musical Brownies, 1932–1937* (Santa Monica, Calif.: Texas Rose Records, 1995).

and his unit and of any number of other long-recognized small jazz ensembles.

Milton Brown, born near Stephenville, Texas, in 1903, was first recorded in 1932 by the Victor company as part of the Fort Worth Doughboys, which included Bob Wills, the more famous exponent of western swing, on fiddle and harmony vocals. After playing over Fort Worth radio stations WBAP and KFJZ between 1930 and 1932, Brown and Wills split up when the sponsor of their radio show, W. Lee "Pappy" O'Daniel, refused to hire Brown's brother Derwood as a guitarist. In 1932 Milton Brown formed his own group, as Wills did in 1933, and the two musicians developed western swing in their separate ways.

Prior to their separation, Brown and Wills's first recorded sides in 1932 represented a transition from the "dry, dusty sound of cowboy vocalists" to "a sophisticated, smoother sound, more associated with the big city," and Brown's vocals resembled those of "jazz/pop singers" rather than cowboy crooners.[7] At this point there were no real improvisations included on the recordings, but these would come when Brown established his Musical Brownies. Indeed, there is a dramatic difference between "Sunbonnet Sue" and "Nancy Jane," the two sides recorded by the Doughboys in 1932, and "Brownie's Stomp," the first side cut by the Musical Brownies on April 4, 1934.[8] Not only do the titles indicate a difference between country songs and a jazz-influenced style, but Cecil Brower on fiddle shows immediately that not only can he swing in a jazz mode but that as a classically trained violinist he can handle his instrument as a pro, not just an amateur picker. Cary Ginell also observes that Brower's "closing melody" is "a variation on [Jelly Roll Morton's] 'Milenburg Joys,'" which indicates the soloist's awareness of the jazz tradition.[9] This piece begins with a tremendous burst of energy that lasts throughout the side, with Ocie Stockard on banjo really tearing it up and Fred "Papa" Calhoun on piano swinging and improvising with élan, even though Calhoun is certainly not in the same class with a jazz pianist like Fats Waller. The next number, another purely instrumental piece, entitled "Joe Turner Blues," demonstrates that from the first Brown and his Brownies would play the blues and could do so with real conviction, with Brower's weepy fiddle and Calhoun's downhearted piano truly capturing the blues feeling. Stockard's banjo powers the opening of "Oh! You Pretty Woman," where Wanna Coffman on string bass backs up Brower's theme statement, while Calhoun's piano stomps and ripples behind Brown's lively vocal. Brower's improvised break is full of swinging trills and rips, and Brown sings with humor and fine rhythmic drive. A sentimental waltz like "My Precious Sonny Boy" must have been popular with the Depression crowd, especially with Brown's western delivery, which includes a straight talking section that yet conveys a rhythmic feel. With the leader's charming vocals and his Brownies' energetic drive, this was from the start a highly appealing group that was rarely equaled by any other western swing unit.

At the annual meeting of the International Association of Jazz Record Collectors, held in San Antonio, Texas, in August 2000, Ron Sweetman of Canada presented a talk entitled "Jazz and Blues Recording Sessions 1928–1938," in which he included the Brownies' "Garbage Man Blues." This side, recorded in San Antonio at the same session of April 4, 1934, starts off with a bang (after a comedy exchange), and Brown's vocal is an example of powerhouse blues—that is, blues in a tempo that is not slow and low-down but fast and furious, full of boom and boisterousness. Brown shouts and almost growls out the repeated line about getting out the can because the garbage man is coming, and as Ginell has suggested, Brown even imitates something of Cab Calloway's tone of voice. Another piece that finds Brown in the Calloway vein is "Four, Five or Six Times," in which the vocalist scats the lyrics in the same style as Cab, echoed at times by the Brownies. The whole group furnishes an easy swing behind the singer, and Stockard takes a fine break on tenor guitar.

Perhaps more typical of the western style of the Brown band is "Where You Been So Long, Corrine?" recorded at the session of August 8, 1934. Here Calhoun's piano obbligato is the jazziest part of this essentially country side. For the most part, the ten sides recorded at this session are more in the country mode, although one piece, "Just Sitting on Top of the World," is blues-tinged, and "Take It Slow and Easy" has to it something of a dixie feel. On the latter, the breaks by Brower on fiddle and Calhoun on piano, especially their stop-time moments, are very much in the dixieland style. "Get Along, Cindy" and "This Morning, This Evening, So Soon" both swing but with a country-western fiddling sound, except for Calhoun's and Brower's breaks on the second side. "Trinity Waltz," "Loveland and You," and "Girl of My Dreams" are country-western waltzes, with the string harmonies quite rich on the first. "Loveless Love" from this recording date contains two of Brower's best solo outings.

As of the session of January 27, 1935, which took place in Chicago for the Decca label, the Brownies included for the first time amplified steel guitarist Bob Dunn, originally a trombonist who was a great admirer of Jack Teagarden. Dunn takes his first solo on "Put On Your Old Grey Bonnet," and though this is a very brief appearance, it is marked by the guitarist's honking, nasal tone quality that indeed suggests a trombone influence. On this session the Brownies also cut a couple of Mexican standards, "In El Rancho Grande" and "Baile en Mi Rancho," revealing something of the wide range of material offered by the group. In his vocal on "Down by the O-Hi-O," Brown again recalls Calloway, while on "I Love You" Brower offers one of his more impressive fiddle solos that sounds somewhat under the influence of jazz violinist Joe Venuti. Dunn takes a full chorus on "Sweet Jennie Lee," and although this is a curiosity not quite in the jazz mainstream, it is the earliest example of extended improvisation on the amplified guitar and is in its way quite fascinating. As sung by Brown, "St. Louis Blues" is not the W. C. Handy song, but it is in the blues mode, with Dunn soloing again, not in the jazz tradition but with his own unique sound and style, including some sudden pinging leaps into the upper register, as is also the case on "The Object of My Affection." Brown's vocal on this last piece is once again quite charming. Brown's brother Derwood croons in a western style on "Love in Bloom," hinting at times in his tone at a certain Fats Waller affinity. Cary Ginell indicates, in fact, that Derwood Brown was "a big Fats Waller fan," which is revealed most fully on Derwood's recording of "Cross Patch" from February 19, 1937.[10]

One of the swingingest sides from the January 27 session is "Chinatown, My Chinatown," with an excellent vocal by Milton Brown, Calhoun pounding it out on the piano, Dunn doing his thing on electric guitar, and Brower turning in another of his splendid fiddle performances. The Brownies' version of "Copenhagen" contains in Brower's "take-off" (the western swing phrase for an improvised break) what Ginell says had become "a staple of Texas string bands": a "'weeping fiddle' and the ubiquitous 'rockin' bow.'"[11] "Brownie Special" is a fun tour of towns on the Texas railroad line, complete with train whistle imitations and Brower's fiddle stoking the fire. "Some of These Days" is not in a class with the 1930 version by Calloway's orchestra, but it swings with an easy rock and Dunn contributes one of his erratic breaks full of unexpected dartings here and there. "Wabash Blues" also swings with a leisurely pulse, with Brower providing obbligato support to Brown's vocal and Dunn utilizing a touch of what Gunther Schuller refers to as the guitarist's "slidy Hawaiian effects, very popular on recordings going back to the late twenties."[12]

On January 28, 1935, the Brownies recorded twenty-two additional sides. From this session comes a number entitled "Taking Off," which features Cecil Brower and Bob Dunn. Jean Boyd writes that "Brower's solo chorus . . . is the product of a jazz musician" and his "solo line, though idiomatic for the violin, is phrased like a horn solo."[13] This is not, however, one of Brower's better efforts, and in fact it is Dunn who is more adventuresome, including a few of his Hawaiian licks along with his usual nasal honk. Another jazz fiddler, J. R. Chatwell, produced on "Hot As I Am," recorded June 23, 1937, what is "still regarded as one of the definitive swing solos" on fiddle, and Chatwell's solo does indeed swing more intensely and inventively than any other such "take-off."[14] A number of the other sides from the Brownies' January 28 session feature tunes that are more traditionally associated with the jazz repertoire, such as "I'll Be Glad When You're Dead You Rascal You," "Sweet Georgia Brown," "Darktown Strutter's Ball," and "Black and White Rag." However, Brower's take-off break on "I'll Be Glad" is in quite a different style from the many jazz versions of this number (such as Waller and Teagarden's "You Rascal, You"), and Brown's phrase, "you dirty dog you," although recalling Waller's aside on "How Can You Face Me," does not carry the same humorous force, despite its being a bit of clowning commentary during the break by Dunn.[15] On "Sweet Georgia Brown," Brower combines traditional breakdown fiddling with a Joe Venuti type of jazz violin swing.

Cary Ginell has noted that "the Brownies' repertoire deemphasized traditional country music in accordance with [their] jazz-oriented interplay between the musicians and the vocals; and with their focus on current popular numbers, classic city blues, and sophisticated jazz instrumentals, the band totally transformed hillbilly music in Texas."[16] Nevertheless, insofar as being up to date in their "jazz-oriented interplay" is concerned, the Brownies were not really, for a piece like "Darktown Strutter's Ball" has more of a dated, dixieland sound, especially with Stockard's banjo taking a leading part. Also, Dunn's guitar lines are extremely stiff, his lines not really so smooth or flowing as those of Eddie Durham and especially not those of Charlie Christian. Of course, Dunn was ahead of the two jazz guitarists chronologically in terms of recording dates, although Durham would record on an amplified guitar later in 1935 and had been using a homemade amplified guitar from as early as 1930. Brower is the most fluid of the Brownies, but even he is into the syncopated style of the 1920s more than the smoother swing of the 1930s. Mainly it is the rhythm section, which is still rooted in a two-beat pattern, that is quite heavy compared to the four-beat swing of the jazz groups of this time period. The Brownies' version of "Black and White Rag" is also a rather backward-looking form of jazz by this date. And certainly the Brownies remained tied to a country idiom in such pieces as "Little Betty Brown," which is in the hoedown category, and "Going Up Brushy Creek," on which Brower plays another fiddle breakdown.

During its next three sessions, recorded in New Orleans on March 3, 4, and 5, 1936—the final dates with Milton Brown as leader—the Brownies cut a tune identified with Jack Teagarden, "The Sheik of Araby."[17] Brown's vocal does not offer so distinctive a rendition as Teagarden's, and here as elsewhere Calhoun's piano seems overly rudimentary, whereas Brower still swings more smoothly than any other sideman. For these New Orleans dates the Brownies added a second fiddle in Cliff Bruner, who at times could be rather fluent but still in a more western style. Cary Ginell considers Brown's singing on "Beale Street Mama" to be "arguably" his "finest hot vocal performance," but by now Brown seems to have lost some of the special gusto that he had exhibited on the 1934 sides.[18] In general, the group has not developed much beyond its first session, although at times Bob Dunn has definitely contributed some unusual breaks, as on the March 3 recording of "Somebody's Been Using That Thing." The difference between Brower and Bruner's fiddle styles is most evident on the March 4 side entitled "When I'm Gone, Don't You Grieve," which Ginell says has "possible origins as a traditional play-party song."[19] Here Bruner retains more of a western fiddle sound and technique, while Brower clearly belongs to the Joe Venuti school of jazz violin.

One thing that can be said for Milton Brown and his jazz-oriented group is that the leader included many tunes associated with jazz-blues performance. Among such pieces are "Beale Street Mama" (sung by Bessie Smith as "Beale Street Papa"), "Cow-Cow" Davenport's "Mama Don't Allow It," Big Bill Broonzy and the Hokum Boys' "Easy Ridin' Papa," "Am I Blue?" (sung by Ethel Waters and Billie Holiday), "Memphis Blues" by W. C. Handy, "Somebody Stole My Gal," "Avalon" (arranged for the Jimmie Lunceford Orchestra by Eddie Durham), and "Sadie Green (The Vamp of New Orleans)." Brown's vocal on "Avalon" is not really jazz singing, but his rendition of "Sadie Green" is. One of his best blues vocals is on "Tired of the Same Thing All the Time," on which Brower on violin does a fine job with the blues and the group turns in a nice jam at the end.

Unfortunately, the title of this tune can be applied to Bob Dunn's guitar take-off, which is very repetitious of the phrases he tended to play over and over. As for Calhoun, his piano break on "Am I Blue?" is certainly one of his strongest efforts. Brower shows his versatility on "I'll String Along with You" when he effectively delivers the melody with a mute and tremolo. He also plays the theme on "Goofus" with a fine jazz rhythm, whereas Bruner is rather stiff and countrified.

Milton Brown's last side was "The Old Grey Mare," on which he and his brother Derwood sing a fine bit of harmony. After Milton's death from an auto accident on April 13, 1936, Derwood kept part of the band together and replaced those who decided to join up with other outfits. Lefty Perkins took over for Dunn, continuing with the same honking, nasal sound on the amplified steel guitar and many of the same licks played by Dunn, although Perkins manages a smoother flow to his lines. "Buck" Buchanan on fiddle replaced Brower and, according to Cary Ginell, "helped usher in a new, more stylish era for western swing."[20] Calhoun and Stockard are their old reliable selves, while Johnny Borowski plays both fiddle and ocarini, the latter to great effect on "Cross Patch," recorded at the new Musical Brownies' only session, on February 19, 1937. Derwood Brown sounds fine on "Bring It on Down to My House Honey" and, as mentioned earlier, does a Fats Waller bit on "Cross Patch," ending the side with a "yas" reminiscent of Fats. On "Louise Louise Blues," Derwood manages a decent job and carries on his brother's tradition of including the blues, but this and a number of the other sides (such as the slow blues entitled "I Just Want Your Stingaree") tend to drag and lack the spirit of the Milton Brown recordings. Some of the sides have lost a truer jazz quality, the two-fiddle sound is more syrupy and whiney, and Calhoun does not drive with the same urgency. Jimmie Davis's vocals on "High-Geared Daddy" and "Honky Tonk Blues" identify these tunes even more with the country mode, although Calhoun's piano takeoffs are not bad, just not as inspired as before. Buchanan's take-off on "Honky Tonk Blues" is rather spiritless and countrified, though at one point in this piece the group does jam nicely.

The only purely instrumental piece recorded by Derwood and the Brownies was "Rose Room," but this version has nothing special to recommend it and perhaps belongs more properly in the country category. Although Calhoun and Buchanan do contribute improvisations, they sound more like honky-tonk music that just happens to be jazz-inflected.

Ultimately, western swing may never be accepted in the jazz camp because it does retain so much of a country sound. Nonetheless, when Milton Brown led his group, especially in 1934, there was an excitement and energy to his music that at times places it squarely in the jazz tradition.

Jean Boyd has claimed that Joaquin Murphy of the Spade Cooley and later the Tex Williams band was in the same class of jazz improvisers with Charlie Christian and Charlie Parker.[21] But it is to be doubted that any western swing player will ever be considered a mainstream or major jazz soloist, for any number of reasons. Perhaps the context may always seem wrong, with a string sound that derives so greatly from the country tradition. Even so, it is possible that with time listeners with jazz-inclined ears will hear individual western swing soloists more sympathetically. Admittedly, in the case of a Texas jazzman like Ornette Coleman, some of his work is country-based, and jazz aficionados have not rejected his music on the basis of such an affiliation. Certainly jazz and western swing both originated primarily as a dance music that eventually incorporated improvisation to the delight of dancers and listeners alike. In the end the level of invention and expressiveness may determine whether western swing improvisers join the ranks of the jazz soloists so admired and emulated by the former. It may also depend on the type of band context in which the soloists perform their takeoffs. In this regard, it seems apparent that a small group like Milton Brown and His Musical Brownies, with its more fully committed policy of performing blues, stomp, rag, dixieland, and swing, best represents the necessary justification for being included in any history of jazz.

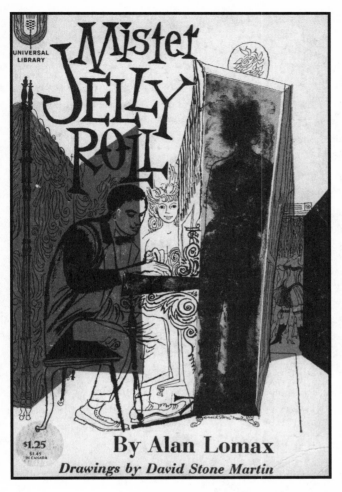

UNIVERSAL
LIBRARY

Mister
JELLY
ROLL

By Alan Lomax
Drawings by David Stone Martin

$1.25
$1.45
IN CANADA

THE INVENTOR OF JAZZ REVISITED
Untangling the Legacy of Jelly Roll Morton and Alan Lomax

n 1938 Alan Lomax, a native of Austin, was serving as "assistant in charge" of the Archive of American Folk Song at the Library of Congress when he recorded on acetate disks the voice and piano virtuosity of Ferdinand "Jelly Roll" Morton, the self-declared inventor of jazz. The library's folk song archive had been established in 1928, and from 1936 to 1943 its curator and consultant was Alan's father, John Avery Lomax, who helped found the Texas Folklore Society and traveled more than 200,000 miles throughout the United States to document and record American folk music. The Lomaxes are famous—or infamous, depending on one's perspective—for their promotion and exploitation of the career of folk singer Huddie Ledbetter and their publication of *Negro Folk Songs as Sung by Leadbelly*, which, at the time of its publication in November 1936, was praised by black poet James Weldon Johnson as "one of the most amazing autobiographical accounts ever printed in America."[1] Studs Terkel, the nonagenarian master chronicler of American society, has acknowledged that his pursuit of oral history was inspired by the example of Alan Lomax, in particular Lomax's *Mister Jelly Roll, The Fortunes of Jelly Roll Morton, New Orleans Creole and "Inventor of Jazz."* If the Lomaxes have had their avid champions as well as their detractors, who have questioned some of their materials and collecting methods, no one has denied to them their place in the sun as dedicated documenters and preservers of some of the most important music that America has yet produced.

Despite the fact that Alan Lomax's father did not approve of jazz, even "professed to loathe" it, the son was determined to explore further the genre of oral biography, which father and son had established with their Leadbelly volume, by interviewing Jelly Roll Morton, widely considered the first great jazz composer.[2] Even though Duke Ellington, acclaimed by most aficionados as the greatest jazz composer of all time, dismissed Morton as nothing more than a big mouth, other commentators have long compared Jelly Roll to Mozart in classical music, primarily, as critic William Russell asserted in 1944, for Morton's "wealth of melodic invention and skill in variation" and "the tremendous swing, which made him a veritable one-man band."[3] All Morton's classic jazz qualities, as well as his penchant for claiming in his colorful recollections that he had invented jazz and swing, were captured by Alan Lomax in May 1938 when he recorded Jelly Roll at the Library of Congress, only three years before his untimely death in 1941. On this occasion, while Morton exhibited his formidable prowess at the keyboard, Lomax elicited from him a rich oral record of the early period of the musician's life and also the beginnings of

PREVIOUS PAGE: Cover of Alan Lomax's *Mister Jelly Roll: The Fortunes of Jelly Roll Morton, New Orleans Creole and "Inventor of Jazz"* (1950). Used by permission of Penguin Group (U.S.A.), Inc.

New Orleans jazz, which Morton proclaimed that he had invented in 1902. Subsequently, in 1949, Lomax published *Mister Jelly Roll*, a biography-autobiography of Morton, based on the interviews Lomax conducted with Jelly Roll and with his contemporary musicians, his wife Mabel, his relatives (including a great-grandmother), and the Melrose brothers, Morton's Chicago publishers. Lomax's interviews and his insightful understanding of Morton's contributions to jazz resulted in a unique volume in the history of the music—one that was reprinted in November 2001 to the same encomiums that greeted it on its first appearance more than fifty years before.

Alan Lomax died in July of 2002, and in the spring of 2003 *Jelly's Blues*, a new "definitive biography" of Jelly Roll Morton, appeared, co-authored by Howard Reich, a writer for the *Chicago Tribune*, and William Gaines, a Pulitzer Prize-winning investigative reporter and a journalism teacher at the University of Illinois.[4] This book, which is based on a series of articles written for the *Tribune* in 1999, is well researched, praiseworthy for once again publicizing Morton's major artistic achievements, and valuable for unearthing facts unavailable to Lomax. For example, through the FOIA (Freedom of Information Act), Reich and Gaines uncovered correspondence between Morton and the Attorney General regarding ASCAP (the American Society of Composers, Authors, and Publishers), which Morton charged with not paying him for performances of his music. But despite its contributions to a more complete Morton story, the Reich-Gaines book is also disingenuous, verges on the unethical, and is ultimately downright shameful. To compete in the bookselling market, the authors seem to have gone out of their way to utilize different sources for the very same information found in Lomax's *Mister Jelly Roll*, even as they purposely ignore, unjustly denigrate, and even at times plagiarize his book. Seeking to appear the first to present accounts already contained in *Mister Jelly Roll*, the authors provide scanty notes and avoid making clear the connection between Lomax's interviews at the Library of Congress and his book, which they occasionally quote without bothering to give proper credit. Not until we come to the endnotes for the fourth chapter of *Jelly's Blues* do we find a reference to Lomax's book, even though many of the quotes in the first three chapters of *Jelly's Blues* are simply identified as "interview, Library of Congress, 1939," without the co-authors' ever disclosing the fact that such quotes exist word for word in *Mister Jelly Roll*. Only in their final chapter do they at last inform the reader that "Alan Lomax turned his

Library of Congress interviews with Morton into *Mister Jelly Roll,* his oral biography of Morton."[5] This is at the very least subterfuge.

When Reich and Gaines do acknowledge Lomax's precedence, they do so grudgingly—then charge the author with having "codified many of the myths that had long gathered around Morton's name."[6] One of these so-called myths involves Morton's pride in proclaiming himself to be a Creole with almost no Negro blood. Reich and Gaines accuse Lomax of fostering this myth and blame the 1993 Broadway musical *Jelly's Last Jam* for having perpetuated it. But if Lomax contributed to the notion that Morton suffered from a type of racism, which apparently was common-place among New Orleans Creoles with more white blood than black, he did so by relying on Morton's own words. In his Library of Congress interviews, Jelly averred that his people had come straight to America "from the shores of France."[7] Moreover, a decade before *Jelly's Blues* was published, Lomax was openly critical of *Jelly's Last Jam* in his 1993 introduction to a third edition of his *Mister Jelly Roll.* There he observed that, among other inaccuracies and shortcomings, the play neglected Morton's "innovative compositions" and substituted "supposedly sophisticated formulas," such as white Chicago jazz recorded in New York in the 1930s.[8] This was my own principal disappointment with the play, rather than its dramatizing of Jelly's rejection by his Creole grandmother Mimi Peché for playing in the bordellos and its criticizing of his desire to be known as Creole instead of black.[9]

Another type of so-called myth is the birth date of Morton, which Lomax gave as 1885. Lawrence Gushee, who wrote an afterword for the 2001 edition of *Mister Jelly Roll,* discovered a baptismal citation that assigned Morton's year of birth to 1890, but Gushee admitted to Reich and Gaines that for various reasons 1890 could be wrong. Nonetheless, they lambaste Lomax for having suggested that Morton may have given 1885 as his birth date in order to appear on the scene in New Orleans earlier than other jazzmen.[10] On the other hand, Reich and Gaines do not reveal that Lomax had essentially verified an 1885 or at least an 1886 birth date when he interviewed Morton's half-sister Amide Colas, who said that she was born in 1897 and Morton was eleven years older. Reich and Gaines refer to an interview with the same half-sister conducted by William Russell, rather than cite Lomax's interview in *Mister Jelly Roll,* and thus avoid having to acknowledge that Lomax had tried to verify the 1885 date as authentic.[11] They even resort to the gratuitous charge that Lomax "may have been the first to accuse Morton of lying about this date."[12] As a matter of fact, throughout Lomax's book he establishes in the reader's mind the view that whatever Morton said was most likely true, since he could back up his claims at the piano and the other musicians interviewed by Lomax corroborated Morton's assertions as to dates, places, perform-ances, styles of music, and his mastery of the keyboard. In their own book, Reich and Gaines try time and again to make the case that only they have appreciated Morton's integrity, his artistic accomplishments, and his deserved place as the first great composer in jazz. All of this, however, was already fully evident in Lomax's *Mister Jelly Roll* of 1949.

An example of Reich and Gaines's handling—or mishandling—of Lomax's material occurs in the second chapter of their book, where they quote one of the most impressive statements ever made by Jelly Roll Morton. The context is a discussion of the composer's discovery of a method for notating jazz, which had not existed prior to his 1915 written score for his "Jelly Roll Blues." Reich and Gaines quote Morton as saying, "I myself figured out the peculiar form of mathematics and harmonics that was strange to all the world but me."[13] There is no citation for a source for this quote, but a version of the same quote appears in Lomax's book in his chapter appropriately entitled "Jelly Roll Blues": "So around 1912 I began to write down this peculiar form of mathematics and harmonics that was strange to all the world."[14] In their third chapter, Reich and Gaines state, "Morton was studded with diamonds, literally pinning them to his under-wear for safekeeping," but Lomax had already entitled one of his chapters "Diamonds on His Underwear"; once again the fact that Lomax had reported Morton's phrase in *Mister Jelly Roll* goes unmentioned in *Jelly's Blues.*[15]

A quote by Reich and Gaines concerning Joe "King" Oliver presented for me a special problem because once more the authors do not cite their source, which is clearly Lomax's book. Since I was working from the 1950 Grosset & Dunlap paperback edition of Lomax's *Mister Jelly Roll*, I found it curious that the authors' quote from Walter Melrose, one of Morton's Chicago publishers, made reference to Oliver as "the old Southern-type nigger."[16] In the Grosset & Dunlap edition, Lomax's reference is to "Joe" as "more the old Southern-type." I wondered if Reich and Gaines had added the "N" word or Lomax or his publishers had silently deleted it. Only after consulting the 1950 Duell, Sloan and Pearce hardback and the 2001 University of California Press reprint did I discover that the "N" word appears in both, but not in the Grosset & Dunlap paperback. Reich and Gaines quote word for word the version of Melrose's full comment on Oliver found in the first and last editions of Lomax's book: "Joe was more the old Southern-type nigger. Like Handy. Didn't want any trouble with anybody."[17] It is evident that the authors rightly wished to underscore, through such a quote, the disreputable character that Morton's publisher became after he had promoted Morton's career by publishing his ragtime tune "The Wolverines" in 1923. Copyrighting Morton's music in both the composer and the publisher's names, Walter Melrose would collect royalties from Morton's music for decades without paying the composer his fair share. Reich and Gaines trace the history of Morton's struggle with Melrose and cite the publisher's claims that without him the composer would have been nothing. But none of this is new. Lomax had already covered the ground thoroughly and had seen Walter Melrose for exactly what he was: a greedy racist full of, in Lomax's words, "myopic self-importance," who had a "comfortable home" and "fat bank account" while "the Negroes who created jazz [had] mostly died broke or had to leave jazz to keep them from starving to death."[18]

In 1941 Morton was back in California for the second time in his career, broke and in very poor health, having been stabbed in the back in 1938 in Washington, D.C., by a disgruntled patron at the Music Box, where he had been performing. Reich and Gaines quote from a letter Morton wrote to his wife Mabel back in New York: "I haven't made any money since I've been gone, although I received the ASCAP check. . . . But this town takes money to live, so that is about all gone."[19] This is straight out of a letter reproduced in Lomax, but no source is given in the notes to *Jelly's Blues*. This kind of casual use of Lomax's materials is in some ways the authors' least egregious practice. More disheartening is the way they vilify Lomax. They allege that he used liquor "to keep the bawdiest anecdotes flowing" and that as Morton's stories "became more colorful, raunchy, and exaggerated," he "didn't realize that by giving Lomax the dirt he wanted, he was helping to soil his own reputation for generations to come."[20] The authors further charge that Lomax did not pay Morton for the recording sessions, nor did he contribute royalties to the Morton estate after the composer's death when *Mister Jelly Roll* was published in 1949. This is a valid issue—precisely the kind of disturbing exploitation that historians and musicians should be questioning. But Reich and Gaines make no attempt to address such issues directly. Instead, in almost every reference to Lomax, they fault both the man and his book through hyperbole and innuendo.

Lomax himself does not hide the fact that he provided Morton with liquor, and indeed the composer himself is quoted by Lomax as saying, "Lord, this whiskey is just lovely!"[21] But the allegation that Lomax was only after "the dirt" is totally contradicted by the focus in *Mister Jelly Roll* on Morton's music and the significance of his contributions to jazz history. As for the accusation that Lomax did not pay Morton, this is left for the reader to wonder about, since neither Lomax himself nor Reich and Gaines discuss the financial arrangement. In contrast, when they refer to Roy Carew, another white man who, like Lomax, befriended Morton in Washington, D.C., the authors are far more charitable. They offer a favorable explanation for the fact that Carew had reported to Morton's estate that the composer "transferred his interest in [their jointly owned] Tempo-Music to Carew to cancel outstanding debts."[22] Although the authors find it "difficult to fathom why Carew told" this to the executor, they nevertheless suggest that perhaps Carew did not want to see the money go to John Ford, a man who inherited all of Morton's ASCAP royalties without knowing or being any kin to the composer.[23] The authors never allow for a similar motive for Lomax, whose research methods and financial dealings they are so quick to condemn.

The accusation that Lomax "grilled Morton about sex, mayhem, and murders" when "Morton wanted to talk about music" distorts the contents of Lomax's book.[24] Moreover, the authors spend a good part of their own first chapter describing the New Orleans red-light district in raunchier detail than anything offered by *Mister Jelly Roll*. Most of what we know about Jelly's views on his and others' music is to be found in Lomax's writings, and much of this information has been silently plowed into the prose narrative of Reich and Gaines. For example, Morton's famous dictum, "If you can't manage to put tinges of Spanish in your tunes, you will never be able to get the right seasoning," was recorded by Lomax and has been repeated subsequently by every commentator on Jelly's music, including Reich and Gaines.[25] It was also Lomax who first revealed that "Jelly abominated jam sessions; they ran counter to his whole approach to jazz."[26] Morton's discussion of tempo, melody, riffs, the break ("like a musical surprise which didn't come in until I originated the idea of jazz, as I told you"), and the notion that "no jazz piano player can really play good jazz unless they try to give an imitation of a band" are fully elaborated in *Mister Jelly*

Roll.[27] Once again, Reich and Gaines pilfer this information without crediting their source in Lomax.

While *Jelly's Blues* has serious flaws, it does contribute something new to what we know about the history of American music. Through the records uncovered in their FOIA requests, the authors recount Morton's efforts to make ASCAP compensate him for all the royalties that the organization had collected for performances of Jelly's compositions, above all his "King Porter Stomp," a tune recorded by almost every major and minor big band of the swing era. They also trace the relationship between Morton and Roy Carew, thanks to an archive compiled by William Russell, a classically trained musician whom Lomax calls in *Mister Jelly Roll* the "most learned of jazz critics."[28] Lomax quotes at length from an article by Russell published in 1944, and throughout *Mister Jelly Roll* Lomax credits Russell and others who made his book possible, among them Thomas Cusack, who helped compile the Morton discography included in the book; Roy Carew, who provided music manuscripts; and such musicians as Bunk Johnson, Johnny St. Cyr, and Omer Simeon, who testified to the fact that "Jelly could back his brags with plenty of money, plenty of red-hot piano and, when necessary, a 'hard-hitting .38.'"[29] But rather than acknowledge this fact, Reich and Gaines pretend that William Russell's archive will revolutionize our understanding of Morton's achievement, even though Lomax's book had already examined the most important issues in the life and art of the pianist-composer-bandleader.

Jelly's Blues is eager to inform its readers that in 1938 William Russell met several times with Morton in D.C., where the great jazzman was "forgotten by the music industry world."[30] And yet nowhere in the book do the authors say a word about Lomax meeting Morton, recording him for over a month, and writing what Lomax himself claims in his preface to the 1973 edition of *Mister Jelly Roll* is, as far as he knows, "the first recorded biography to be made into a book."[31] In his 1993 preface to *Mister Jelly Roll*, Lomax asserts that "a more significant outcome was the establishment of recorded history as a literary and historical genre of its own."[32] Lomax also reports in this preface that his book "turned many people on to the idea of 'oral history.' Among these was Studs Terkel, who interviewed me on the radio about the book when it appeared, and who has since used this 'oral history' approach to create a fresh and democratic vision of American life."[33] Lomax's 1973 and 1993 prefaces to reprints of his book are both included in the 2001 edition of *Mister Jelly Roll*, but only the 1950 edition is ever mentioned in *Jelly's Blues,* as if the book were out of print and obsolete.

In their description of a number of the most vital recordings of Morton's music, Reich and Gaines present a somewhat different take from Lomax's. An example is their *imagined* rendering of the scene in the Victor studio when Morton's Red Hot Peppers immortalized his "Black Bottom Stomp":

> Between refrains, each of the players took a brief, improvised solo, Ory's whinnying trombone riffs, Mitchell's searing cornet lines, and Simeon's elaborate clarinet phrases dispatched at a break-neck clip. St. Cyr, meanwhile, played comparably aggressive solos on banjo, his hand strumming faster than the eye could see. Morton, for his part, turned in a leonine solo, his buoyant left hand and fast-flying right producing a nearly orchestral burst of sound.[34]

Some of the references here should recall musicians and theories familiar from the pages of *Mister Jelly Roll.* Although Lomax does not engage in descriptions of specific recordings, even so, he frequently evokes Morton's music in quite knowing terms, as when he considers Morton's claim of having "personally originated jazz in New Orleans in 1902."[35] Lomax follows Jelly's declaration with the following, well-considered observations:

> He wished he had somehow copyrighted jazz and he groaned because he could not sue the white band leaders who were making their fortunes with "my ideas."
>
> The facts justify Morton to some extent. Although he neither originated jazz nor "composed" *Tiger Rag,* he was the first true composer of jazz, not only an original, competent, and prolific creator, but an aggressive organizer and self-advertiser. Jazzmen often disliked him personally, but always respected his talent professionally. What Jelly Roll did was to absorb the complex currents of the music of his hometown and, very early, to set about organizing and ripening them into a system of music. His compositions were inventions in the New Orleans style, reflections of what a whole musical community had to say: His "band piano style" brought together on the keyboard the polyphonic weave of voices in Storyville dance bands; his powerful

left hand, with its constantly shifting riffs, reflected the polyrhythmic style of those bands; so, although it suited Jelly Roll to feel that he walked alone, actually a generation of inspired New Orleans musicians always marched by his side.[36]

Elsewhere, Lomax provides firsthand accounts of the recording sessions through his interviews with Morton's sidemen, Omer Simeon and Johnny St. Cyr. These accounts are invaluable evidence of Morton's working methods and have been a source for innumerable commentaries on the pianist-composer-bandleader and what some have labeled his "arranged jazz." As clarinetist Omer Simeon recalled,

> He was exact with us. Very jolly, very full of life all the time, but serious. We used to spend maybe three hours rehearsing four sides and in that time he'd give us the effects he wanted, like the background behind a solo—he would run that over on the piano with one finger and the guys would get together and harmonize it. . . .
>
> The solos—they were ad lib. We played according to how we felt. Of course, Jelly had his ideas and sometimes we'd listen to them and sometimes, together with our own, we'd make something better.
>
> . . . Now Jelly was a very, very agreeable man to cut a record with and I'll tell you why . . . he'd leave it to your own judgment, say, "You take a break here," . . . and "Clarinet'll take a break here." That's what cause his records to have more variety than you find on Joe Oliver's records, for instance.[37]

As for Reich and Gaines, they frequently glean kernels from Lomax's interviews, as in the case of Morton's story of his 1907 visit to Texas, though rarely if ever adding anything of significance.[38] Even in their retelling of the Texas visit, Reich and Gaines fail to mention one important fact revealed by Lomax, which is that the only pianist in Texas whom Morton remembered, a George W. Smith, admitted that "Morton carved everybody, including himself."[39] When Reich and Gaines appropriate an insightful passage in the Lomax book, such as the view that in Morton's music "the left hand occasionally fired off a series of driving octaves, recalling the tailgate trombone that young Ferd had first heard as a youth, when his father played around the house," they don't bother to credit Lomax for having already observed that it was from Morton's father, who "played a slidin' trombone," that the composer had developed "in almost every line . . . bass figures in tailgate style" and that "trombone phrasing is the Jelly Roll trademark."[40] Unlike Reich and Gaines, jazz critic Gunther Schuller, in his 1968 study *Early Jazz*, pays grateful tribute to Lomax for being the first to arrive at this important perception about the influence of the father's trombone on the son's jazz compositions.[41]

In addition to the information on ASCAP that is new in *Jelly's Blues*, Reich and Gaines disclose in their discussion of Morton's later compositions that jazz critic and historian William Russell rescued a group of works from the composer's last years. According to the authors, these compositions were "no longer elaborating in the ornate polyphonic style that had made him famous in the 1920s, no longer relying on the two-beats-to-the-bar stomps and lazy blues dirges that epitomized New Orleans-Chicago jazz. Instead, Morton's music had become sleek and streamlined."[42] The authors single out a tune entitled "Ganjam" as venturing into "the kinds of unabashedly dissonant chords and exotic Eastern scales that were not to be heard in jazz for at least another decade, with the experiments of Charles Mingus in the 1950s."[43] Apparently, these compositions were unavailable to Lomax in 1949, and at that point Mingus had not yet developed his experimental work that did in fact owe something to Morton's music, as evinced by the titles of two Mingus pieces: his "Jelly Roll" and "My Jelly Roll Soul."[44] One can only hope that Morton's later compositions will soon be recorded by a qualified repertory jazz ensemble. But even if they prove that Morton was continuing to develop as an artist, it seems hard to believe that they will change the indelible image of a vital New Orleans creator whose personality, cultural roots, trials and tribulations, and contributions to jazz were first captured most fully in Alan Lomax's *Mister Jelly Roll*.

Any reader who desires to hear this great jazz artist in his own words and to envision him in his milieu will still want to consult Lomax before and after any other volume that contends for the title of definitive biography. It is unfortunate that Reich and Gaines could not bring themselves, as Lawrence Gushee does in his afterword to the 2001 edition of Lomax's book, to render homage to Morton's first biographer, especially when the authors are so undeniably indebted both to Lomax's interviews and to his published book. Reich and Gaines would have established an ethos of trust and fair play had they echoed the tone of Gushee's tribute: "*Mister Jelly Roll* makes Morton so interesting as a person that one can lose sight of the fact that he was an authentic genius whose music continues to mesmerize and charm. Finally, the book surely established Jelly Roll's position in jazz history, which in 1950 was far from certain. For these and other reasons, our hypothetical hats should be doffed at Lomax's pioneering achievement."[45]

THE BASS
SAXOPHONE
JOSEF SKVORECKY

PICADOR

15

DISCOGRAPHIES AND TEXAN JAZZ

n arriving at value judgments, students of jazz have long
relied on specific information regarding performances
and performers, in particular the solos by individual
artists. Knowing who is playing a solo may not be necessary
for assessing its artistry, and perhaps all listening should be
a sort of Blindfold Test of the kind conducted by Leonard
Feather in *Metronome* and *Down Beat* magazines. In his tests
administered to leading jazz figures, Feather demonstrated

that without seeing a musician, even a trained listener may not recognize the performer's race or gender and is therefore forced to judge the performance purely on the basis of its aural effect.[1] Nonetheless, knowledge of who is performing on a recording has been important for determining the relationship of one solo to other solos by the same musician, for comparing and contrasting these with solos by other musicians (especially improvisations on the same tune), and for evaluating the performer at that precise moment and in comparison with other periods in or throughout his or her career. Recognition of an individual performer and his or her peculiar style has indeed been crucial to the appreciation of each artist's creativity and development over time.

Although critical commentary on jazz began before the first discographies appeared in France in 1936, the publication in that year of Charles Delaunay's *Hot Discography* marked the beginning of serious attention to the personnel, dates, and matrix numbers of recordings. So important was this event that even Josef Skvorecky alludes to it in his fictional account of life in Czechoslovakia during World War Two. In his jazz novel *The Bass Saxophone*, Skvorecky writes that "after the war, a German officer in occupied Paris named Schulz-Koehn became a legend—he had concealed an escaped black POW in his apartment, who along with Charles Delaunay, in the shadow of the German High Command, put together *Hot Discography*."[2] The irony of a German officer promoting a music that the Nazis condemned as degenerate is both figuratively telling and perhaps literally true, since even SS and Gestapo members are said to have loved and listened to jazz on the sly.

In studying Texan jazz, I myself have been deeply indebted to discographies compiled by Brian Rust and Tom Lord, and to bio-discographies on the bands of Fletcher Henderson and Count Basie produced by Walter C. Allen and Chris Sheridan, respectively. For me the primary significance of such discographies has resided in their identification of the many Texans who recorded—and in particular soloed—with the leading bands and combos from the 1920s through the 1960s. In conjunction with discographies, I have also made use of jazz encyclopedias and John Chilton's *Who's Who of Jazz*, which have aided me as well in identifying

PREVIOUS PAGE: Cover of *The Bass Saxophone*, by Josef Skvorecky (1980). Illustration by Ian Pollock.

musicians who were Texas-born. With biographical information in hand, I have been able to seek out the names of Texans among the personnel list- ed in discographies and among the names of unit members provided on record jackets or CD insert notes, thereby making it possible to appraise their performances and their roles as leaders, sidemen, soloists, arrangers, and composers.

The sheer number of recordings on which Texans have participated reveals in itself the enormous influence of the state's musicians on every period of jazz history. According to jazz historian Ross Russell, the more than 1,000 recordings on which Texas trombonist Jack Teagarden appears—100 alone in 1929—make the Teagarden discography "one of the most extensive in jazz, comparable to [those of] Louis Armstrong, Fats Waller, Duke Ellington, and Coleman Hawkins."[3] Many others of the state's musicians also generated an impressive number of recordings for the major periods and movements of jazz, among them, in the 1920s and 1930s, trumpeter Lammar Wright; in the 1930s and 1940s, pianist Teddy Wilson, reedman-composer-arranger Budd Johnson, and guitarist-trombonist-composer-arranger Eddie Durham; from the 1940s to the 1960s, bassist Gene Ramey and trumpeter Kenny Dorham; from the 1950s through the 1970s, pianist Red Garland and reedman-composer Jimmy Giuffre; and from the late 1950s up to 2005, reedman-trumpeter-violinist-composer Ornette Coleman.[4]

In "Discography: The Thankless Science," Dan Morgenstern, director of the Institute of Jazz Studies at Rutgers University, traces the history of jazz discography up to 1966 and pays tribute to its tireless, "unsung breed of researchers and enthusiasts" who have "made it possible for the begin- ning student of jazz to become, in a short time, as well informed about who played what chorus on an important record as the expert of yesterday was after years of devoted studies."[5] In addition to Charles Delaunay's *Hot Discography* and Brian Rust's *Jazz Records, 1897–1942* (the latter consid- ered by Morgenstern to be "the most thoroughgoing and complete approach to jazz discography hitherto accomplished" and its "scope and accuracy . . . not likely to be surpassed"), Morgenstern also discusses discographies "limited to the work of a single artist."[6] As examples of the single-artist discography, he mentions the work of four compilers: Kurt Mohr of Switzerland, who produced various volumes on "lesser-known artists," such as Texas trumpeter Hot Lips Page; Benny H. Aasland's *The*

Wax Works of Duke Ellington, published in Sweden in 1954; D. Russell Connor's *B.G.: Off the Record*, published in 1958; and Howard A. Waters' *Jack Teagarden's Music: His Career and Recordings* of 1960, this last volume called by Morgenstern an "outstanding work" that is "staggering to contemplate," but like almost all discographies, "the book made no profit."[7] Since the 1966 cutoff date for Morgenstern's history, innumerable discographies have seen the light of day, most comprehensive of all being Canadian Tom Lord's monumental thirty-four-volume compilation of 150,000 recordings, which is available as a CD-ROM that includes the same information as on the 20,000 pages of the print version.[8]

Howard Waters's discography of Jack Teagarden is especially outstanding for one reason: he himself listened to every recording listed. Whether this is true for the Tom Lord discography is unclear to me, but so far as I can ascertain, Lord's data is dependably accurate. Certainly any discography is only as valuable as its information is reliable. For purposes of illustrating but one type of service rendered by the Tom Lord discography, I will consider a single cut from a 1956 quintet session that included Texan Kenny Dorham on trumpet. The leader of the quintet on this occasion was tenor saxophonist Hank Mobley, with whom Dorham recorded frequently when both were founding members of drummer Art Blakey's Jazz Messengers; not incidentally, the two albums recorded in July 1956 with Mobley as leader are entitled *Hank Mobley's Message* and *Hank Mobley's Second Message*. This period and the style of the jazz on these albums have been designated hard bop, and some of this movement's characteristics include the influence of black church or soul music and extended solos that may be less technically spectacular but can be more passionate or emotive than those of the bebop era.[9]

The insert notes to *Hank Mobley: Messages*, a composite CD containing all the tunes from both recording sessions of July 20 and 27, 1956, attribute the trumpet part on the tune "These Are the Things I Love" to Donald Byrd, whom Dorham replaced for the July 27 date.[10] The insert notes are confusing as to who is on trumpet on which tunes because they state that Byrd performs on the first six numbers and Dorham appears on tunes 7 through 12, "except on 'These Are the Things I Love,'" which is tune 6.[11] My own ear told me that the trumpet on this tune was actually that of Kenny Dorham and not Donald Byrd, but I could not feel certain that my self-trained hearing was to be trusted. It was only while scrolling through the Lord CD in search of Dorham albums of which I might not have been aware that I noticed that Dorham was credited as the trumpeter on "These Are the Things I Love." This confirmed for me my recognition of Dorham's special turns of phrase and what Ira Gitler aptly terms his "smoky tone," in contrast to the fuller sound, smoother execution, but, for me, less inventive approach of Donald Byrd.[12]

Even though Kenny Dorham possessed a readily identifiable sound and phrasing, it can be especially difficult to know positively if he is playing when there are two trumpets sharing solo time on the same tune. An example is the album entitled *The Birdland Stars on Tour, Volumes 1 & 2*, on which Dorham is paired with trumpeter Conte Candoli.[13] Before I consider this specific instance, it is germane to comment on the pairing of Dorham and Candoli. It is curious to me that a Texas jazzman like Dorham, who developed his very personal style from working with Charlie Parker, Dizzy Gillespie, Fats Navarro, and other important bebop-era leaders and sidemen of the 1940s, could work so effectively with a fellow jazzer like Candoli, a native of Mishawaka, Indiana, who began his career with the Woody Herman Orchestra and in the 1950s became a member of the West Coast "School" on joining the Lighthouse all-stars at Hermosa Beach, California. Prior to the Birdland Stars recording, Candoli had performed almost exclusively with all-white bands, and Dorham had played largely with all-black groups.

Candoli's work with a number of West Coast units included his appearance on the 1955 album entitled *The Five*, with arrangements written by Shorty Rogers, which is one of my favorite Candoli outings.[14] As for Dorham, he had recorded with a wide variety of groups prior to collaborating with Candoli, but no matter with what ensemble he performed, Dorham's lovely ballad interpretations and his up-tempo choruses are to me endlessly satisfying.[15] Despite their differing backgrounds, races, and associations, the two men proved more than compatible on the bandstand, which is so often the case in jazz. Although a discography may not account for a listener's taste and pleasure and may not reveal biographical facts about the musicians (whereas album notes often do so), by surveying the careers of two such jazzmen as Dorham and Candoli, a discography does make clear the backgrounds and experiences that the musicians bring to bear on their performances. Furthermore, a discography may not explain why two jazzmen from different regions will be able to perform together successfully, but it may go a long ways toward doing so by providing the personnel and the types of music performed by the various groups with which a musician has recorded. Both Dorham and Candoli were essentially products of bop-inspired outfits, and both were technically secure on their instrument.

In listening to Dorham and Candoli on the 1956 Birdland Stars recording, and in particular to the tune entitled "Two Pairs of Aces," it is not difficult to recognize each trumpeter when he plays his extended solo, but once the two musicians begin to trade four bars apiece, it is more problematic to identify who is playing when. The two men seem to try to match each other's sound, and this is fairly easy for them to do, since in fact both share at times a similar tone production and both exhibit a "running" style and a use of ornamental figures and half-valve effects. Because they can sound very similar, they definitely perform well together and can blend as one horn when they execute passages in unison. Again, whereas it is not difficult to distinguish the two during their solos, since Dorham's have more of a unified shape and concept than Candoli's and less technique for its own sake, the challenge comes with the four-bar exchanges. Although one can count off the bars in 4/4 time in order to know when a player begins or ends his part in the "chase" sequence, the fact remains that it does require an effort to tell them apart.

Unfortunately, perhaps, discographies do not furnish listeners with a full account of which musician is playing for how long during an exchange like the one engaged in by Dorham and Candoli, although at times insert notes do mention the number of bars involved or whether the player performs for a half chorus, a full chorus, or more than one chorus. But then something should be left to the listener in terms of discovering distinctions, since the ability to recognize an artist's unique qualities is one of the special joys of listening to any music, especially to improvised jazz. And since discographies already provide an invaluable service in supplying the names of personnel, the recording label, the date and place of the performance, and the song titles and the alternate takes, such data should be enough for any researcher or aficionado, particularly when one realizes, as Dan Morgenstern has pointed out, that discographical research has almost never paid for itself.

Another use that I have made of discographies for research into Texan jazz relates to the single-artist compilations done for Kenny Dorham by

Claude Schlouch and Bo Raftegard. Although Tom Lord includes all the performances by Dorham that Schlouch and Raftegard list in their respective discographies, *The Unforgettable Kenny Dorham* (1977; 1983) and *The Kenny Dorham Discography* (1982), it was only after looking closely at these single-artist compilations that I discovered information that I might not have noticed otherwise. For years I had wondered to myself if Kenny Dorham ever performed with Eddie Durham, the fellow Texan whose name is so similar to Dorham's. The first item listed in Schlouch's discography is a fall 1945 recording session with Frank Humphries and His Orchestra, and here in fact I found Eddie Durham listed on trombone along with Dorham on trumpet. Not only did I find the two men together, but I discovered that this 1945 session was Kenny Dorham's very first recording. It also occurred to me that as a result of Eddie Durham, the veteran of many a swing-era historic recording session, having joined on this occasion with Dorham, one of the soon-to-be stars of the bebop revolution, this recording represented a meeting of two generations of Texans and of two vital jazz movements.

In listening to Frank Humphries and His Orchestra's version of "After You've Gone" from their 1945 session, I was disappointed that I could not distinguish Kenny Dorham from the other four trumpets, including the leader, who is the only featured soloist (and vocalist).[16] It is not clear that the brief but attractive trombone break is by Eddie Durham, since George Stevenson is also listed as "probably" on trombone. The big-band arrangement of the classic song is credited to Durham and is fairly typical of the swing era, whereas both it and Humphries' grandstanding trumpet solo differ greatly from the more cerebral mode of bebop as represented by Dorham's trumpet work on recordings with the Be-Bop Boys of 1946.[17] Despite my disappointment in not being able to identify Dorham among the trumpets or to be certain that Durham was the trombone soloist, this recording did fulfill my desire to know that two generations of Central Texas jazzmen had actually performed together, uniting, in a sense, the swing and bebop eras. This gratifying answer to the question I had posed to myself was owing, once again, to Morgenstern's "unsung" discographers.

Although I could have found the Frank Humphries recording in the Lord discography, it was the earlier Schlouch compilation that brought to my attention the presence of the two Texans as sidemen on this 1945 session. And even though the Bo Raftegard discography does not include this first Dorham recording, the compiler's introduction furnished me with important, if doleful, information on the Texas jazzman through its quotation of a commentary by baritone saxophonist Cecil Payne, a frequent session mate of Dorham's. Payne reveals something of the admirable, unself-pitying character of Kenny Dorham in his final year when he was dying of kidney disease. Payne recalls the last time he saw Dorham:

> [It] was at a Jazz mobile rehearsal studio a few weeks before he passed. Anyone could tell he was very sick, because his skin colour was *very* dry. We (Curtis Fuller, Jimmy Owens, Paul West and other musicians) were standing in a group talking and complaining about the sad state of the jazz musician economically. During all that time, about a half hour, Kenny just stood holding his horn, not saying a word. Just listening to our gripes.
>
> I talked to him on the phone the next day and told him that he should be able to get some money from the local 802 musicians union for blood transfusions. He called back and told my wife Ruth that he couldn't get the money because his union card had expired.[18]

Additionally, Raftegard himself provides insight into his reasons for compiling his discography when he recounts his first hearing at age four of a 45 rpm single with Dorham and the Jazz Messengers performing Horace Silver's tune "The Preacher." Raftegard explains, "The tune really got me. Most attractive to me was the funky piano [of Silver] and the cold trumpet [of Dorham]. Yes, The Preacher was like a children's song for me."[19]

Even though a "very unpretentious work" like Bo Raftegard's type-written, self-published discography may not be a complete listing, and even when it mistakenly follows the personnel for the Hank Mobley *Second Message* album (which fails to credit Dorham as the performer on "These Are the Things I Love"), such a labor of love still serves as a reward-ing source of information on a musician like Kenny Dorham, who, as Raftegard points out, may not have been a big "star," but achieving such recognition "is not necessarily due to the musical or artistical value" of his playing.[20] In the case of Raftegard and other listeners, the music of this native Texan has obviously spoken to them deeply, and as Raftegard testifies, "Ever since I first heard him I have loved his music—and that's almost as far back as I can remember."[21] As a Swedish jazz fan and a compiler of a work for "private use," Raftegard has not only made an important contribution to our knowledge but his work stands as another testament to the international impact of Texan jazz.

SAN MARCOS IN JAZZ HISTORY

uring the 1930s and 1940s, the town of San Marcos, now on the Interstate 35 corridor between Dallas-Fort Worth and San Antonio, reached out like tree roots to nourish a number of the major developments in jazz history—through its native son, multi-instrumentalist and composer-arranger Eddie Durham. Having first heard jazz in high school, I was aware of the music of Eddie Durham from listening over the years to recordings made by bands like those of Jimmie Lunceford and Count Basie, but not until 1989 did I learn that Eddie Durham was from Texas. This discovery led me first to write an article on his career for the *Southwestern Historical Quarterly*, which appeared in 1993, and subsequently to write *Texan Jazz*, published in 1996. But these publications did not end my interest in this seminal figure. As I have continued to listen to his music and to research more about his life, I have uncovered facts regarding his early days in San Marcos that reveal the sources for his becoming, as we say in Texas, a breed apart.

Like the proverbial acorn, from whose small beginnings will grow a giant Texas live oak, Eddie Durham lived in Central Texas a simple, essentially rural life that perhaps surprisingly prepared him to develop into a leading light during the rise of the big bands and of the small experimental combos that would influence jazz for decades to come. The tree analogy also applies to the Durham genealogy, since other members of the family played prominent roles in Eddie's musical career and therefore in the evolution of jazz.[1]

When I was working on my book on Texans in jazz history, I wanted very much to see the transcript of an interview with Eddie Durham conducted in 1978 by Stanley Dance and his wife, Helen Oakley. At the time, however, I could not afford a trip to Washington, D.C., to view this document held by the Smithsonian Institution. Fortunately, a copy of the interview is now housed in San Marcos in the special collections library at Texas State University, as it should be. This priceless document demonstrates what an articulate man Eddie Durham was, discloses how well he remembered and how much he understood life in his native state during the early part of the twentieth century, and, most significantly, provides insight into the musician's boyhood in San Marcos, which accounts in large part for his success as the first jazzman to record on an amplified guitar and as one of the swing era's truly outstanding composer-arrangers.

Eddie's father, Joe Durham, was a farmer and professional bronco-buster, who Eddie said was never thrown from a horse. His father also played the fiddle, entertaining as many as a hundred people at a time as they danced to the music that he made on his catgut strings. On occasion Eddie would accompany Joe by beating on his father's fiddle strings with

---

PREVIOUS PAGE: Three members of the 101 Ranch Band, ca. 1922. Pictured from left to right are Edgar Battle, Valentine Billington, and Eddie Durham. Used by permission of Marsha Durham.

a lady's hatpin while Joe was performing with his homemade, horsehair bow. Eddie's hatpin kept time, he said, like a drum, but still allowed his father's melody to come through loud and clear. Eddie also speaks of making fiddles out of cigar boxes that he acquired in downtown San Marcos. What is especially prophetic of his later historic development of the amplified guitar is his memory of hunting rattlesnakes, shooting them, and drying out their rattles to sell to local musicians who would put them down the holes of their fiddles so that, in his words, "when you hit the fiddle, boy, them rattles would sound . . . like an amplifier."[2]

In about 1930 Eddie would place a tin pie plate inside an acoustic guitar and wire it to a resonator, making it possible for him to create the first amplified jazz solos. In 1935 the Jimmie Lunceford Orchestra recorded Durham's tune "Hittin' the Bottle," and on this same piece, which Eddie arranged, he solos on his resonator-amplified guitar. Later, in about 1938, Eddie would introduce fellow Texan Charlie Christian to the amplified guitar (by then electrified). By 1940, when Charlie Christian recorded "Gone with What Draft" with the Benny Goodman Sextet, Charlie would not only quote Eddie's amplified guitar break from his 1935 Lunceford recording of "Avalon" but, through his revolutionary playing of the electric guitar, influence the creation of bebop. Here, indeed, is the sprouting of a kind of Jack's beanstalk from a handful of tiny San Marcos seeds.

Just as Eddie Durham's early experience with rattlesnake amplification led to his experiments with an amplified jazz guitar, his formative training in music theory during his boyhood years in San Marcos would also enable him to climb to jazz fame on such golden hit arrangements as his "Swinging the Blues," "Moten Swing," "Harlem Shout," "Lunceford Special," and, one of my personal favorites, "Runnin' a Temperature." Although Eddie's father instilled in him and his three brothers a love of music, Joe Durham could not read music and even told his son that he didn't want to see any notes because people "couldn't hear you read; they hear you play."[3] Nevertheless, Eddie's oldest brother, also named Joe, took correspondence courses in music theory, and it was he who would keep after Eddie to be serious about learning to read and to understand music instead of just playing it.

Eddie started out on trombone and guitar simultaneously, and his brother Joe, as Eddie said, "taught him from the beginning."[4] Joe himself played violin, cello, bass, and trumpet, among other instruments, performed for a time as a member of the first Nat King Cole trio, and was a sideman with such bands as the Dixie Ramblers, Jap Allen's band, and Blanche Calloway's orchestra. Eddie's other brothers were Earl, who played clarinet and saxophone, and Roosevelt, the youngest, who played piano and, as Eddie reported, sang and played like stride pianist Fats Waller. Clyde, a cousin, who also lived with the Durham family, would play bass with Gene Coy's Happy Black Aces out of Amarillo; trombonist Allen Durham, another cousin, recorded with Andy Kirk's Twelve Clouds of Joy; and Herschel Evans, yet another cousin, was a star tenor saxophonist with the great Count Basie band of the late 1930s. Both Herschel and Eddie would write classic tunes for the Basie unit, including Herschel's "Texas Shuffle" and "Doggin' Around" and Eddie's "Swinging the Blues," "Blue and Sentimental," "Every Tub," "John's Idea," "Out the Window," and "Time Out."[5]

Something that I did not know until I could read Stanley Dance and Helen Oakley's 1978 interview with Eddie Durham is that Edgar Battle, who was born in Atlanta, Georgia, in 1907, also lived with the Durham family as a pre-teen and later traveled in territory bands with Eddie when they were both teenagers. Battle, along with Eddie and his brothers Joe, Earl, and Roosevelt, formed the Durham Brothers band, and all five were also members of the Dixie Ramblers in the mid-1920s. In time Eddie worked with such name bands as those of Bennie Moten, Jimmie Lunceford, Count Basie, Artie Shaw, and Glenn Miller. The Moten recording session of 1932 is considered one of the greatest of the entire swing era, and Eddie contributed to the Moten recordings as arranger, trombonist, and guitarist. Edgar Battle has mistakenly been credited with co-writing "Topsy," Eddie Durham's highly popular tune that was first recorded in 1937 by the Basie band.[6] Later, in 1941, Eddie's "Topsy" was important in the development of bebop, since it served as the basis for a jam session recording entitled "Swing to Bop," which included such founders of the bebop movement as Dizzy Gillespie, Thelonious Monk, and Charlie Christian.

As a boy in San Marcos, Eddie took, at the insistence of his brother Joe, theory lessons by mail. These lessons would later lead him to score for the big bands in three-part harmony, then five-part, and finally six-part, which was beyond anything being done by the major arrangers of the mid-1930s. It was in fact Eddie who taught many of the successful arrangers of the day to score for six parts and to create riffs that, as he noted, were good melodies, not just repeated phrases that lacked any inherent musical value. Eddie's expansion of the harmonic range in jazz can also be attributed to a mind that, as he himself said, liked to create, "to find something bigger and more exciting."[7] He never stayed that long with any one band because he was never satisfied to stick with the same old patterns. Like many other Texas jazz musicians, Eddie Durham was his own man.

In describing himself, Eddie said that he was a rolling stone and a lone wolf, clearly attributes of a Texan who grew up making his own instruments, who was a crack shot with a rifle, who, when he hunted rattlesnakes, wore his boots and looked where he was going, and who shared with his fellow musicians all that he had learned, having grown up in a family that worked and played together. He never cared that much for gaining credit for what he had done; having his music performed was his main concern. He was philosophical in believing that "as soon as you write [a hit], you go back and write something else. If you can write another one, you don't worry too much [about who gets the credit or the money]."[8] Above all, as he once remarked, he was interested in "that Western idea of getting [the] tempo down right."[9]

Wherever Eddie Durham's tunes and solos are heard, whether on radio or reissued on CDs, his American music is loved around the world and carries with it a touch of his Central Texas hometown. And this should make the people of San Marcos, including the students and faculty members of the city's Texas State University, deeply proud of Eddie Durham's jazz legacy and of the part played in his career by his immediate and extended family. Appropriately, on February 6, 2004, the University's jazz ensembles presented a program of Eddie Durham compositions in a splendid tribute to the community's internationally acclaimed native son. Thinking of Eddie Durham's legacy, I am reminded of lines in a sonnet from World War One by English poet Rupert Brooke, which, if applied to Eddie, might read: "there's some corner in foreign lands / That is forever San Marcos and her Durhams."

NOTES

JAZZ MAVERICKS OF THE LONE STAR STATE

This essay was previously published in *Texas Highways* 51, no. 4 (April 2004): 50–57.

1. *The Complete OKeh & Brunswick Bix Beiderbecke, Frank Trumbauer & Jack Teagarden Sessions, 1924–1936* (Mosaic Records, MD7-211, 2001).
2. Giddins, *Riding on a Blue Note*, p. 75.
3. Dorham, "Fragments of an Autobiography," p. 30.
4. "Dorham's Epitaph" is included on Kenny Dorham's *Whistle Stop* (Blue Note CDP 7243 8 28978 2 8, 1994).
5. Jimmy Giuffre, Paul Bley, and Steve Swallow, *Conversations with a Goose* (Soul Note 121258-2, 1996). All of Giuffre's late recordings were made in Europe, this one produced in Italy. Early recordings by this particular trio were *Fusion* (1961) and *Thesis* (1962). For a discussion of these two albums, see my *Texan Jazz*, 303–304.
6. For a full discussion of John Carter's *Roots and Folklore*, see my *Texan Jazz*, pp. 350–360.
7. In 1988 Giuffre performed at the Jazz Festival Willisau in Lucerne, Switzerland. One piece included on the program was his improvisation for solo soprano entitled "Momentum," but it was in a duet with André Jaume on bass clarinet, entitled "Sequence," that Giuffre achieved perhaps his loveliest lines on soprano sax. See *Jimmy Giuffre & André Jaume: Momentum, Willisau 1988* (Hat Hut Records, hatOLOGY 508, 1997). Giuffre and Jaume had performed "Sequence" the year before in Paris, but I greatly prefer the Willisau version. See *Jimmy Giuffre/André Jaume: Eiffel, Live in Paris* (Harmonia Mundi, France, CELP.C6, HM 85, 1987).

THE ROOTS OF TEXAN JAZZ

This essay was previously published as "Texan Jazz 1920–1950" in *The Roots of Texas Music*, ed. Lawrence Clayton and Joe W. Specht (College Station: Texas A&M University Press, 2003): 37–65. Reprinted by permission of the Texas A&M University Press, copyright © 2003 by the Texas A&M University Press.

1. See, for example, E. Simms Campbell's "Blues," in *Jazzmen*, ed. Ramsey and Smith, p. 112.
2. Blesh, *Shining Trumpets*, p. 184. Bunk Johnson is said to have played in Dallas in 1904, Sidney Bechet in Plantersville in 1911, and Jelly Roll Morton a few years later in Houston and "more towns" than he could remember, while King Oliver toured Texas in 1914. See my *Texan Jazz*, pp. 86, 88.

3. José Hosiasson, liner notes, *Jazz and Hot Dance in Chile, 1926–1959* (Harlequin HQ 2083, 1991).

4. *Jazz in Texas, 1924–1930* (Timeless Records, CBC 1-033, 1997). Ross Russell, in his *Jazz Style in Kansas City and the Southwest*, claims that "there is no record of an outstanding band in the Houston area during the twenties" (p. 59), but this Fatty Martin side, as well as another of "Jimtown Blues," on which Martin takes a fine piano solo, suggests that perhaps Russell was unaware of this band.

5. Pablo Garrido, "Recuento integral del Jazz in Chile," *Para todos* (vol. 1, no. 29 [June 10, 1935]: 40), quoted in Hosiasson, *Jazz and Hot Dance in Chile, 1926–1959.*

6. Kirk, *Twenty Years on Wheels*, p. 46.

7. According to Jim Fisher, former curator of the O'Henry Museum in Austin, there was a band playing jazz in Taylor, Texas, in 1904. Fisher told me in conversation that he had seen more than one reference to this band but could not recall where. In Austin a number of groups were active from 1920 on.

For a 1925 article entitled "'Fire Hall Five,'" a survey of popular bands of the period that appeared in the University of Texas student newspaper, author Lyra Haisley interviewed bandleader William Besserer, whose group had played in 1918 and 1919 for the University's German Club dances. Besserer remembered that in 1920 "along came the jazz—and Paul Whiteman and his 'tin-can' orchestra." Haisley observes that since Besserer's group "did not realize what jazz was all about," it "disbanded, and Shakey's orchestra, directed by Jack Tobin, became the ruling favorites in University circles. If it wasn't Shakey's, according to some, it wasn't jazz. Jack and his men played the unadulterated, primitive jazz." Haisley then reports that "About 1920, Pharr's Fire Hall Five, directed by Blondy Pharr, was quite well-known for its particular kind of 'jazzmania.'" After this, Haisley writes, "Jimmie's Joys, directed by Jimmy Maloney, was the leading campus dance band for about two years. In 1921–22, six brothers formed Howell's Moonshiners and played for some of the dances" (p. 6).

Another campus group, the Texas Collegians Varsity Peacocks, traveled as far as Laredo to perform. One member of this group was drummer Jay "Bird" Thomas, who, as we shall see, in 1930 also formed part of Fred Gardner's Texas University Troubadours, which recorded four sides that feature cornetist Tom Howell. (The reference to "six brothers" may be an error, since there were only five Howell brothers.)

For making me aware of Haisley's article, I am indebted to Berry, "Student Life and Customs," 2:598.

8. Hadlock, *Jazz Masters of the Twenties*, p. 174.

9. In *Texan Jazz*, I give Teagarden's birth date as August 29, following the standard sources, but this has been corrected by archivist Joe Showler of Toronto, who gives the day as August 20.

10. Quoted in Waters, *Jack Teagarden's Music*, p. 3.

11. Smith and Len Guttridge, *Jack Teagarden*, p. 42.

12. Hadlock, *Jazz Masters of the Twenties*, p. 183.

13. The music for this radio series is now available from Showler's CD label, Vernon Music. See *Jack Teagarden—1930 with Ben Pollack and his Orchestra: Whiz Radio Programs* (Vernon Music, VMCD-62901, 2001). Most of the music on this CD is not jazz, and unfortunately Teagarden is heard from infrequently.

14. *Jack Teagarden and His Band—1951: Live at the Royal Room, Hollywood* (Vernon Music, VMCD-83199, 1999).

15. Ed Steane, liner notes, *Bennie Moten's Kansas City Orchestra, 1923–1929* (Historical Records, vol. 9, ASC-5829-9, n.d.).

16. Schuller, *The Swing Era*, p. 336.

17. Brian Rust, insert notes, *Jazz in Texas, 1924–1930*.

18. Ibid.

19. See *Lillian Glinn: Complete Recorded Works in Chronological Order, 1927–1929* (Document Records, COCD-5184, 1993). The most impressive side by Glinn is entitled "Shake It Down," recorded in New Orleans in April 1928 with an unidentified ensemble.

20. *Blue Rhythm Stomp: Texas Jazz* (Jazz Greats CD 073, 1999). Since so many jazz musicians tended to be kin to one another, one would think that John Hardee of Wichita Falls, who recorded extensively in the mid-1940s, might have been related to Stanley Hardee.

21. Schuller, *Early Jazz*, p. 296.

22. John McDonough, "A Century with Count Basie," *Down Beat* 57 (January 1990): 36.

23. Schuller, *Early Jazz*, p. 316.

24. *Jazz in Texas, 1924–1930*.

25. Rust, insert notes, *Jazz in Texas, 1924–1930*. See also Rust, comp., *Jazz Records, 1897–1942*, 1:595–596.

26. *The Cactus*, p. 357.

27. Chester Seekatz is listed in *Jazz in Texas, 1924–1930* as Chester Skeekatz.

28. *Matchless Milam*, pp. 134–135. For more on Tom Howell and his family, see my entry on the musician in *The Handbook of Texas Music*, pp. 145–146.

29. *Texas & Tennessee Territory Bands* (Retrieval Recordings, RTR 79006, 1997).

30. *Jazz Records, 1897–1942*, p. 343. Rust reports in this discography that "Sunny Clapp himself claims that Bix Beiderbecke is on 'Come Easy, Go Easy Love,' but he is not on the issued take of this number, and there is no evidence of his presence on any of the other sides from the three sessions at which this was recorded" (p. 343).

31. See *Jazz Records, 1897–1942*, p. 342, as well as Lord's *The Jazz Discography*, 4:344.

32. "Come Easy, Go Easy Love" is a song credited to Hoagy Carmichael and Sunny Clapp, with a vocal by Carmichael. There is a truly impressive trombone solo on "When I Can't Be with You," but again no trombonist is listed in the CD insert notes, while Rust identifies the trombonist as Lee Howell. Also included on *Texas & Tennessee Territory Bands* are four sides by Phil Baxter and his Orchestra, recorded at the Park Hotel Ballroom in Dallas on October 20, 1929. One of the trumpets here, either Roy Nooner or Al Hann, takes an excellent solo on "Down Where the Blue Bonnets Grow," and the accordionist, Davy Crocker, also solos wonderfully. The alto soloist on "Honey Child," either Ken Naylor or Jack Jones, has a very professional sound and flow. All four songs were written by Baxter, who is perhaps best known in Texas music circles as the composer of "I'm a Ding Dong Daddy from Dumas."

33. *The Real Kansas City* (Columbia/Legacy CK 64855, 1996).

34. These three sides were reissued on *Louis Armstrong: The Complete RCA Victor Recordings* (BMG Classics, 09026-68682-2, 1997).

35. Schuller, *The Swing Era*, p. 184.

36. Keg Johnson can be heard soloing on "Blue Lou" with the Benny Carter Orchestra from 1933, as reissued on *Benny Carter and His Orchestra, 1933–1936* (Classics 530, 1990). He was with the Fletcher Henderson Orchestra of 1934 but does not solo on the sides reissued on *Fletcher Henderson & His Orchestra: The Father of the Big Band, 1925–1937* (Jazz Archives No. 137, 159352, 1998). Keg was with the Calloway orchestra from 1936 to the 1940s and is present on numerous recordings reissued for those years by the Classics CD series. Hear, for example, his solo on "At the Clambake Carnival," recorded on March 23, 1938 (Classics, 576, 1991).

37. *Earl Hines—Piano Man: Earl Hines, His Piano and His Orchestra* (RCA Victor Bluebird 6750-2-RB, 1989).

38. *Earl Hines Live at the Village Vanguard* (Columbia, CK 44197, 1988).

39. Schuller, *The Swing Era*, p. 285.

40. Russell, *Jazz Style in Kansas City and the Southwest*, p. 74.

41. Schuller, *Early Jazz*, p. 298.

42. "Baby, Look at You" is included on *The Real Kansas City*.

43. *Hot Lips Page and His Band, 1938–1940* (Classics, 561, 1991). Parker's first full-length solos appear on *Early Bird: Charlie Parker with Jay McShann and His Orchestra* (Stash Records, St-CD-542, 1991). One poorly recorded side from August 1940 is also included on this CD and may contain a solo by Parker.

44. Quoted in Gitler, *Swing to Bop*, p. 60.

45. Christian's birthplace has always been given as Dallas, but in Govenar and Brakefield's *Deep Ellum and Central Track*, the authors identify his birthplace as Bonham (p. 121).

46. Hear Durham's guitar on "New Vine Street Blues," which is included on *Count Basie in Kansas City: Bennie Moten's Great Band of 1930–1932* (RCA

Victor, LPV-514, 1965). "Hittin' the Bottle" is on *Swingsation: Jimmie Lunceford* (GRP Records, GRD-9923, 1998), and "Time Out" is included on *One O'Clock Jump: An Album of Classic "Swing" by Count Basie and His Orchestra 1937* (Decca, MCA-42324, 1990).

47. See Boyd, *The Jazz of the Southwest*, which quotes from an interview with Leon McAuliffe, who recalled that he had "learned to play Hawaiian music because that's what the steel guitar was primarily used for" (p. 117).

48. *The Complete Recordings of the Father of Western Swing: Milton Brown and the Musical Brownies, 1932–1937* (Texas Rose Records, TXRCD1-5, 1995).

49. *Bob Wills and His Texas Playboys: 'The King of Western Swing' 25 Hits, 1935–1945* (Living Era, AJA 5250, 1998).

50. *Charlie Christian Volume 6, 1940–1941* (Média 7, MJCD 68, 1994).

51. Christian, "Guitarmen, Wake Up and Pluck!"

52. *Jimmie Lunceford 2: "Harlem Shout" (1935–1936)* (MCA Records, 1305, 1980).

53. Simon, "Charlie Christian," p. 318.

54. Schuller, *The Swing Era*, p. 563.

55. *Solo Flight: The Genius of Charlie Christian* (Columbia, CG30779, 1972).

56. "Swing to Bop," with Charlie Christian and Thelonious Monk, was recorded May 1941. This piece is essentially a retitled version of Eddie Durham's "Topsy," and Christian's solo work here has been called "a condensed history of jazz as riff after riff from the swing age are laid down until the complex [bebop] phrases are reached" (Tudor and Tudor, *Jazz*, p. 144). The side is included on *Charlie Christian—Guest Artists: Dizzy Gillespie and Thelonious Monk* (Everest Records, FS-219, n.d.).

57. François Billard, insert notes, *Casa Loma Orchestra, 1930/1934* (Jazz Archives No. 54, 157692, 1992).

58. Smith's sides with Lester Young are included on *Count Basie, Harry James: Basie Rhythm* (HEP Records, 1032, 1991).

59. Much of James's work with Goodman is reproduced on two CDs, *The Harry James Years, Volume 1* (Bluebird, 66155-2, 1993), and *Wrappin' It Up: The Harry James Years Part 2* (Bluebird, 66549-2, 1995).

60. Some of Herschel's most memorable solos, such as those on "Blue and Sentimental," "Jumpin' at the Woodside," and his own tune "Doggin' Around," can be heard on *Count Basie: His Best Recordings, 1936–1944* (Best of Jazz, 4026, 1995).

61. "I Got Rhythm" is included on *Casa Loma Orchestra: Stompin' Around* (HEP, CD 1062, 1999).

62. *Giants of the Tenor Sax: Lester "Prez" Young & Friends* (Commodore, CCD 7002, 1988).

63. *Jazz in Texas, 1924–1930*.

64. Russell, *Jazz Style in Kansas City and the Southwest*, pp. 56–57.

65. A later exponent of this tenor style was Don Wilkerson, who attended Houston's Jack Yates High School in the late 1940s, recorded with the Ray Charles Orchestra in 1954, and made three albums with Blue Note in the early 1960s. See *Don Wilkerson: The Complete Blue Note Sessions* (Blue Note, 24555, 2001).

66. "Seventh Avenue Express" is included on *Count Basie: Kansas City Powerhouse* (Bluebird, 09026-63903-2, 2002).

67. McCarthy, *Big Band Jazz*, p. 109.

68. Lomax, *Mister Jelly Roll*, p. 145. In his classic version of Morton's biography, Lomax reports that in Morton's account of his life and times he mentioned having been active in Memphis during 1908 before his travels started again, at which point "Jelly Roll's story began to move so fast that we gave up trying for exact chronology" (p. 143n). After touring the East Coast and ending up in Jacksonville, where Morton stayed for about two months, he returned to Memphis and then traveled with a show that was stranded in Hot Springs, Arkansas, after which he accepted an offer to appear at the Pastime Theatre in Houston (p. 145).

69. For a fuller account of these figures, see my *Texan Jazz*, especially chapter 3 on classic blues and chapter 4 on boogie-woogie.

70. Driggs, "Kansas City and the Southwest," p. 223.

71. Leonard Feather, liner notes, *Lionel Hampton "Steppin' Out," Vol. 1, 1942–1945* (Decca Records, DL 79244, n.d.).

72. See my *Texan Jazz*, p. 226, pp. 411–412, notes 34 and 35. "Flying Home No. 2" is included on *Lionel Hampton "Steppin' Out," Vol. 1, 1942–1945*.

73. Kenneth Randall, liner notes, *The Wild Man From Texas: Arnett Cobb* (Home Cooking Records, HCS-114, 1989).

74. Maurice Simon was born in Houston on March 26, 1929. In *Texan Jazz*, I mention his participation in the Illinois Jacquet recording of "Hot Rod," commenting that he engages in a "high-speed chase" sequence with Jacquet (p. 225), but I did not realize at the time that Simon was a Texan.

75. "The Jitney Man" is included on *Kenny Dorham: Blues in Bebop* (Savoy, SVY-17028, 1998).

76. Ibid., liner notes, p. 4. Two albums by Dallas natives James Clay and David "Fathead" Newman are entitled *Wide Open Spaces* and *Return to the Wide Open Spaces*. See my *Texan Jazz*, pp. 313–314.

77. *New Sounds: Art Blakey's Messengers/James Moody & His Modernists* (Blue Note, CDP 7 84436 2, 1991).

78. For more on Dorham's career, see "Texas Bebop Messengers to the World: Kenny Dorham and Leo Wright," a subsequent essay in this volume.

79. George Corley can be heard on *Boots and His Buddies, 1935–1937* (Classics, 723, 1993) and *Boots and His Buddies, 1937–1938* (Classics, 738, 1993).

80. For a full discussion of Bowman and the Fort Worth source of his most famous tune, see my *Texan Jazz*, p. 29.

81. *Glenn Miller: Moonlight Serenade* (Bluebird, 61072, 1992).

82. Quoted by Michael James, liner notes, *Seeking: The New Art Jazz Ensemble* (Revelation Records, REV-9, 1969).

83. Evans, interview with Dewey Redman.

84. Tony Baldwin, liner notes, *Hot Violins* (ABC Records, 836 049-2, 1988).

85. Duke Ellington, *Liberian Suite* (CBS Records, France, CBS 62686, 1973). Only after the publication of *Texan Jazz* did I notice in the liner notes to Erroll Garner's *Concert by the Sea* (Columbia CL 883, ca. 1956) that one of the tunes recorded by Garner, "How Could You Do a Thing Like That to Me," called by George Avakian "something of a classic," was written by Tyree Glenn.

86. Ervin and Handy's "duel" on the Mingus recording of "No Private Income Blues" (on *Jazz Portraits: Mingus in Wonderland* [Blue Note, CDP7243 8 27325 2 5, 1994]) is an amazing performance unmatched by anything of its kind.

87. Among Texas women instrumentalists, trumpeter Clora Bryant, who was born in Denison, Texas, on May 30, 1929, was a member of an all-girl orchestra at Prairie View A&M before establishing herself in Los Angeles as "one of the most respected trumpet players on the West Coast" (Placksin, *American Women in Jazz*, p. 152). Bryant's one album, issued originally in 1957, is *Clora Bryant . . . Gal with a Horn* (Mode 106, V.S.O.P. #42, 1995). Her autobiographical sketch is included in Bryant et al., eds., *Central Avenue Sounds*.

FROM BEBOP TO HARD BOP AND BEYOND

This essay was previously published in *Juneteenth Texas: Essays in African-American Folklore,* ed. Francis E. Abernethy, Patrick B. Mullen, and Alan B. Govenar (Denton: University of North Texas Press, 1996): 153–164.

1. *The Last of the Blue Devils,* dir. Ricker.

2. Clifford Brown, *Jazz Immortal* (Pacific Jazz, PJ-3, 1960).

3. *Thelonious Monk: Genius of Modern Music,* vol. 2 (BST-81511, [1952]).

4. Quoted by Chris Albertson, liner notes, *Budd Johnson and the Four Brass Giants* (Riverside Records, 343, 1960).

5. The best firsthand account of the music program at Wiley College, as far as I am aware, is bebop drummer Roy Porter's autobiography, *There and Back.*

6. From Nat Hentoff's "Jazz Messengers Blazing a Spirited Trail," an interview with Art Blakey, in *Down Beat* 23, no. 4 (February 22, 1956): 10; cited by George Avakian, liner notes, *The Jazz Messengers* (Columbia, CL 897, [1956]). Blakey also comments that "the spirit in good music is sometimes stronger than the spirit in a church meeting." He notes too that a piece like

Kenny Dorham's "Minor's Holiday" represents a "more intellectual, more up-to-date" form of jazz, "but still with feeling" (p. 10).

7. *Kenny Dorham: New York 1953–1956 & Oslo 1960* (Landscape, LS2-918, 1992).

8. Ornette Coleman, quoted by Martin Williams, liner notes, *The Shape of Jazz to Come* (Atlantic 1317-2, 1959).

TEXAS BEBOP MESSENGERS TO THE WORLD

This essay was previously published as "Kenny Dorham and Leo Wright: Texas Bebop Messengers to the World" in *Journal of Texas Music History* 1, no. 1 (Spring 2001): 15–23.

1. Poe, "Some Words with a Mummy," p. 543. Coincidentally, in writing about the effect of jazz according to "an elite predatory audience of white hunters," i.e., white writers on black jazz, David Meltzer, in his *Reading Jazz*, has employed a battery metaphor similar to Poe's: "The slave music bags its hunters, turns them into pale-skinned savages in wild spasms juiced by galvanic bolts of electricity à la *Frankenstein*; the victim is hurled back into a primal state of being and, as such, repudiates the progress dynamo for the tom-tom of regress" (p. 22).

2. Mark Gardner, insert notes, *The Kenny Dorham Memorial Album* (Xanadu Records, XCD 1235, 1975, 1995). According to Gardner's notes, Dorham's statement about his youthful ambition was taken from his *Fragments of an Autobiography*, but Gardner does not reveal where it was published. Later I discovered, thanks to another CD entitled *Kenny Dorham: Blues in Bebop* (Savoy, SVY-17028, 1998), that this autobiographical work appears in the *Down Beat Music Yearbook* for 1970.

3. See Massey's preface to *Black Cowboys in Texas*, where she writes that it is "plausible that the total number of African American cowboys herding cattle up the trail 1866–1895 was 8,700, or twenty-five percent" of all the cowboys involved, white, Mexican, and African American (p. xv).

4. It may be that Dorham had been inspired by an earlier version of "I'm an Old Cowhand" by his fellow jazzman Sonny Rollins, who recorded the Mercer tune for his 1957 album entitled *Way Out West* (Contemporary, OJCCD-337-2, 1988). Dorham appears with Rollins on a 1954 recording entitled *Moving Out* (Prestige Records, OJCCD-058-2, 1987), and the trumpeter's playing on this occasion is truly superb.

5. [Traill], "Boppin' in Paris," p. 16. Traill remarks of Kenny Dorham that he "was one of the best bop trumpeters, a musician who had an immediately identifiable sound and more than the average quota of original ideas. His brisk 'running' style was a good foil for Parker's lucidity, and it has always seemed true that Dorham was one of Bird's better trumpet partners."

6. *Bird in Paris* (Yard Records, CP3, n.d.).

7. *Kenny Dorham: The Complete Savoy Recordings* (DRCD11156, 1999). Dorham probably heard the phrase he plays from "On the Trail" on one of the Philip Morris Cigarette Company's popular radio programs, which used Grofé's music as their theme. Composed in 1931, "On the Trail" served as the Philip Morris theme for at least twenty-five years—from 1934, when the company sponsored the Ferde Grofé Show, until 1959, when NBC Radio aired a half-hour program celebrating the twenty-fifth anniversary of the company's use of both the phrase "Call for Philip Morris" and the "On the Trail" theme. The combination of the "call" and the musical theme was employed on over fifty radio programs sponsored by the cigarette manufacturer.

It is also possible that Dorham simply picked up the Grofé theme from other beboppers, such as Dizzy Gillespie, who definitely had a penchant for incorporating quotes from diverse sources. Although I am not aware of Gillespie using the Grofé theme prior to Dorham's 1949 recording of "Hilo," Gillespie does quote "On the Trail" in his solo on "All the Things You Are," recorded May 15, 1953, with Charlie Parker, Bud Powell, Max Roach, and Charles Mingus. See *The Quintet: Jazz at Massey Hall* (Debut, OJCCD-044-2, 1989).

8. Feigin, comp. and ed., *Russian Jazz*, p. 2.

9. One of the most impressive "Scandinavian" performances by Dorham that I have heard is a 1963 Stockholm radio broadcast that unfortunately was not issued, but as a taped transcription it was made available to me by a friend, trumpeter Dave Laczko. Three tunes were performed on this occasion, with a group of Swedish musicians and the American baritone saxophonist Sahib Shihab (Edmund Gregory). The three tunes are Dorham's own "Short Story," the lovely ballad "I Concentrate on You," and "Not Yet." Dorham's playing on the ballad is one of his finest performances ever, as is his work on the uptempo "Not Yet." This unissued sextet performance is indexed in Lord's *The Jazz Discography*.

10. Kenny Dorham Quintet, *Scandia Skies* (SteepleChase, SCCD 36011, 1993).

11. *Kenny Dorham: New York 1953–1956 & Oslo 1960* (Landscape, LS2-918, 1992). The Oslo session was recorded in January at the Metropole Jazz Club.

12. *Miles Ahead: Miles Davis + 19*, orchestra directed by Gil Evans (Columbia, CL 1041, 1957; reissued as CK 651121, 1997).

13. *Kenny Dorham: The Complete Savoy Recordings*.

14. "Osmosis" is on *Kenny Dorham Quintet* (Debut Records, DLP-9, 1953; reissued as OJCCD-113-2, 1993).

15. "Minor's Holiday" and "Basheer's Dream" are on *Kenny Dorham: Afro-Cuban* (Blue Note, BLP 1535 and 5065; reissued as CDP 7 46815-2, 1987); "The Theme" is on *The Jazz Messengers at the Café Bohemia*, Vol. 1 (Blue Note, BLP 1507, 1955; reissued as CDP 7 46521 2, 1987); "Man of Moods" is on *Kenny Dorham: Blues in Bebop* (originally on Signal LP 1203, 1956; reissued

by Savoy as SVY-17028, 1998); two takes of "Mexico City" are included on
Kenny Dorham: 'Round About Midnight at the Café Bohemia (Blue Note, BLP
1524, 1956; reissued as CDP 7243 8 333576 2 8, 1995); and "Why Not?" is on
Kenny Dorham: West 42nd Street (Black Lion, BLP 60119, 1961; reissued as
BLCD 760119, 1989).

16. See *Swingin' the Classics* (Viper's Nest Records, CD-VN-1010, 1996).

17. See Gillespie's autobiography, *To Be or Not . . . to Bop*, p. 415.

18. Collier, *Benny Goodman and the Swing Era*, p. 233.

19. The lecture was delivered on December 4, 1997, as part of the Union
Distinguished Speakers Series at the University of Texas at Austin.

20. *Thelonious Monk: Genius of Modern Music*, Vol. 2 (Blue Note,
BST-81511, n.d.).

21. See Owens, *Bebop*, pp. 34–35.

22. One version of "Swedish Schnapps," from August 8, 1951, is included
on *Bird's Best Bop on Verve* (Polygram Records, 314 527 452-2, 1995).

23. Duke Ellington, "Serenade to Sweden," is included on *The Ellington
Era, 1927–1940, Volume Two* (Columbia, C3L39, n.d.); Stan Getz, "Dear Old
Stockholm," on Miles Davis, *'Round About Midnight* (Columbia, CJ 40610,
1956). Davis first recorded "Dear Old Stockholm" in 1952 with his All-Stars,
reissued on *Miles Davis: Volume 1* (Blue Note, 7243 5 32610 2 3, 2001).

24. A different type of personal connection with Norway is found in
Dorham's association with Randi Hultin, a jazz buff in Oslo whose account
of her relationship with and hospitality toward jazz musicians is recorded
in her book *Born under the Sign of Jazz*. Hultin's book comes with a CD
that includes her home taping of Dorham playing piano and singing "Fair
Weather," his own song that was used in the 1986 movie *'Round Midnight*,
starring tenor saxophonist Dexter Gordon. Hultin's 1964 taping of Dorham
was the only time that he ever performed his song, for which he wrote the
lyrics as well. Hultin also mentions that Texas reedman Leo Wright visited
her home and was amazed by her young daughter, who did improvised
dancing to jazz. See pp. 227–228 for Dorham and p. 132 for Wright.

25. Max Harrison et al., p. 18.

26. Chris Sheridan, insert notes, *Kenny Dorham: Short Story*
(SteepleChase, SCCD 36010, 1993).

27. "Short Story" is included on *Kenny Dorham: New York 1953–1956
& Oslo 1960* and *Kenny Dorham: Short Story*.

28. Kenny Dorham, *Hot Stuff From Brazil* (West Wind, 2015, 1988).

29. Michael Cuscuna, insert note, *Kenny Dorham: Una más* (Blue Note,
BLP 4127, 1963; reissued as CDP 0777 7 46515 2 0, 1995).

30. Heitor Villa-Lobos's "Prelude" (recorded in November 1961) is
included on *Kenny Dorham: Matador/Inta Somethin'* (Blue Note, CDP 7
844602 2, 1991); "Manha de Carnaval" (recorded on December 19, 1963) is
included on *Kenny Dorham: Short Story*. Of one performance of "Manha de
Carnaval," Dorham noted in an article in *Down Beat* that he wrote about the

Longhorn Jazz Festival, held in Austin on April 28–30, 1967, at which he was the featured soloist, that the piece was "frolicking and basking in the Brazilian-Texas sun. I have a special affection for this music—seems to be the music of many languages—internationale" ("With K. D. in Texas," p. 29).

31. "Una más" (first recorded in November 1961) is included on *Kenny Dorham: Matador/Inta Somethin'* and (as recorded on April 1, 1963) on *Kenny Dorham: Una más*; "Blue Bossa," along with Dorham's "La Mesha" (recorded on June 3, 1963), is included on *Joe Henderson: Page One* (Blue Note, 84140, 1963; reissued as 7243 4 98795 2 2, 1999); "São Paulo" is included on *Kenny Dorham: Una más*; "Afrodisia" is on *Kenny Dorham: Afro-Cuban*; and "Pedro's Time" (recorded on September 9, 1963) is on *Joe Henderson: Our Thing* (Blue Note, BLP 4152, 1963; reissued as 84152, 2000).

32. Quoted in insert notes, *The Kenny Dorham Memorial Album*.

33. "Monaco" is on *Kenny Dorham: 'Round About Midnight at the Café Bohemia*; "Bombay" (recorded on August 23, 1946) is on *"Opus de Bop"* (Savoy MG 12114, 1991) and *Kenny Dorham: Blues in Bebop*; and "Tahitian Suite" (recorded on April 4, 1956) is on *Kenny Dorham and The Jazz Prophets, Vol. 1* (Chessmates, GRD-820, n.d.). This last album is one of Dorham's very finest recordings, with his solo work on his own tune "The Prophet" a marvelous piece of improvisation and his "pecking" with tenorist J. R. Monterose a thrilling interchange between these two highly complementary hornmen.

34. Although Boots and His Buddies recorded during the 1930s, Mel Wright was not in the band at the time of the group's recording sessions. Two CDs by the Clifford "Boots" Douglas band are now available: *Boots and His Buddies, 1935–1937* (Classics, 723, 1993) and *Boots and His Buddies, 1937–1938* (Classics, 738, 1993). Leo Wright recalled that his father taught him a great deal: "two things he used to say I'll never forget. . . . 'learn your horn' and 'don't forget what came before.' . . . And believe it or not, one of the first altos I became conscious of was Jimmy Dorsey—my father used to play his records" (quoted by Morgenstern, "Introducing Leo Wright," p. 26).

35. Buddy Tate can be heard soloing on "Tickle Toe" (the apparent source for Dorham's "Short Story") and "Super Chief" from 1940 (included on *Count Basie and His Orchestra, 1937–1943: Jumpin' at the Woodside* [Jazz Roots, CD 56015, 1991]) and on "Seventh Avenue Express" from 1947 (included on *Count Basie: Kansas City Powerhouse* [Bluebird, 09026-63903-2, 2002]).

36. See *The Complete Blue Note Forties Recordings of Ike Quebec and John Hardee* (Mosaic Records, MR4-107, 1984).

37. So far as I am aware, Dorham and Wright never recorded together, even though Dorham did record with most of the major and minor saxophonists of postwar jazz, among them Pepper Adams, Cannonball Adderley, Joe Alexander, Rocky Boyd, Al Cohn, George Coleman, John Coltrane, Junior Cook, Charles Davis, Eric Dolphy, Frank Foster, Coleman Hawkins, Frank Haynes, Jimmy Heath, Joe Henderson, Ernie Henry, Clifford Jordan, Musa Kaleem, Harold Land, Jackie McLean, Charles McPherson, Hank

Mobley, James Moody, J. R. Monterose, Oliver Nelson, Charlie Parker, Cecil Payne, Sonny Rollins, Sahib Shihab, Zoot Sims, Sonny Stitt, Ernie Thompson, and Lucky Thompson. Dorham appears in a photograph on stage with Ornette Coleman during the November 1960 Newport Rebels concert in New York City, organized by the Jazz Artists Guild in protest of the regular Newport Jazz Festival of the same year. But so far as I know, Kenny and Ornette never recorded together. Dorham does appear on piano on a recording from the Newport Rebels concert but does not perform with Coleman (*Newport Rebels* [Candid, CCD79022, 1991]).

38. Chris Sheridan, insert notes, *Dizzy Gillespie Quintet: Copenhagen Concert* (SteepleChase, SCCD 36024, 1992).

39. *Four Jazz Legends: Live at Newport 1960* (Omega, OCD 3025, 1994); *The Dizzy Gillespie Big Band: Carnegie Hall Concert* (Verve, V6-8423, 1961; reissued as part of Dizzy Gillespie and His Orchestra, *Gillespiana* [Verve, MGV83914] by Polygram Records [314 519 809-2, 1993]).

40. Gillespie is quoted as having said, "I know the blues, but Hot Lips Page is a blues man. When he plays trumpet, he plays it like a blues player would play. My music is not that deep—not as deep as his—not as deep as Hot Lips Page or Charlie Parker, because Yard knew the blues" (*To Be or Not to . . . Bop*, p. 310).

41. Quoted by Mark Gardner, insert notes, *An Electrifying Evening with the Dizzy Gillespie Quintet* (Verve, V6-8401, 1961; reissued by Polygram Records, 314 557 544-2, 1999).

42. Ibid.

43. Duke Ellington, quoted by Stanley Dance, album notes, *The Ellington Era, 1927–1940, Volume One* (Columbia, C3L27, 1963). It is fascinating to me that not only Gillespie the bebopper was attracted to Ellington's "The Mooche," but, as I point out in "The Roots of Texan Jazz," even the white University of Texas Troubadours recorded in 1930 their own version of this 1928 masterpiece.

44. For a discussion of jazz from this period, see Rosenthal, *Hard Bop*.

45. Dizzy Gillespie and His Orchestra, *Gillespiana*. In the original liner notes to the album, Gunther Schuller refers to the work as "one of the few successful *large-scale* attempts to blend authentic South American rhythms and sonorities with those of jazz" and as being "in the eighteenth century 'Suite' form . . . namely the *Concerto grosso* format, as exemplified in this instance by a quintet featured within a large accompanimental brass and percussion group."

46. Joel Dorn, note on video box, *Dizzy Gillespie: Ralph Gleason's Jazz Casual* (Rhino, R3 2586, 1995).

47. Both "Dionysos" and "A Felicidade" are included on Leo Wright's *Suddenly the Blues* (Koch Jazz, KOC CD-8544, 2000; originally Atlantic, 1393, 1962). An additional side on this album that has ties with another culture is "Tali," a piece composed by Tom McIntosh, titled after the name of an Iranian

friend—Tali meaning "dawn" in Persian. In Kenny Dorham's *Down Beat* article entitled "With K. D. in Texas," he speaks of performing "A Felicidade" and also refers to Art Blakey as his favorite drummer because, in Dorham's own Spanish, Blakey exhibits *"Fuerte y mucho fuego"* (pp. 26, 28).

48. Leo Wright, *Blues Shout* (Atlantic, 1358, 1960; reissued on *Hank Crawford, The Soul Clinic/Leo Wright, Blues Shout* [Collectables, COL-CD-6281, 1999]).

49. Leonard Feather, liner notes to the 1960 *Blues Shout*, reproduced in the Collectables reissue.

50. Red Garland, *I Left My Heart . . .* (Muse, 5311, 1978; reissued by 32 Jazz, 32107, 1999). Earlier Wright recorded an album entitled *Soul Talk* (Vortex 2011, 1964; reissued by Water Records, 146, 2005), which also contains an excellent example of his expert handling of a pop song, in this case Hoagy Carmichael and Johnny Mercer's "Skylark." Once again, the blues predominate on this album (from Wright's tune "Blue Leo" for flute to his "Blues Fanfare" for alto), but it also includes the moving spiritual "Sometimes I Feel Like a Motherless Child," as well as a fine original by Wright entitled "Poopsie's Minor," with the rhythm section backing up the soloist with a type of Brazilian beat.

51. See Feather's insert notes to *Blues Shout.*

52. Quoted by Morgenstern, "Introducing Leo Wright."

BRITISH ACOLYTES OF JAZZ AND ITS TEXAS CONTINGENT

1. The idea for this essay originated when I rather facetiously suggested to Professor Roger Louis, who has presided over the Faculty Seminar on British Studies at the University of Texas at Austin since its inception in 1975, that I should give a talk on the British and jazz. To my surprise and delight, he immediately took me up on the offer and scheduled the talk for the spring semester of 1996. I am deeply grateful to Roger and feel honored that he listed my talk on jazz, along with so many distinguished presentations on the British Empire, British literature, and the Royal Society, in the seminar's twenty-fifth anniversary publication, *British Studies at the University of Texas, 1975–2000*, p. 46.

2. For information on Lammar Wright and his career, see my *Texan Jazz*, pp. [85]–90.

3. Bell, *Since Cezanne*, p. 219.

4. Ibid., p. 216.

5. Ibid., pp. 116–117.

6. Ibid., p. 214.

7. Ibid., p. 224.

8. Ibid., p. 226.

9. Ibid., pp. 226–227.

10. Godbolt, *A History of Jazz in Britain 1919–1950*, p. 161 (caption).

11. Wilmer, *Jazz People*, p. 2. Jake Trussell, who was born in Kingsville in 1915 and died in Corpus Christi in 1971, also reviewed for U.S. magazines, such as *Down Beat* and *Jazz Quarterly* (1942–1946), both published in Chicago, although the latter was edited during its last years by Trussell and printed in Kingsville. Trussell had two radio programs in his hometown, a morning show called *Jam for Breakfast* and an afternoon program billed as *Jazz with Jake*. His son Philip remembers their home being filled with jazz musicians who stayed "until the wee hours of the morning," to quote from Jake Trussell's foreword to his *After Hours Poetry*. Trussell's poetry on jazz, as collected in this volume, includes one piece that originally appeared in Britain in *Jazz Music*.

The titles of some of Trussell's prose writings that appeared in *Jazz Quarterly* include "Blues in the Texas Night," "Dostoyevsky on Jazz," and "Hot Wax: Duke's Music," the last of these listed in *Jazz Index*. One prose piece that reveals Trussell's attitude toward British critic Leonard Feather, who was living in the United States, is entitled "Nicksieland by a Mile" and includes the following remarks: "The next time Leonard Feather slanders Nicksieland Jazz somebody should buy him a ticket back to London. And may God have mercy on London" (*Jazz Quarterly* 2, no. 1 [ca. 1943]: 29). Trussell was an early critic of Leonard Feather; later writers have also found fault with the Brit for factual errors in his biographical entries, for leaving out figures that he did not rate as important, and for categorizing musicians on the basis of his own stylistic biases. "Nicksieland" is a reference to both Dixieland and Nick's, a nightspot on 52nd Street in New York, which Trussell visited on occasion to listen to jazz and meet the musicians.

12. McCarthy, *Big Band Jazz*.

13. Godbolt, *A History of Jazz in Britain 1950–1970*.

14. Ibid., pp. 277–278.

15. Ibid., p. 279.

16. Bell, *Since Cezanne*, p. 229.

17. Harrison et al., *The Essential Jazz Records*.

18. Harrison et al., *Modern Jazz*.

19. Douglass Parker, "'Donna Lee' and the Ironies of Bebop," in *The Bebop Revolution in Words and Music*, ed. Oliphant, pp. 161–201.

20. Harrison, review of *The Bebop Revolution in Words and Music*, p. 80.

21. Godbolt, *A History of Jazz in Britain 1919–1950*, p. 3.

22. John R. McMahon, "Unspeakable Jazz Must Go! It is Worse than Saloon and Scarlet Vice, Professional Dance Experts—Only a Few Cities Are Curbing the Evil," *Ladies Home Journal*, December 1921, p. 34; cited in Richard Lawn, introduction to *The Bebop Revolution in Words and Music*, ed. Oliphant, p. 14.

23. Godbolt, *A History of Jazz in Britain 1919–1950*, p. 284.

24. Ibid. More recently, Robert Walser, the editor of *Keeping Time*, asserts that "there are probably already more anthologies devoted to jazz

than to any other twentieth-century musical genre" (p. ix); cited in *Riffs & Choruses*, ed. Clark, p. [1]. Relatedly, it has been observed that since 1991 "the expansion of jazz titles among scholarly presses and academic journals [is] attributable to the growing acknowledgment that jazz has affected twentieth-century world culture in numerous ways not yet completely understood" (Christopher Harlos, "Jazz Autobiography," in *Representing Jazz*, ed. Gabbard, p. 132).

25. Jim Godbolt has selected and introduced a companion 4-CD box set of recordings, entitled *Jazz in Britain, 1919–1950* (Proper Records Ltd., England, Properbox 88, 2005). The first recording is by the ODJB from their London performance of "At the Jazz Band Ball" on April 16, 1919.

26. Godbolt, *A History of Jazz in Britain 1919–1950*, p. 9.

27. British poet Philip Larkin alludes to this practice in his poem "For Sidney Bechet" when he writes of the "scholars *manqués*" who "nod around unnoticed / Wrapped up in personnels like old plaids" (Larkin, *Collected Poems*, p. 83).

28. Godbolt, *A History of Jazz in Britain 1950–1970*, p. 296.

29. Ibid., p. 84.

30. Ibid., p. 85.

31. Ibid.

32. Bell, *Since Cezanne*, pp. 222–224.

33. Godbolt, *A History of Jazz in Britain 1919–1950*, p. 89.

34. Ibid., p. 90.

35. Ibid., p. 93.

36. Ibid., p. 96.

37. Ibid., pp. 98–99.

38. Ibid., p. 100.

39. Ibid., p. 101.

40. Ibid., pp. 104 and 114. This early British adulation, so often phrased in religious terms, would apply equally to American "followers" of the jazz "prophets." Leonard traced this tendency in *Jazz: Myth and Religion*.

41. Ibid., pp. 109–110.

42. Ibid., p. 111.

43. Ibid., p. 112.

44. Ibid., p. 274; also Godbolt, *A History of Jazz in Britain 1950–1970*, p. 299.

45. Godbolt, *A History of Jazz in Britain 1950–1970*, p. 293.

46. For the Feather-Page session, see my *Texan Jazz*, p. 191; for the Feather-Hughes recording, see *Weary Blues: With Langston Hughes, Charles Mingus, and Leonard Feather* (Verve 841 660-4, 1990), for which Feather wrote the liner notes.

47. Godbolt, *A History of Jazz in Britain 1950–1970*, p. 280.

48. Ibid., pp. 281–282.

49. Ibid., p. 279.

50. For Larkin's "For Sidney Bechet" and "Reasons for Attendance," see his *Collected Poems,* pp. 80 and 83.

51. A copy of this interview is in the Department of Special Collections, Alkek Library, at Texas State University in Durham's hometown of San Marcos.

52. See Ward and Burns, *Jazz,* pp. 234, 236.

53. Helen Oakley (Dance), "The Ellington Orchestra at the Apollo (1936)," in *The Duke Ellington Reader,* ed. Tucker, p. 126.

54. "A Landmark in Ellington Criticism: R. D. Darrell's 'Black Beauty,'" in *The Duke Ellington Reader,* p. 59.

55. "Constant Lambert on Ellington," in *The Duke Ellington Reader,* p. 110.

56. Ibid., p. 111.

57. Ibid., p. 112. In this regard, Appel, in his *Jazz Modernism,* cites the 1934 remarks on Ellington's 1928 "Hot and Bothered" by English composer and critic Constant Lambert, who averred that he knew "nothing in Ravel so dextrous in treatment as the varied solos in the middle . . . and nothing in Stravinsky more dynamic than the final section." Appel goes on to note that, according to Gunther Schuller, this was an "extravagant" claim and that Schuller doubted "that Ellington had even heard of Ravel at this point." Appel continues: "But highbrow praise such as Lambert's and Percy Grainger's (he ranked Ellington with Bach and Delius) set the tone and trajectory of subsequent commentary on Ellington" (p. 215).

58. Wilmer, *Mama Said There'd Be Days Like This,* p. 27.

59. Bell, *Since Cezanne,* p. 224.

60. Wilmer, *Mama Said There'd Be Days Like This,* p. 27.

61. Ibid., p. 133.

62. Ibid., p. 261.

63. Ibid., pp. 241, 243.

64. Ibid., p. 186.

65. Quoted in ibid., p. 149. In Duke Ellington's autobiography, *Music Is My Mistress,* he traces the Garvey influence back to Nanton's native West Indies: "Tricky and his people were deep in the West Indian legacy and the Marcus Garvey movement. . . . It's the same now with the Muslim movement, and a lot of West Indian people are involved in it. There are many resemblances to the Marcus Garvey schemes. Bop, I once said, is the Marcus Garvey extension" (pp. 108–109); quoted in *The Jazz Cadence of American Culture,* ed. O'Meally, p. 594.

66. Ibid., p. 187.

67. Ibid., p. 23.

68. Ibid., p. 24.

69. See my *Texan Jazz,* p. 32.

70. *The Duke Ellington Reader,* p. 65.

71. Wilmer, *Mama Said There'd Be Days Like This*, p. 218.

72. Ibid., p. 220. Coleman was in fact photographed by Wilmer, and two images of the Texan appear in her book *The Face of Black Jazz*, n.p.

73. Also included in *The Face of Black Jazz* are photographs of Gene Ramey, Dewey Redman, and, as noted earlier, Ornette Coleman. Leroy Cooper's career is mentioned in my *Texan Jazz*, pp. 232, 314, and 434. However, I failed to include him in my discussion of the album entitled *The Legendary Buster Smith*, on which he plays several very impressive choruses. See *Texan Jazz*, p. 188. Another baritone saxophonist mentioned in *Texan Jazz* is Maurice Simon, who was a sideman with Ray Charles in 1967 and before that appeared in 1950 with Houstonite Illinois Jacquet on a tune entitled "Hot Rod." In *Texan Jazz* I praise Simon's playing (p. 225) but did not realize at the time that he too was a Texan, born in Houston in 1929. Wilmer's photograph of Eddie Durham appears at the beginning of the first essay in this volume, "Jazz Mavericks of the Lone Star State."

74. See my *Texan Jazz*, p. 386, n. 56.

75. Wilmer, *Mama Said There'd Be Days Like This*, p. 42.

76. Ibid.

77. Ibid., p. 43.

78. Ibid., pp. 84–85.

79. Wilmer, *As Serious As Your Life*.

80. Wilmer, *Mama Said There'd Be Days Like This*, pp. 305–306.

THE WISCONSIN-TEXAS JAZZ NEXUS

This essay was previously published in *Journal of Texas Music History* 4, no. 1 (Spring 2004): 8–17.

1. Schuller, *The Swing Era*, p. 562.

2. A shorter, preliminary version of this essay was presented at Lakeland College in Sheboygan, Wisconsin, on October 1, 2003. I wish to thank Karl Elder and Lakeland College for inviting me to speak as part of their Krueger Fine Arts Lecture Series. One of the first Wisconsin musicians that I am aware of having heard, without knowing at the time that he was a Wisconsin native, was Joe Dodge of Monroe, drummer with the early Dave Brubeck Quartet. I began my lecture at Lakeland College "with a bang not a whimper," to paraphrase T. S. Eliot, by playing Dodge's bass-drum thud that opens "Take the 'A' Train" on Brubeck's 1954 *Jazz Goes to College* (Columbia Records, CK 45149). Although there was no connection between Dodge and Texas musicians that I know of, it was my own personal memories of listening with pleasure to Dodge and the early Brubeck Quartet that was my excuse for beginning the talk with an example of Dodge typically "kicking" his bass drum in so many of the quartet recordings. It was only after

researching Wisconsin jazz musicians for the talk at Lakeland College that I discovered, over forty years after first hearing Dodge, that he too was from the thirtieth state.

3. In *The Folk Songs of North America*, Lomax writes: "No subject, not even the little dogie, has produced so much good American music as the railroad" (p. 406). Quoted in Ann Miller Carpenter, "The Railroad in American Folk Song, 1865–1920," in *Diamond Bessie & The Shepherds*, ed. Hudson, p. 103.

4. See Faulkner's *Intruder in the Dust*, p. 194.

5. For a discussion of Texas boogie-woogie musicians in Chicago, see my *Texan Jazz*, pp. 74–81.

6. In writing *Texan Jazz*, I was not aware that percussionist Jasper Taylor (1894–1964) was a native of Texarkana, or that in June 1923 he had recorded two tunes with Jelly Roll Morton, "Big Fat Ham" and "Muddy Water." See *The Immortal Jelly Roll Morton* (Milestone MLP 2003, n.d.). Taylor also recorded with Freddy Keppard and Johnny Dodds in 1927. See *Johnny Dodds 1927* (Classics 603, 1991).

7. Dupuis, in his *Bunny Berigan*, gives Berigan's place of birth as Hilbert, Wisconsin, but Berigan grew up in Fox Lake. See Appendix E (n.p.).

8. Chilton, *Who's Who of Jazz*, p. 143.

9. *Jimmie Joy and His Orchestra* (Arcadia Records, 2017D, n.d.), recorded ca. September–October 1923. I am beholden to Dave Laczko of Austin for making me aware of this important recording. The notes to the album identify the musicians on "Bugle Call Rag" as Jimmie Maloney, clarinet; Rex "Curley" Preis, cornet; Jack Brown, trombone; Lynn "Son" Harrell, piano; Smith "Sykes" Ballew, banjo; and Dick Hamel, drums. Smith Ballew, known primarily as a vocalist, was born in Palestine, Texas, and went to high school in Sherman, attended the University of Texas from 1920 to 1922, and has been credited with organizing Jimmie's Joys. Later, in 1926, he fronted Dick Voynow's Wolverines, which had previously included the legendary Bix Beiderbecke. In 1929 Ballew formed his own orchestra, which in 1932 included Bunny Berigan. See Dupuis, *Bunny Berigan*, pp. 57–58, and also Slate's entry on Ballew in *The Handbook of Texas Music*, ed. Barkley, p. 15.

10. *Jazz at the Philharmonic* (Verve Records, VE-2-2504, 1976).

11. *New Orleans Rhythm Kings and Jelly Roll Morton* (Milestone Records, M-47020, 1974). I am grateful to Morton Stine, my longtime musician friend from Wichita Falls, now at East Carolina University, for going back and listening to the NORK recording after I asked him why he thought the trombonist with Jimmie's Joys and Red Callender on the JATP recording would both quote from "Yankee Doodle Dandy." I am also indebted to a student at Diamond Hill–Jarvis High School in Fort Worth who identified "Yankee Doodle Dandy" when I could recognize the tune but couldn't place it by name. I asked the students filling their school auditorium to listen for a familiar tune being quoted in the Jimmie's Joys recording, thinking that

they would all easily recognize "The Eyes of Texas," but one young man on the front row yelled out "Yankee Doodle Dandy," and I knew immediately that he had heard the trombonist's quotation and was correct as to its source.

I later contacted Robert Botello of the Fine Arts Department of Diamond Hill–Jarvis High School and asked if he could give me the name of the student who had identified "Yankee Doodle Dandy." He checked with the other teachers in attendance and reported that the student was Adelaida Robles. This meant to me that more than one student had recognized "Yankee Doodle Dandy," since the student that I heard yell the title was a young man just down from where I was speaking on the stage. I was impressed by the student body and pleased that they responded so enthusiastically to the jazz that I played for them. On hearing Glenn Miller's "In the Mood," with the trumpet solo by Fort Worth native Clyde Hurley, some of the students began to dance in front of their seats and a few moved into the aisles to "cut a rug," just as the jitterbugs had done almost sixty-five years before when the piece was first recorded in 1939.

12. Callender and Cohen, *Unfinished Dream*, p. 61. For the list of tunes Callender recorded with Bunk Johnson, see p. 195. Les Paul was a member of the Red Callender Six in Los Angeles in 1945, and another Wisconsin connection exists for Callender in the mid-forties when he led a trio in Kenosha, Wisconsin (see pp. 56, 59). Also, in 1947, Callender teamed up with Texan Jimmy Giuffre for a recording with the Red Norvo Septet (p. 204). Finally, Callender was on some of the classic bebop sides recorded in 1947 by the Charlie Parker All-Stars for Dial records (see pp. 76–79).

13. *The Golden Horn of Jack Teagarden* (Decca Records, DL4540, n.d.).

14. *Bunny Berigan: His Best Recordings, 1935–1939* (Best of Jazz, 4021, 1995).

15. Ibid.

16. *Meet the Band Leaders* (Hollywood, Calif.: Swingtime Video, ca. 1984).

17. Dupuis, *Bunny Berigan*, pp. 163, 181.

18. *Bunny Berigan: The Pied Piper, 1934–40* (RCA Bluebird, 66615-2, 1995).

19. *Bunny Berigan: His Best Recordings, 1935–1939.*

20. *Woody Herman and His Orchestra, 1936–1937* (Classics Records, 1042, 1999).

21. Joop Visser, notes, *The Woody Herman Story* (Proper Records, Properbox 15, 4 CD set, 2000), p. 15.

22. Ibid., p. 12.

23. In 1941 the Herman Herd recorded "Blue Flame," which would replace "Blue Prelude" as the band's theme song and "would remain its theme to the end" (Visser, notes, *The Woody Herman Story*, p. 17,). Steady Nelson was also in the band when "Blue Flame" was recorded, but there is no trumpet solo. On "Bishop's Blues," also from 1941, Nelson was still with the band but the trumpet solo here is taken by Cappy Lewis of Brillion,

Wisconsin. Yet another blues on which Nelson solos is the classic "Farewell Blues," and on "Bessie's Blues" he vocalizes with Herman. Nelson also is heard singing the phrase "Beat me, papa" to end the popular tune "Beat Me Daddy, Eight to the Bar." See Kriebel's *Blue Flame*, p. 43.

24. Information on Steady Nelson's later years was supplied to me by his niece, Lucy Carriker, who also informed me that her uncle was the vocalist on two sides recorded by the Herman Herd: "Oh Caldonia," a song that pre-dated the 1945 "Caldonia," which the famous First Herd recorded with such instrumental stars as trombonist Bill Harris and bass player Chubby Jackson; and "Whatcha Know, Joe." Neither of these tunes is included on *The Woody Herman Story*, which does include the 1945 "Caldonia." Robert Kriebel also credits Nelson with a vocal on "Rosetta."

25. Visser, notes, *The Woody Herman Story*, p. 22.

26. In 1963 the Herman Herd appeared on *Jazz Casual*, a television program hosted by jazz critic Ralph J. Gleason, and the band's use of three tenors and a baritone sax can be seen from the video of this appearance, released under the title *Woody Herman and the Swingin' Herd* (Rhino Home Video, R3 970024, 2000).

27. Simon Korteweg, liner notes, *Woody Herman and His Orchestra: Early Autumn* (Capitol Jazz Classics Vol. 9, M-11034, 1972).

28. *The Swinging Mr. Rogers: Shorty Rogers and His Giants* (Atlantic Records, 1212, n.d.).

29. *Jazz on a Summer's Day* (New Yorker Video, NYV 16590, ca. 1987).

30. *Woody Herman: The Second Herd, 1948* (Storyville Records, STCD 8240, 1997).

31. *Bird and Chet: Inglewood Jam* (Fresh Sound Records, FSR-CD 17, 1991); *Laurindo Almeida Quartet Featuring Bud Shank* (Pacific Jazz Records, PJ-1204, 1955).

32. See Visser's insert notes, *The Woody Herman Story*, p. 43. Parker's solo on "Dark Shadows" can be heard on *The Legendary Dial Masters, Vol. 1* (Stash ST-CD-23, 1989). According to Clancy, in his *Woody Herman*, the Rogers transcription inspired Med Flory, the founder in 1972 of the group Supersax, "to build a library of arrangements based on Parker solos from various sources, voicing them for a five-man saxophone section" (p. 119).

33. The 1948 performances of "I've Got News for You" are included on *Woody Herman: The Second Herd, 1948*.

34. Terkel, in his *Giants of Jazz*, characterizes Herman as a leader who had a "lifelong faith in artists 'on their own,'" quoting him as saying that he "let the boys think up things to do" (p. 144).

35. Quoted by Nat Hentoff, liner notes, *Woody Herman '58* (Verve Records, MG V-8255, 1958).

36. Ibid.

37. "Woodsheddin' with Woody" is included on *The Woody Herman Story*.

38. *Return to the Wide Open Spaces* (Amazing Records, AMC-1021, 1990). See my *Texan Jazz*, pp. 314, 434–435.

39. Quoted by Ralph J. Gleason, liner notes, *The Woody Herman Quartet: Swing Low, Sweet Clarinet* (Philips Records, PHM 200-004, 1962).

40. Prior to joining Giuffre for the 1956 session, Clark had been a member of the Tex Beneke Orchestra from 1950 to 1954. Beneke, a tenor saxophonist and singer from Fort Worth, was a featured sideman with the Glenn Miller Orchestra in the late 1930s and early 1940s.

41. *Lennie Niehaus Volume 5: The Sextet* (Contemporary Records, C3542, 1956).

42. This same type of writing is found in Texas arranger-composer Eddie Durham's arrangement of "Runnin' a Temperature" for the Jimmie Lunceford Orchestra of 1936. In an interview with Stanley Dance, Durham reports that he would combine the string bass and baritone, "Sometimes, in some spots, like Running A Temperature. . . . [Q]uite a few bands out West now that are doing it. Not all the time, but they'll find a place where they play bass with that baritone" (Dance, "Oral History—Eddie Durham," p. 55 of sides 1–2). A copy of this interview is available in the Department of Special Collections, Alkek Library, Texas State University, San Marcos.

43. *The Jimmy Giuffre 3* (Atlantic 7 90981-2, 1988).

44. Visser, notes, *The Woody Herman Story*, p. 14. Visser goes on to mention an incident that occurred with regard to the Herman band's playing of the blues at the Rice Hotel in Houston, a disappointing but not surprising example of racism at the end of the 1930s. Visser reports that around 1938 the hotel manager sent a note to Herman saying, "Will you kindly stop singing and playing those nigger blues" (p. 14), a request that fortunately Herman ignored.

JAZZ IN LITERATURE

1. Poem 17 from *Spring and All* (Dijon, France: Contact Publishing Co., 1923) is included in *The Collected Poems of William Carlos Williams*, ed. Litz and MacGowan, 1:216. Under the title "Shoot it Jimmy!" the poem appears in *The Collected Earlier Poems of William Carlos Williams* (New York: New Directions, 1951), p. 269. One very curious feature of this poem is its reference to "Banjo jazz / with a nickel-plated / amplifier." Recordings of amplified jazz first date from the mid-1930s, notably one with Texan Eddie Durham performing in 1935 with the Jimmie Lunceford Orchestra on "Hittin' the Bottle." There is still a nickel-plated resonator banjo in use today, and this was probably the type of instrument that Williams knew at the time that he wrote the poem, which would have been prior to the 1923 publication date of *Spring and All*. In this regard as well, Williams's poem is historically significant since it documents the early use of amplification in jazz, even before it became a fixture of the music beginning in the 1930s and continuing to the present day.

Also in 1923, Langston Hughes published his "Jazzonia," which has been discussed at length in a very perspicacious essay by Camille Paglia in her *Break, Blow, Burn* (New York: Vintage Books, 2005), pp. [141]–144. As Paglia acknowledges, Hughes's poem does not describe or consider directly the music itself, "the poem functioning instead, through mood and syncopation, as a transposition of the music" (p. 142).

One wonders what jazz groups Williams and Hughes would have heard at this early date. The Original Dixieland Jazz Band first recorded a form of jazz in 1917 and for several years thereafter, but this group did not include a banjo. In 1922 the Friars Society Orchestra (later known as the New Orleans Rhythm Kings, or NORK) did record with banjoist Lew Black as part of the group. In 1923 the Texas band called Jimmie's Joys also recorded with a banjo, played by Smith "Sykes" Ballew, but it would be a stretch to imagine that Williams knew of this group or could have had it in mind, especially since Jimmie's Joys did not record until the fall of 1923. Whatever jazz Williams heard, it seems clear that he understood quite early on that it was a new American form of original, artistic expression.

2. For information on Bunk Johnson, see David Stuart's "How We Recorded Bunk!" insert notes, *Bunk Johnson and His Superior Jazz Band* (Good Time Jazz, GTJCD-12048-2, 1991). Three of the same musicians on this recording from 1942 were members of Johnson's band when Williams heard it in 1945.

3. Donley, in her valuable article entitled "William Carlos Williams and 'Ol' Bunk's Band,'" traces the poet's use of rifflike phrases and also discusses the idea that as a writer the poet may have been drawn in particular to the polyrhythms of jazz. However, Donley does not believe that "jazz influenced Williams' poetic innovations, at least not before 1946" (p. 16). Apparently she was not aware of Williams's 1923 poem on jazz, "Shoot it Jimmy!" Donley does quote, but disagrees with, biographer Paul Mariani, who claims that "the central analogue . . . for the jagged patterns that distinguish Williams' poetic lines . . . is black jazz" (Mariani, *William Carlos Williams*, p. 716). It would seem that, in light of Williams's 1923 poem, Mariani is closer to the mark.

4. Section II of Hart Crane's "For the Marriage of Faustus and Helen" is included in *The Second Set*, ed. Feinstein and Komunyakaa, pp. 31–32. Crane's use of the word "soothings" echoes Williams's line in "Shoot it Jimmy!" that speaks of jazz being able to ""soothe / the savage beast," which itself seems drawn from William Congreve's often misquoted line that music can charm "a savage breast."

5. Mina Loy, "The Widow's Jazz," in *The Jazz Poetry Anthology*, ed. Feinstein and Komunyakaa, pp. 133–134.

6. Ibid.

7. A perfect example of a list of names is Ted Joans's "Jazz Must Be a Woman," which simply catalogs some 208 musicians, out of which 14 are

from Texas. The poem is dedicated "to all the jazzmen that I fail to include." Prominent among the Texans that Joans left out are guitarist Charlie Christian and trombonist Jack Teagarden. Joans's poem is in *The Jazz Poetry Anthology*, ed. Feinstein and Komunyakaa, pp. 105–106.

8. John Sinclair's "humphf," Kazuko Shiraishi's "Dedicated to the Late John Coltane," Melvin B. Tolson's "Mu [From *Harlem Gallery*]," and Fred Chappell's "The Highest Wind That Ever Blew: Homage to Louis" are included in *The Jazz Poetry Anthology*; ed. Feinstein and Komunyakaa, pp. 202, 198, 210, and 33, respectively. A poem by Russian poet Yevgeny Yevtushenko, entitled "Saints of Jazz," is representative of an international hagiographic attitude toward jazz musicians and their music. See Yevtushenko's poem in *The Second Set*, ed. Feinstein and Komunyakaa, pp. 188–189.

9. Langston Hughes, "Trumpet Player," in *Selected Poems of Langston Hughes*, pp. 112–113. Nicholas M. Evans provides a thorough analysis of the poem in his "Langston Hughes as Bop Ethnographer in 'Trumpet Player: 52nd Street,'" in *The Bebop Revolution in Words and Music*, ed. Oliphant, pp. 119–135.

10. Julio Cortázar, "The Pursuer," in *Hot and Cool*, ed. Breton, p. 281. Ellipses are Cortázar's.

11. Ibid., p. 219.

12. Miller Williams, "The Death of Chet Baker," in *The Second Set*, ed. Feinstein and Komunyakaa, p. 184.

13. Eudora Welty, "Powerhouse," in *Hot and Cool*, ed. Breton, pp. 29–43. For an excellent critical analysis of Welty's short story, see Leland H. Chambers, "Improvising and Mythmaking in Eudora Welty's 'Powerhouse,'" in *Representing Jazz*, ed. Gabbard, pp. 54–69.

14. Welty, "Powerhouse," p. 31.

15. Donald Barthelme, "The King of Jazz," in *Hot and Cool*, ed. Breton, pp. 234–238. In my course on jazz and literature, this story serves to introduce the amazing trombonist Dickie Wells as an illustration of the story's main character, trombonist Hokie Mokie. For an oral report, I assign a student to read the chapter entitled "The Romantic Imagination of Dickie Wells," in Hodeir's *Jazz*, pp. 63–76.

16. McSloy, "Jack Teagarden, " *For Jazz*, p. 45. As it turns out, Teagarden shared an interest in "engineering" with his fellow native, trombonist-guitarist Eddie Durham. See my discussion of Durham's mechanical inventions in "San Marcos in Jazz History."

17. James McKean's poem and his commentary in a contributor's note are included in *The Second Set*, ed. Feinstein and Komunyakaa, pp. 132–133, 221–222.

18. Joel "Yehuda" Wolk, "Elegy for Kenny Dorham," in *The Jazz Poetry Anthology*, ed. Feinstein and Komunyakaa, p. 239.

19. Hayden Carruth, "Paragraphs," in *The Jazz Poetry Anthology*, ed. Feinstein and Komunyakaa, p. 29.

20. Jack Kerouac, "239th Chorus [From *Mexico City Blues*]," in *The Jazz Poetry Anthology*, ed. Feinstein and Komunyakaa, p. 116.

21. Kerouac, *On the Road*, p. 241.

22. C. W. Smith, "The Plantation Club," in *Hot and Cool*, ed. Breton, p. 204.

23. "Charlie Parker's Sax," p. 2. Julio Cortázar, in his short story "The Pursuer," also touches on this motif when he has his narrator, Bruno, comment on the playing of the protagonist-saxophonist Johnny Carter (based on Charlie Parker): "Nobody knew how many instruments had already been lost, pawned, or smashed up. And on all of them he played like I imagine only a god can play an alto sax, given that they quit using lyres and flutes" (in *Hot and Cool*, ed. Breton, p. 271).

24. Smith, "The Plantation Club," p. 207.

25. Ibid., p. 204.

26. Steve Jonas, "One of Three Musicians," in *The Jazz Poetry Anthology*, ed. Feinstein and Komunyakaa, p. 108.

27. Excerpts from Kenneth Rexroth's "Written to Music" are in *The Jazz Poetry Anthology*, ed. Feinstein and Komunyakaa, pp. 174–178. Two of Coleman's fellow musicians from Fort Worth, Dewey Redman and Julius Hemphill, have also had poems written on their forms of jazz. See Jim Brodey, "On Dewey Redman's Ascending Zither, I Rose Unarmed in Vast Intelligent Light," in *Reading Jazz*, ed. Meltzer, pp. 291–292: "vast intelligent light, the likes / of which / I've scarcely ever seen before"; and Jane Cortez, "Hemphill Tonight," *Jazz Fan Looks Back*, p. 102: "Texas Dogon A.D. Coon Bid'ness stint of / nomad flint on firefly wings."

28. John Taggart's "Coming Forth by Day" and Gillian Conoley's "The One" are in *The Jazz Poetry Anthology*, ed. Feinstein and Komunyakaa, pp. 39–40, 207–208.

29. In my course on jazz and literature I have used such plays as Edward Albee's *The Death of Bessie Smith*; George C. Wolfe and Susan Birkenhead's *Jelly's Last Jam*; and August Wilson's *Ma Rainey's Black Bottom*. As for novels, I have used, above all, Josef Skvorecky's *The Bass Saxophone*, set (as is his fine short story "Eine Kleine Jazzmusik") in Czechoslovakia during the Nazi occupation; Michael Ondaatje's *Coming Through Slaughter*, based on the life of legendary New Orleans cornetist Buddy Bolden, about whom there are a number of poems in print; and Jack Fuller's *The Best of Jackson Payne*, whose extremely violent and drug-and-sex-laden plot does include some meaningful discussions of jazz. Poet and novelist Frederick Turner, who resides in Dallas, has written a novel entitled *1929*, which is based on the life of Bix Beiderbecke, who was first treated in jazz literature by Dorothy Baker in her novel *Young Man with a Horn*, published in 1938.

Skvorecky's novel touches in particular on the theme of the religiosity of jazz adherents: "I raised the bass saxophone; it glowed like a rainbow in the white dusty light; it seemed to me that they [the band members] all sighed, as if they had seen something sacred" (p. 158). Also, Wolfe and

Birkenhead's play echoes the theme of improvisation vs. sheet music found in Williams's "Shoot it Jimmy!" When the young Jelly Roll Morton tells Buddy Bolden that he can play "The Miserere" from *Il Trovatore*, Bolden replies: "That ain't no music; the notes is written out, tellin' ya what's gon' come next" (p. 28). In this same vein, Studs Terkel, in his *Giants of Jazz*, imagines King Oliver thinking, "There is more to jazz than following what is written on a sheet of paper, note for note. He knew the feeling of freedom must be there" (p. 5).

30. Vassar Miller, "Dirge in Jazz Time," in *The Jazz Poetry Anthology*, pp. 154–155.

31. Lewis, *Splendor in the Short Grass*, ed. Reid and Stratton.

32. Lorenzo Thomas, "Historiography," in *The Second Set*, ed. Feinstein and Komunyakaa, p. 170.

33. Susan Wood, "Strange Fruit," *Asunder*, pp. 58–60.

34. Betty Adcock, "Poem for Dizzy," *Intervale*, pp. 163–164.

35. Rosemary Catacalos, "The Lesson in 'A Waltz for Debby,'" in *After Aztlan*, ed. González, pp. 29–30.

36. Harryette Mullen, "Playing the Invisible Saxophone *en el combo de las estrellas*," in *The Jazz Poetry Anthology*, ed. Feinstein and Komunyakaa, p. 159.

37. Harryette Mullen, commentary on *Muse & Drudge*, in *Roundup: An Anthology of Texas Poets from 1973 until 1998*, ed. Dave Oliphant (Cedar Park, Tex.: Prickly Pear Press, 1999), p. 129; *Muse & Drudge* (Philadelphia: Singing Horse, 1995). For an extensive study of Mullen's *Muse & Drudge*, see Huehls, "Spun Puns (and Anagrams)."

THE ALCHEMY OF JAZZ

This essay was previously published as "The Alchemists of Jazz" in the *Texas Observer* 95, no. 9 (May 9, 2003): 24–25, 29.

1. For examples of such recordings, see my study *The Early Swing Era*, especially pp. 10–15.

2. Appel, *Jazz Modernism*; Terkel, *Giants of Jazz*.

3. Peter Townsend, in his forthcoming study "Pearl Harbor to the Paramount: Change in American Jazz and Popular Music in the Early 1940s" (University Press of Mississippi), objects to the idea that pop songs were second-rate productions and argues that they were often the inspiration for complex forms of jazz and could be in themselves sophisticated creations. Appel and Terkel primarily point to the lyrics of such pop songs as being sappy, but many lyrics were also quite artful and unforgettable.

4. Appel, *Jazz Modernism*, pp. 179–180. Teagarden also recorded with Fats Waller, when the two musicians collaborated at a studio session that

produced what critic Richard B. Hadlock considers "among the most notable records of 1929." See Hadlock's insert notes, *Fats Waller: Fats and His Buddies* (Bluebird 07863-61005-2, 1992). In 1931 Waller joined Teagarden on six sides, including "That's What I Like About You," on which the two musicians sing the lyrics and then Waller plays some of his sparkling piano. Both Waller and Teagarden especially shine in their soloing on "China Boy" and "Tiger Rag." All of these 1931 sides are reproduced on *Jack Teagarden and His Orchestra, 1930–1934* (Classics 698, 1993).

5. Appel, *Jazz Modernism*, p. 182. Appel's book has "multiculturism" rather than the expected "multiculturalism," which may or may not be a typo. Earlier the text has "multicultural" in reference to Teagarden's singing, as quoted at the end of the present paragraph. See pp. 180, 182.

6. Ibid. Appel even applies his cowboy-multiculturalism motif to the bebop master, Charlie "Bird" Parker, claiming that he was "a bona fide multiculturalist long before the politically charged word was coined." As evidence, Appel recounts how Parker "moved Texas roustabouts, cowboys, and rough women when he sat in with a country-and-western band in a Dallas roadhouse and played 'Home on the Range' straightforwardly, as a dirge—'sounding like a bagpipe,' according to the [Austin] bass player Gene Ramey" (p. 49).

7. Ibid.

8. Ibid., p. 180.

9. Ibid., pp. 114, 136. "Tom foolery" is in reference to Fats Waller's verbal antics. Budd Johnson's scatting of the lyrics to "Sweet Sue, Just You" are referred to by Armstrong as "the viper's language," which both Appel and Morgenstern explain is code for marijuana users. For Morgenstern's explanation of Johnson's chorus as "sung in pig latin scat," see his insert notes to *Louis Armstrong: The Complete RCA Victor Recordings* (RCA Victor, BMG Classics, 09026-68682-2, 1997), p. 25.

10. Appel, *Jazz Modernism*, pp. 78–79.

11. Ibid., p. 70.

12. Ibid., p. 235.

13. Ibid.

14. Ibid., pp. 102 and 111.

15. Ibid., p. 112.

16. Ibid., pp. 106 and 206.

17. Terkel, *Giants of Jazz*, p. 62.

18. Ibid., p. 63.

19. Ibid., pp. 63–64.

20. Ibid., p. 72.

21. Ibid., p. 177.

22. Appel, *Jazz Modernism*, p. 84.

23. Terkel, *Giants of Jazz*, pp. 182, 189.

ORNETTE COLEMAN'S HARMOLODIC LIFE

This essay was previously published as "Ornette Coleman: A Harmolodic Life" in the *Texas Observer* 85, no. 23 (November 26, 1993): 20–21.

1. Leonard Feather, *Encyclopedia of Jazz* (New York: Horizon Press, 1960). Later editions of Feather's *Encyclopedia* would add musicians from the 1960s and 1970s. The most recent edition is *The Biographical Encyclopedia of Jazz*, comp. Feather and Gitler.

2. Litweiler, *Ornette Coleman*, p. 15.

3. Ibid., p. 204.

4. Ibid., p. 195. Quoted from Larry Rohter, "Ornette Coleman Takes His Quartet Home," in the *New York Times*, September 10, 1990, C15.

5. Litweiler, *Ornette Coleman*, pp. 196, 105.

6. Ibid., p. 94. Quoted from Schuller, preface to *A Collection of the Compositions of Ornette Coleman*, p. [1].

7. Litweiler, *Ornette Coleman*, p. 26. Quoted from Nat Hentoff, "Ornette Coleman: Biggest Noise in Jazz," *Esquire* 55, no. 3 (March 1961): 84; reprinted in Hentoff, *The Jazz Life*, p. 233.

8. Litweiler, *Ornette Coleman*, p. 27.

9. Ibid., p. 37.

10. Ibid., p. 27. Quoted from Wilmer, *As Serious as Your Life*, p. 67.

11. Litweiler, *Ornette Coleman*, p. 32.

12. Ibid., p. 28.

13. Ibid., p. 29.

14. Ibid., p. 31.

15. Ibid., p. 66.

16. Ibid., p. 89. Quoted from T. E. Martin, "The Plastic Muse, Part 2," p. 15.

17. Litweiler, *Ornette Coleman*, p. 152.

18. Ibid., pp. 152–153.

19. Ibid., p. 167.

20. Ibid., pp. 114–115.

21. Ibid., pp. 127–128. Quoted from McRae, *Ornette Coleman*, p. 52.

22. Litweiler, *Ornette Coleman*, p. 81. Quoted from Hentoff, *The Jazz Life*, p. 231.

23. Litweiler, *Ornette Coleman*, p. 67.

24. Ibid., pp. 134–135.

25. Ibid., p. 57. Quoted from Keith Raether, "Ornette: Bobby Bradford's Portrait of an Emerging Giant," *Jazz*, Spring 1977.

26. Litweiler, *Ornette Coleman*, p. 159. Quoted from Cliff Tinder, "Jamaaladeen Tacuma: Electric Bass in the Harmolodic Pocket," *Down Beat* 49, no. 4 (April 1982): 21.

27. Litweiler, *Ornette Coleman*, pp. 148–149.

28. Ibid. pp. 112, 173.

29. Ibid., p. 198.

30. Ibid., p. 75. Quoted from Martin, "Plastic Muse, Part 1," p. 14.

31. Litweiler, *Ornette Coleman*, p. 61. Quoted from John Tynan, record review of Ornette Coleman's *Something Else!* in *Down Beat* 25, no. 22 (October 30, 1958): 25.

A JAZZ MASTER'S DIAMOND JUBILEE

This essay was previously published in the *Texas Observer* 97, no. 6 (March 18, 2005): 22–23, 27.

1. Ornette Coleman, liner notes, *This Is Our Music* (Atlantic 1353, 1960).

2. Ornette Coleman, liner notes, *Change of the Century* (Atlantic SD-1327, 1959).

3. Julio Cortázar, "The Pursuer," in *Hot and Cool,* ed. Breton, p. 317.

4. Ornette Coleman, insert notes, *Skies of America*, with the London Symphony Orchestra conducted by David Measham (Columbia/Legacy, CK63568, 1972).

5. Ibid.

A TEXAS TAKE ON KEN BURNS'S *JAZZ*

This essay was previously published as "A Texas Take on *Jazz*" in the *Texas Observer* 93, no. 4 (March 2, 2001): 20–23.

1. This phrase comes from the Ken Burns PBS broadcast of his *Jazz*, available on cassette and DVD. The phrase may also appear in Ward and Ken Burns's *Jazz*, although I did not come across it in my reading of this companion volume to the TV series.

2. Coulter, "Billie Holiday," pp. 164–165.

3. Schuller, *The Swing Era*, p. 242.

4. *The Best of Ken Burns Jazz* (Columbia/Legacy, CK 61439, 2000).

SWINGING THROUGH TEXAS ON A SCOTTISH AIR

This essay was previously published in *Texas Books in Review* 18, no. 2 (Summer 1998): 8–9.

1. McLean, *Lone Star Swing*, p. 93.

2. Ibid., p. 212.

3. Ibid., p. 24.

4. Ibid., p. 95. Much later in the book, McLean elaborates on this idea: "While playing with Milton Brown, an avowed pop and jazz lover, Bob developed his ideas about combining these more modern sounds with the traditional fiddle style he had learned from his father. . . . Interestingly, Bob could never play jazz fiddle himself: he loved it, he could hear what he wanted, but the old melodies and fingerings were too deeply ingrained for him to be able to fly free of them into improvised take-offs" (p. 236).

5. Ibid., p. 272.

6. Ibid., pp. 284–285.

7. Ibid., p. 111.

8. Ibid.

9. Ibid., p. 268.

10. Ibid., p. 240.

11. Ibid., p. 171.

12. Ibid., p. 177.

13. Ibid., p. 87.

14. Ibid., p. 93.

15. Ibid., p. 96.

16. Ibid., p. 191.

17. Ibid., p. 193.

18. Ibid., p. 243.

19. Ibid., p. 285.

20. Ibid.

THE BIRTH OF WESTERN SWING

This essay was previously published in *The Early Swing Era, 1930 to 1941* (Westport, Conn.: Greenwood Press, 2002): 361–367, copyright © 2002 by Greenwood Press. Reproduced with permission of Greenwood Publishing Group, Inc.

1. Richard B. Hadlock, insert notes, *Fats Waller: Fats and His Buddies* (Bluebird 07863-61005-2, 1992). Except for this first introductory paragraph, the rest of this essay was originally included in my study *The Early Swing Era*, pp. 361–367, 394–395.

2. Fats Waller formed part of Jack Teagarden's studio orchestra in October and November of 1931 when it recorded six tunes, including "You Rascal, You" and "That's What I Like About You" (both with vocal banter by Waller and Teagarden), as well as two especially swinging versions of "China Boy" and "Tiger Rag." Most recently, these are included in the box set *The Complete OKeh and Brunswick Bix Beiderbecke, Frank Trumbauer, and Jack Teagarden Sessions (1924–1936)* from Mosaic Records (MD7-211, 2001). "Us on a Bus" is included on *Fats Waller: Us On A Bus* (Early Bird EBCS 1008, 1995).

3. Cary Ginell, insert notes, *The Complete Recordings of the Father of Western Swing: Milton Brown and the Musical Brownies, 1932–1937* (Texas Rose Records, TXRCD1-5, 1995). Ginell also writes in his book-length study, *Milton Brown and the Founding of Western Swing,* that Brown's "energetic vocals, affecting recitations, and Roaring Twenties 'hotcha' style suggest Ted Lewis or Cab Calloway on jazz tunes and Fred Astaire on Tin Pan Alley songs" (p. xxi). One tune not recorded by the Brownies but which Brown's brother Roy Lee reported the leader "put extra words to" was "What's the Reason (I'm Not Pleasin' You)," which Waller recorded on March 6, 1935. Milton's brother Derwood sang "There'll Be Some Changes Made," which was cut by Waller on June 24, 1935, with Derwood's version recorded with the Musical Brownies in 1937 after Milton's accidental death.

4. Ginell, *Milton Brown and the Founding of Western Swing,* p. xxvi.

5. Boyd, *The Jazz of the Southwest.*

6. Schuller, *The Swing Era,* p. 564, note 33.

7. Ginell, *Milton Brown and the Founding of Western Swing,* pp. 63–64.

8. All sides by Milton Brown and the Musical Brownies are included on the five-CD set *The Complete Recordings of the Father of Western Swing.*

9. Ginell, *Milton Brown and the Founding of Western Swing,* p. 281.

10. Ibid., p. 309.

11. Ibid., p. 289.

12. Schuller, *The Swing Era,* p. 564, note 33.

13. Boyd, *The Jazz of the Southwest,* p. 41.

14. John Morthland, insert notes, *Texas Music Vol. 2: Western Swing & Honky Tonk* (Rhino, R2 71782, 1994).

15. Fats Waller's "How Can You Face Me" is included on *Handful of Keys* (Properbox B0002DSA1G, 2004).

16. Ginell, p. xxii.

17. Jack Teagarden's 1930 version of "The Sheik of Araby" is included on *Jack Teagarden: I Gotta Right to Sing the Blues* (Living Era CD AJA 5059, 1989).

18. Ginell, *Milton Brown and the Founding of Western Swing,* p. 296.

19. Ibid., p. 301.

20. Ibid., p. 309.

21. Boyd, *The Jazz of the Southwest,* p. 127.

THE INVENTOR OF JAZZ REVISITED

This essay was previously published in the *Texas Observer* 95, no. 17 (September 12, 2003): 6–9, 19.

1. Quoted in Porterfield, *The Last Cavalier,* p. 398.

2. Ibid., p. 285.

3. Russell, "Jelly Roll Morton and the *Frog-i-more Rag*," pp. 35–36.

4. Reich and Gaines, *Jelly's Blues*. The "definitive" claim appears on the front inside flap of the dust jacket.

5. Ibid., p. 236.

6. Ibid.

7. Lomax, *Mister Jelly Roll* (1950 ed.), p. 3.

8. Lomax, preface to *Mister Jelly Roll* (1993 ed.), p. ix.

9. Whitney Balliett also objected to the music in the play: "The worst of Wolfe's distortions in 'Jelly's Last Jam' involves Morton's music. Apparently believing that it was not 'black' enough or emotional enough, he hired the arranger-composer, Luther Henderson, to write a homogenized 'modern' score. The result is a tasteless stew on which float largely unrecognizable bits and pieces of Morton compositions" (Balliett, "The Real Jelly Roll," p. 790).

10. Reich and Gaines, *Jelly's Blues*, p. 237.

11. In May 2005, Mike Meddings reported on his Monrovia Sound Studio Web site that Morton's newly discovered Mexican visa revealed in the composer's own hand the date of 1890 as the year of his birth: "What we are ultimately left with is a number of inconsistent birth dates: 1885 (for the Library of Congress and *Down Beat* magazine), 1886 (his great-grandmother's recollection, reported by his sister), 1888 (the date on his insurance policy), 1889 (the date on his death certificate), and 1890 (the date on his baptismal certificate, Mexican Visa, and gravestone)." See http://www.doctorjazz.freeserve.co.uk/index.html

12. Ibid., *Jelly's Blues*, p. 271.

13. Ibid., p. 48.

14. Lomax, *Mister Jelly Roll* (1950 ed.), p. 147.

15. Reich and Gaines, *Jelly's Blues*, p. 65; Lomax, *Mister Jelly Roll*, pp. 170–172.

16. Reich and Gaines, *Jelly's Blues*, p. 205.

17. Ibid.; Lomax, *Mister Jelly Roll*, p. 190.

18. Lomax, *Mister Jelly Roll*, pp. 188, 186–187.

19. Reich and Gaines, *Jelly's Blues*, p. 226; Lomax, *Mister Jelly Roll*, p. 255.

20. Reich and Gaines, *Jelly's Blues*, p. 154.

21. Lomax, *Mister Jelly Roll*, p. 41. Much later in his book, Lomax has this to say about Morton and the liquor he imbibed: "Protesting that the blues were 'lowdown, illiterate' music, he nevertheless moaned the blues by the hour, ladling down the cheap whiskey I could afford to buy, warming up his dusty vocal chords and discovering in himself a singing style as rich as Louis Armstrong's" (p. 241).

22. Reich and Gaines, *Jelly's Blues*, p. 242.

23. Ibid.

24. Ibid., p. 154.

25. Ibid., p. 16; Lomax, *Mister Jelly Roll*, p. 61.

26. Lomax, *Mister Jelly Roll*, p. 245.

27. Lomax, *Mister Jelly Roll*, p. 63. Elsewhere Morton comments further on his "band" approach in his "Wolverines": "in the last strain I put all the instruments in the band together and made the piano sound as much like a band as possible" (p. 176).

28. Ibid., p. 290.

29. Ibid., p. 105. A similar claim reads: "Jelly . . . could back up everything he *said* by what he could *do*" (p. 220).

30. Reich and Gaines, *Jelly's Blues*, p. 246.

31. Lomax, preface to the 1973 edition of *Mister Jelly Roll* (reprinted in the 2001 edition), p. [xv].

32. Lomax, preface to the 1993 edition of *Mister Jelly Roll* (reprinted in the 2001 edition), pp. xiii–xiv.

33. Ibid., p. xiv.

34. Reich and Gaines, *Jelly's Blues*, p. 118.

35. Lomax, *Mister Jelly Roll*, p. 68.

36. Ibid., pp. 68–69.

37. Ibid., pp. 194–195.

38. Reich and Gaines, *Jelly's Blues*, pp. 33–34. In their rather uninformative citation, Reich and Gaines refer to their source for a quote on Morton's Texas trip as deriving from "Notes of unrecorded portions of Morton interview, Library of Congress, 1939" (p. 253). It remains unclear whether this is Lomax's interview, a vagueness apparently intentional on the authors' part.

39. Lomax, *Mister Jelly Roll*, p. 145 and footnote. A full account of this Texas pianist and cornetist is contained in Stearns's "George Washington Smith Rocks Cradle of Jazz," p. 13. Stearns reports that Smith was a member of the W. H. Hawkins Brass Band, "the pride of San Antonio," and that this "solid cornetist . . . could get it off if he had the chance." But Smith preferred a Houston outfit called Sid Isles' Ragtime Band because it "didn't 'pay no mind' to music reading." Smith, born in San Antonio in 1882, had begun on piano; before he switched to cornet, Jelly Roll Morton came to the Alamo City, and it was there that Smith heard Jelly play his "Jelly Roll Blues" and his "specialty, 'De Lion Roar, and Broke Down the Door.'" Smith was "frank to admit" that in a competition with local pianists "Morton carved everybody, including himself."

40. Reich and Gaines, *Jelly's Blues*, p. 36; Lomax, *Mister Jelly Roll*, p. 34.

41. Schuller, *Early Jazz*, p. 148.

42. Reich and Gaines, *Jelly's Blues*, p. 248.

43. Ibid., p. 249.

44. The working method of Mingus is reminiscent of Morton's: he lays out his composition part by part, takes into consideration "each man's particular style," keeps his "own compositional flavor," yet allows "individual freedom" (quoted by Balliett, "Mingus," p. 119).

45. Lawrence Gushee, afterword to *Mister Jelly Roll,* by Lomax (2001 ed.), pp. 338–339.

DISCOGRAPHIES AND TEXAN JAZZ

1. Leonard Feather began his column "The Jazzman as Critic: The Blindfold Test" in 1946 in *Metronome* magazine and beginning in 1951 continued it for many years in *Down Beat.* See his discussion of the history of his "aural blindfold tests" in his *Encyclopedia of Jazz* (New York: Bonanza Books, 1960) and in his insert notes to *Conte Candoli: Modern Sounds from the West* (Lonnie Hill Jazz LHJ10166, 2005; from the original album notes, ca. 1956). Excerpts from some of Feather's blindfold tests of musicians listening to recordings by their fellow musicians appear in his 1960 *Encyclopedia*; for example, in one test he reports that "Roy Eldridge made a bet with me that he would be able to distinguish white musicians from Negroes. He did not even guess the 50% to which the law of averages entitled him" (p. 477). Eldridge had this to say about a recording by a quartet led by black pianist Billy Taylor: "Couldn't tell who was colored and who was white. They could be Eskimos for all I know" (p. 478). Reactions to Texas jazzman Ornette Coleman include one by tenorist Zoot Sims, who commented that "the alto player sounded like he was playing *slide* alto! Both he and the trumpet player [Don Cherry] sounded like the changes were too much for them, and the tempo. . . . They never got off the ground" (p. 479). Later, Feather gave a blindfold test to alto saxophonist Richie Cole, who recognized Ornette Coleman's music and called it "very good. Coleman went out on a limb when he made these kind of things during his time. He was very much a trendsetter. . . . He did just what he believed, and time has shown that it is a very valid form of music" (*Down Beat* 49, no. 4 [April 1982]: 51).

For the double album *Conte Candoli: Modern Sounds from the West,* Feather states in his notes that this "collection of West Coast Jazz performances . . . brings to fans the first use on records of that celebrated institution known as 'The Blindfold Test.'" He explains, "For years the musicians have entertained the fans by undergoing these tests; now it is their turn to blindfold the fans. . . . Although most of [the musicians on the album] had no contractual commitments, several did, and for this reason it was decided to omit the names of the musicians altogether[, r]ealizing that it would give the records a mysterious aspect."

2. Skvorecky, *The Bass Saxophone,* p. 152.

3. Russell, *Jazz Style in Kansas City,* p. 127; for the number in 1929, see Hadlock, *Jazz Masters of the Twenties,* p. 183. In Lord's *The Jazz Discography,* numbers for Teagarden performances, including appearances on screen and in interviews, do not match the claim by Russell. Lord lists 493 items, but

this is comparable to Armstrong with 593 and Hawkins with 570. However, Ellington exceeds all of these with 1,158, as does Benny Goodman with 1,053.

4. A selected discography for Gene Ramey is included in Addis's "The 'Baptist Beat' in Modern Jazz," pp. 8–21; two discographies are available for Kenny Dorham: Schlouch's *The Unforgettable Kenny Dorham* and Raftegard's *The Kenny Dorham Discography;* and a discography up to 1991 is included in Litweiler's biography, *Ornette Coleman*.

5. Morgenstern, *Living With Jazz*, ed. Meyer, pp. 545–546.

6. Ibid., pp. 552–553.

7. Ibid., pp. 553–554.

8. Lord, *The Jazz Discography*.

9. An account of the founding of the Jazz Messengers appears in Cuscuna's "The Blue Note Story": "[I]n late 1954 [Alfred] Lion [owner of Blue Note Records] felt that Horace [Silver] should do a record with horns. He and the pianist discussed the personnel. Reaching for the sky, Horace laid out an ideal grouping that he thought was impossible to secure for the date: Kenny Dorham, Hank Mobley, Doug Watkins, and Art Blakey. To Horace's surprise Alfred agreed and assured him that this would be no problem. The date went so well that these five men decided on a common purpose and formed a cooperative band called The Jazz Messengers. The group's idea was to present soulful modern jazz that incorporated the language of be-bop, without the virtuosic clichés of its second-generation followers, and the soulful, warm roots of blues and gospel music. It worked! And it became the Blue Note style" (xiv–xv). A revised and enlarged 2001 edition of this discography deletes and adds to some of the information in this paragraph. It is noteworthy that the Blue Note label served as a major outlet not only for the hard-bop performances by Kenny Dorham but also for the avant-garde ensembles of Ornette Coleman.

10. *Hank Mobley: Messages* (Prestige, PCD24063-2, 1989).

11. Ibid., insert notes.

12. Ibid.

13. *Birdland Stars on Tour, Volumes 1 & 2* (Collectables, COL-CD-2802, DRC 12894, 2001). Another album on which it is at times difficult to identify the trumpeter is *Scandia Skies* (SteepleChase, SCCD36011, 1993), on which Dorham splits the soloing time with trumpeter Rolf Ericson.

14. *The Five* (RCA Victor, LPM-1121, 1955). The personnel for this recording, along with Candoli, is Pete Jolly on piano; Mel Lewis on drums; Bill Perkins on tenor; and Wisconsin-born Buddy Clark on bass. One of the happiest pieces on this album is the Shorty Rogers arrangement of "Whistle While You Work," from the Walt Disney film *Snow White*. John S. Wilson in his liner notes reveals that Rogers wrote each arrangement just before "The Five" recorded it. Candoli's playing is especially fine on "Lullaby of the Leaves," on which he performs with a mute.

15. This essay was originally presented before a meeting of the ARSC (Association for Recorded Sound Collections) on March 31, 2005, in Austin. On this occasion I played for the group Kenny Dorham's gorgeous version of "This Love of Mine" (credited to F. Sinatra, S. Parker, and H. Sanicola), from his 1960 album, *Jazz Contemporary* (Time, ST2001, 2003).

16. "After You've Gone" is included on *Trumpet Royalty* (Vintage Jazz Classics, VJC-1009-2, 1990). This CD credits the arrangement to Eddie Durham, whereas neither Lord's *The Jazz Discography* nor Schlouch's *The Unforgettable Kenny Dorham* mentions an arranger.

17. *Kenny Dorham: The Complete Savoy Recordings* (DRCD11156, 1999).

18. Raftegard, *The Kenny Dorham Discography*, pp. V–VI.

19. Ibid., p. I.

20. Ibid.

21. Ibid.

SAN MARCOS IN JAZZ HISTORY

1. This essay was originally a talk presented on February 6, 2004, at Texas State University, San Marcos, for the Eddie Durham Jazz Legacy Night. I am grateful to TSU and Professor Gene Bourgeois of the university's History Department for inviting me to participate in this special celebration, along with jazz critics Stanley Crouch and Loren Schoenberg, as well as Marsha Durham, daughter of the honored musician.

2. Dance, "Oral History—Eddie Durham," sides 5–6. The quotation appears on page 72 of the transcript corresponding to these sides. A copy of the interview is available in the Department of Special Collections, Alkek Library, Texas State University, San Marcos.

3. Siegel and Obrecht, "Eddie Durham," p. 56. This idea of unwritten music being superior to written music is a theme running through several of the essays in this book. See especially "From Bebop to Hard Bop and · Beyond: The Texas Connections" and "Jazz in Literature."

4. Dance, "Oral History—Eddie Durham," p. 5 of sides 1–2.

5. It is possible that Eddie Durham was the composer-arranger of "Doggin' Around." See the insert notes to *The Best of Early Basie* (Decca GRD-655, 1996), p. 14; the personnel for the recording session of June 6, 1938, credits "Doggin' Around" to Edgar Battle/Herschel Evans or E(ddie) D(urham).

6. Eddie Durham reported to Stanley Dance that Edgar Battle did not co-write "Topsy," setting the record straight in the following comments: "And when I got there [Albany, New York], I wrote Topsy on the train, on the way there. Sat down and just thought it, wrote it up and got there, and they was already in rehearsal, out at the park. And I went out there and I had— couldn't make no score because I didn't have time. And Harry Edison, those

guys sat down and—I made some score and they struck it off. And that's why they—all embarrass Edgar so when they see him, because they wonder, how did he get on this sort of music?" ("Oral History—Eddie Durham," p. 24 of sides 3–4). Marsha Durham has explained that Edgar Battle assisted with having "Topsy" copyrighted, but that Battle's own daughter acknowledges that her father had nothing to do with writing the tune and that the rights to this important piece of music properly belong to the Durham Estate.

7. Ibid., p. 90 of sides 1–2.
8. Ibid., p. 26 of sides 3–4.
9. Ibid., p. 36 of sides 3–4.

BIBLIOGRAPHY

Adcock, Betty. *Intervale*. Baton Rouge: Louisiana State University Press, 2001.

Addis, Cameron. "The 'Baptist Beat' in Modern Jazz: Texan Gene Ramey in Kansas City & New York." In *Journal of Texas Music History* 4, no. 2 (Fall 2004): 8–21.

Appel, Alfred, Jr. *Jazz Modernism: From Ellington and Armstrong to Matisse and Joyce*. New York: Alfred A. Knopf, 2002.

Balliett, Whitney. "Mingus." In *Collected Works: A Journal of Jazz, 1954–2000*, pp. 117–121. New York: St. Martin's Press, 2000.

Barkley, Roy R., et al., eds. *The Handbook of Texas Music*. Austin: Texas State Historical Association, 2003.

Bell, Clive. *Since Cezanne*. New York: Harcourt, Brace, 1922.

Berry, Margaret Catherine. "Student Life and Customs, 1883–1933." Ph.D. diss., Columbia University, 1965.

Blesh, Rudi. *Shining Trumpets: A History of Jazz*. New York: Alfred A. Knopf, 1946. Reprint, New York: Da Capo Press, 1980.

Boyd, Jean A. *The Jazz of the Southwest: An Oral History of Western Swing*. Austin: University of Texas Press, 1998.

Breton, Marcela, ed. *Hot and Cool: Jazz Short Stories*. New York: Plume/Penguin Books, 1990.

British Studies at the University of Texas, 1975–2000. Introduction by William Roger Louis. Austin, Tex.: Harry Ransom Humanities Research Center, 2000.

Bryant, Clora, et al., eds. *Central Avenue Sounds: Jazz in Los Angeles*. Berkeley: University of California Press, 1998.

Cactus, The [yearbook of the University of Texas]. Austin: Texas Student Publications, Inc., 1929.

Callender, Red, and Elaine Cohen. *Unfinished Dream: The Musical World of Red Callender*. London: Quartet Books, 1985.

Carpenter, Ann Miller. "The Railroad in American Folk Song, 1865–1920." In *Diamond Bessie & The Shepherds*. Ed. Wilson M. Hudson. Publication of the Texas Folklore Society 36. Austin, Tex.: Encino Press, 1972.

"Charlie Parker's Sax." Transcript, *History Detectives*, episode 11, 2004. http://www.pbs.org/opb/historydetectives/pdf/211_sax.pdf.

Chilton, John. *The Song of the Hawk: The Life and Recordings of Coleman Hawkins*. Ann Arbor: University of Michigan Press, 1990.

———. *Who's Who of Jazz: Storyville to Swing Street*. 4th ed. New York: Da Capo Press, 1985.

Christian, Charlie. "Guitarmen, Wake Up and Pluck!" *Down Beat*, July 10, 1969, p. 19. Reprinted from the December 1, 1939, issue.

Clancy, William D. *Woody Herman: Chronicles of the Herds*. New York: Schirmer Books, 1995.

Clark, Andrew, ed. *Riffs & Choruses: A New Jazz Anthology*. London: Continuum, 2001.

Collier, James Lincoln. *Benny Goodman and the Swing Era*. New York: Oxford University Press, 1989.

Cortázar, Julio. *Blow-Up and Other Stories*. Trans. Paul Blackburn. New York: Pantheon Books, 1967; rpt., 1985.

Cortez, Jane. *Jazz Fan Looks Back*. Brooklyn: Hanging Loose Press, 2002.

Coulter, Glenn. "Billie Holiday." In *The Art of Jazz: Essays on the Nature and Development of Jazz*. Ed. Martin T. Williams. New York: Grove Press, 1960.

Cuscuna, Michael. "The Blue Note Story." Preface to *The Blue Note Label: A Discography*. Comp. Michael Cuscuna and Michel Ruppli. New York: Greenwood Press, 1988.

Dance, Stanley. "Oral History—Eddie Durham." Smithsonian Institution, Washington, D.C., August 1978. A copy is available in the Department of Special Collections, Alkek Library, Texas State University, San Marcos.

———. *The World of Count Basie*. New York: Charles Scribner's Sons, 1980.

———. *The World of Duke Ellington*. New York: Charles Scribner's Sons, 1970.

———. *The World of Earl Hines*. New York: Scribner, 1977.

Donley, Carol. "William Carlos Williams and 'Ol' Bunk's Band.'" In *William Carlos Williams Review* 15, no. 2 (Fall 1989): 9–16.

Dorham, Kenny. "Fragments of an Autobiography." In *Down Beat Yearbook* (1970): 30–34.

———. "With K. D. in Texas." In *Down Beat,* June 15, 1967, pp. 26–29.

Driggs, Frank. "Kansas City and the Southwest." In *Jazz: New Perspectives on the History of Jazz by Twelve of the World's Foremost Jazz Critics and Scholars*. Ed. Nat Hentoff and Albert McCarthy. New York: Holt, Rinehart and Winston, 1959; reprint, New York: Da Capo Press, 1975.

Dupuis, Robert. *Bunny Berigan: Elusive Legend of Jazz*. Baton Rouge: Louisiana State University Press, 1993.

Ellington, Duke. *Music Is My Mistress*. Garden City, N.Y.: Doubleday, 1973.

Evans, Christopher. Interview with Dewey Redman. *Fort Worth Star-Telegram,* February 13, 1994, secs. A & E.

Faulkner, William. *Intruder in the Dust*. New York: Random House, 1948; reprint, 1972.

Feather, Leonard. "The Jazzman as Critic: The Blindfold Test." *Metronome* (1946–1951).

———. *The New Edition of the Encyclopedia of Jazz*. New York: Bonanza Books, 1962.

———, and Ira Gitler, comps. *The Biographical Encyclopedia of Jazz*. Compiled with the assistance of *Swing Journal,* Tokyo. New York: Oxford University Press, 1999.

Feigin, Leo, comp. and ed. *Russian Jazz: New Identity*. London: Quartet Books Limited, 1985.

Feinstein, Sascha, and Yusef Komunyakaa, eds. *The Jazz Poetry Anthology.* Bloomington: Indiana University Press, 1991.

———. *The Second Set: The Jazz Poetry Anthology, Volume 2.* Bloomington: Indiana University Press, 1996.

Gabbard, Krin, ed. *Representing Jazz.* Durham, N.C.: Duke University Press, 1995.

Garber, Frederick. "Fabulating Jazz." In *Representing Jazz.* Ed. Krin Gabbard. Durham, N.C.: Duke University Press, 1995.

Garrido, Pablo. "Recuento integral del Jazz in Chile." In *Para todos,* June 10, 1935, I/29.

Giddins, Gary. *Riding on a Blue Note: Jazz and American Pop.* New York: Oxford University Press, 1981.

Gillespie, Dizzy, with Al Fraser. *To Be or Not . . . to Bop.* New York: Doubleday, 1979; reprint, New York: Da Capo Press, 1985.

Ginell, Cary. *Milton Brown and the Founding of Western Swing.* Urbana: University of Illinois Press, 1994.

Gitler, Ira. *Swing to Bop.* New York: Oxford University Press, 1985.

Godbolt, Jim. *A History of Jazz in Britain, 1919–1950.* London: Quartet Books, 1984.

———. *A History of Jazz in Britain, 1950–1970.* London: Quartet Books, 1989.

González, Ray, ed. *After Aztlan: Latino Poets of the Nineties.* Boston: David D. Godine, 1992.

Govenar, Alan, and Jaye Brakefield. *Deep Ellum and Central Track: Where the Black and White Worlds of Dallas Converged.* Denton: University of North Texas Press, 1996.

Hadlock, Richard. *Jazz Masters of the Twenties.* New York: Macmillan, 1965; reprint, New York: Collier Books, 1974.

Haisley, Lyra. "'Fire Hall Five' One of Many Former Campus Jazz Orchestras of Varsity." *Daily Texan,* April 21, 1925, p. 6.

Harrison, Max. Review of *The Bebop Revolution in Words and Music,* ed. Dave Oliphant. *IAJRC Journal* 28, no. 1 (Winter 1995): 80.

Harrison, Max, et al. *The Essential Jazz Records.* Vol. 1, *Ragtime to Swing.* London: Mansell, 1984; reprint, New York: Da Capo Press, 1988.

———. *Modern Jazz: The Essential Records.* London: Aquarius Books, 1975.

Hentoff, Nat. *The Jazz Life.* New York: Da Capo Press, 1975.

Hodeir, André. *Jazz: Its Evolution and Essence.* Trans. David Noakes. New York: Grove Press, 1956.

Huehls, Mitchum. "Spun Puns (and Anagrams): Exchange Economies, Subjectivity, and History in Harryette Mullen's *Muse & Drudge.*" *Contemporary Literature* 44, no. 1 (2003): 19–46.

Hughes, Langston. *Selected Poems of Langston Hughes.* New York: Random House Vintage Books, 1990.

Hultin, Randi. *Born under the Sign of Jazz: Public Faces, Private Moments.* Trans. Tim Challman. London: Sanctuary, 1998.

Kelley, Robin D. G. "People in Me: On the Polycultural Nature of Blackness." Lecture delivered at the University of Texas at Austin, December 4, 1997, as part of the Union Distinguished Speakers Series.

Kerouac, Jack. *Mexico City Blues.* New York: Grove Press, 1959.

———. *On the Road.* New York: Viking, 1957; reprint, New York: Penguin Books, 1991.

Kirk, Andy. *Twenty Years on Wheels.* Ann Arbor: University of Michigan Press, 1989.

Kriebel, Robert C. *Blue Flame: Woody Herman's Life in Music.* West Lafayette, Ind.: Purdue University Press, 1995.

Larkin, Philip. *All What Jazz: A Record Diary.* New York: Farrar Straus Giroux, 1985.

———. *Collected Poems.* New York: Farrar, Straus and Giroux, 2000.

Last of the Blue Devils, The. Directed by Bruce Ricker. New York: Rhapsody Films, 1979.

Leonard, Neil. *Jazz: Myth and Religion.* New York: Oxford University Press, 1987.

Lewis, Grover. *Splendor in the Short Grass: The Grover Lewis Reader.* Ed. Jan Reid and W. K. Stratton. Austin: University of Texas Press, 2005.

Litweiler, John. *Ornette Coleman: A Harmolodic Life.* New York: William Morrow, 1992.

Lomax, Alan. *The Folk Songs of North America.* New York: Doubleday, 1960.

———. *Mister Jelly Roll: The Fortunes of Jelly Roll Morton, New Orleans Creole and "Inventor of Jazz."* New York: Grosset & Dunlap, 1950; reprint, New York: Pantheon Books, 1993; Berkeley: University of California Press, 1973, 2001.

Lord, Tom. *The Jazz Discography.* West Vancouver, Canada: Lord Music Reference, 1992–2004.

McCarthy, Albert. *Big Band Jazz.* London: Barrie and Jenkins, 1974.

McDonough, John. "A Century with Count Basie." *Down Beat* 57 (January 1990): 36.

McLean, Duncan. *Lone Star Swing.* London: Jonathan Cape, 1997; New York: W. W. Norton, 1998.

McMahon, John R. "Unspeakable Jazz Must Go! It is Worse than Saloon and Scarlet Vice, Professional Dance Experts—Only a Few Cities Are Curbing the Evil." *Ladies Home Journal,* December 1921, p. 34.

McRae, Barry. *Ornette Coleman.* London: Apollo Press, 1988.

McSloy, Pete [Peter Townsend]. *For Jazz: 21 Sonnets.* Lafayette, Calif.: Hit & Run Press, 1995.

Mariani, Paul. *William Carlos Williams: A New World Naked.* New York: W. W. Norton, 1990.

Martin, T. E. "The Plastic Muse, Part 1." *Jazz Monthly,* May 1964, p. 14.

———. "The Plastic Muse, Part 2." *Jazz Monthly,* June 1964, p. 15.

Massey, Sara R. *Black Cowboys in Texas.* College Station: Texas A&M University Press, 2000.

Matchless Milam: History of Milam County, Texas. Comp. and ed. Milam County Heritage Preservation Society. Texas Sesquicentennial Edition. 1984.

Meltzer, David, ed. *Reading Jazz.* San Francisco: Mercury House, 1993.

Morgenstern, Dan. "Introducing Leo Wright." *Metronome* 78, no. 1 (1961): 26.

———. *Living with Jazz.* Ed. Sheldon Meyer. New York: Pantheon Books, 2004.

Oliphant, Dave. *The Early Swing Era, 1930 to 1941.* Westport, Conn.: Greenwood Press, 2001.

———. *Texan Jazz.* Austin: University of Texas Press, 1996.

Oliphant, Dave, ed. *The Bebop Revolution in Words and Music.* Austin, Tex.: Harry Ransom Humanities Research Center, 1992.

O'Meally, Robert G., ed. *The Jazz Cadence of American Culture.* New York: Columbia University Press, 1998.

Owens, Thomas. *Bebop: The Music and the Players.* New York: Oxford University Press, 1995.

Placksin, Sally. *American Women in Jazz, 1900 to the Present: Their Words, Lives, and Music.* New York: Putnam Wideview Books, 1982.

Poe, Edgar Allan. "Some Words with a Mummy." In *The Complete Tales and Poems of Edgar Allan Poe.* New York: Modern Library, 1938.

Porter, Roy, with David Keller. *There and Back.* Baton Rouge: Louisiana State University Press, 1991.

Porterfield, Nolan. *The Last Cavalier: The Life and Times of John A. Lomax, 1867–1948.* Urbana: University of Illinois Press, 1996.

Raftegard, Bo. *The Kenny Dorham Discography.* Karlstad, Sweden: privately printed, 1982.

Ramsey, Frederic, Jr., and Charles Edward Smith, eds. *Jazzmen.* London: Sidgwick and Jackson, 1958.

Reich, Howard, and William Gaines. *Jelly's Blues: The Life, Music, and Redemption of Jelly Roll Morton.* Cambridge, Mass.: Da Capo Press, 2003.

Rohter, Larry. "Ornette Coleman Takes His Quartet Home." *New York Times,* September 10, 1990, p. C15.

Rosenthal, David H. *Hard Bop: Jazz & Black Music, 1955–1965.* New York: Oxford University Press, 1992.

Russell, Ross. *Jazz Style in Kansas City and the Southwest.* Berkeley: University of California Press, 1971.

Russell, William. "Jelly Roll Morton and the *Frog-i-more Rag.*" In *The Art of Jazz: Essays on the Nature and Development of Jazz.* Ed. Martin T. Williams. New York: Grove Press, 1960.

Rust, Brian, comp. *Jazz Records, 1897–1942.* 2 vols. London: Storyville, 1975.

Schlouch, Claude. *The Unforgettable Kenny Dorham: A Discography.* N.p., privately printed, December 1977; reprint, 1983.

Schuller, Gunther. *A Collection of the Compositions of Ornette Coleman.* New York: MJQ Music, 1961.

———. *Early Jazz: Its Roots and Musical Development*. New York: Oxford University Press, 1968.

———. *The Swing Era: The Development of Jazz, 1930–1945*. New York: Oxford University Press, 1989.

Siegel, J. A., and J. Obrecht. "Eddie Durham: Charlie Christian's Mentor, Pioneer of the Amplified Guitar." *Guitar Player* 13 (August 1979): 56.

Simon, Bill. "Charlie Christian." In *The Jazz Makers: Essays on the Greats of Jazz*. Ed. Nat Shapiro & Nat Hentoff. New York: Holt, Rinehart and Winston, 1957; reprint, New York: Da Capo Press, 1979.

Skvorecky, Josef. *The Bass Saxophone*. Trans. Kaca Polackova-Henley. Hopewell, N.J.: Ecco Press, 1994.

Slate, John H. "Ballew." In *The Handbook of Texas Music*. Ed. Roy R. Barkley et al. Austin: Texas State Historical Association, 2003.

Smith, Jay D., and Len Guttridge. *Jack Teagarden: The Story of a Jazz Maverick*. London: Cassell, 1960.

Stearns, M. W. "George Washington Smith Rocks Cradle of Jazz: Three Years Older Than Jelly-Roll He Carved Regulation Cats in Texas." *Down Beat* 5, no. 4 (April 1938): 13.

Stewart, Rex. *Jazz Masters of the Thirties*. New York: Macmillan, 1972.

Terkel, Studs, with Milly Hawk Daniel. *Giants of Jazz*. New York: New Press, 2002.

Tinder, Cliff. "Jamaaladeen Tacuma: Electric Bass in the Harmolodic Pocket." *Down Beat* 49, no. 4 (April 1982): 19–21, 71.

[Traill, Sinclair.] "Boppin' in Paris." *Jazz Journal* 26, no. 1 (1973): 14–17.

Trussell, Jake. *After Hours Poetry*. Kingsville, Texas: privately printed, 1958.

———. "Hot Wax: Duke's Music." In *Jazz Index: Duke Ellington Biography & Bibliography, 1941–1949*. http://www.darmstadt.de/kultur/musik/jazz/Jazzindex/index-ellington-40s.htm.

Tucker, Mark, ed. *The Duke Ellington Reader*. New York: Oxford University Press, 1993.

Tudor, Dean, and Nancy Tudor. *Jazz*. Littleton, Colo.: Libraries Unlimited, 1979.

Tynan, John. "Jazz Records." Review of Ornette Coleman's *Something Else!* *Down Beat* 25, no. 22 (October 30, 1958): 24–25.

Walser, Robert, ed. *Keeping Time: Readings in Jazz History*. New York: Oxford University Press, 1999.

Ward, Geoffrey C., and Ken Burns. *Jazz: A History of America's Music*. New York: Alfred A. Knopf, 2000.

Waters, H. J., Jr. *Jack Teagarden's Music: His Career and Recordings*. Stanhope, N.J.: Walter C. Allen, 1960.

Williams, William Carlos. *The Collected Poems of William Carlos Williams*. 2 vols. Ed. A. Walton Litz and Christopher MacGowan. New York: New Directions, 1986.

Wilmer, Valerie. *As Serious As Your Life: The Story of the New Jazz*. London: Allison and Busby, 1977.

———. *The Face of Black Jazz*. New York: Da Capo Press, 1976.

———. *Jazz People*. London: Allison & Busby, 1970; reprint, London: Quartet Books, 1977.

———. *Mama Said There'd Be Days Like This: My Life in the Jazz World*. London: Women's Press, 1989.

Wood, Susan. *Asunder*. New York: Penguin, 2001.

INDEX